A Social Psychology of Group Processes for Decision-Making

and Hunt encouraged me to remain fundamental in my approaches to the social psychology of group process by allowing me to conduct our interdepartmental seminar in face-to-face groups. Professor Snyder not only supplied research space in our Department of Political Science to house our efforts, but aided me in seeing that the development of this book was complemental to my responsibilities as Co-Director of our International Relations Program, with its emphasis on decision-making (Snyder et al., 1962).

But our deepest acknowledgment is to our many colleagues in social psychology who have developed a body of knowledge from which we could draw in formulating this segment of a social psychology of group processes for decision-making. Short quotations are footnoted throughout the text; the following publishers graciously granted us permission to use the longer passages in the following works: Academic Press for material from *Systematic Error on the Part of Human Links in Communication Systems*, by D. T. Campbell. Chandler Publishing Company for material from *Formal Organizations: A Comparative Approach*, by P. M. Blau and W. R. Scott. Harcourt, Brace and World for material from *Social Behavior: Its Elementary Forms*, by G. C. Homans. Houghton Mifflin for material from *Psychology in Industry*, by N. R. F. Maier. *Human Relations* for material from L. Coch and J. R. P. French, Jr., "Overcoming Resistance to Change"; J. R. P. French, Jr., J. Israel, and D. Ås, "An Experiment on Participation in a Norwegian Factory: Interpersonal Dimensions of Decision-making"; H. B. Gerard, "The Effect of Different Dimensions of Disagreement on the Communication Process in Small Groups"; W. C. Schutz, "What Makes Groups Productive?" and H. Guetzkow and J. Gyr, "An Analysis of Conflict in Decision-making Groups." The Industrial Management Association for D. G. Marquis, "Individual Responsibility and Group Decision Involving Risk." The Institute of Management Sciences for material from H. Guetzkow and H. A. Simon, "The Impact of Certain Communication Nets upon Organization and Performance in Task-Oriented Groups." *The Journal of Conflict Resolution* for material from H. C. Kelman, "Compliance, Identification, and Internalization: Three Processes of Attitude

Change"; and M. Deutsch, "Trust and Suspicion." The Journal Press for material from J. D. Frank, "Experimental Study of Personal Pressure and Resistance: I"; and M. E. Shaw, "Some Effects of Varying Amounts of Information Exclusively Possessed by a Group Member upon His Behavior in the Group." Personnel Psychology, Inc. for material from E. A. Fleishman and E. F. Harris, "Patterns of Leadership Behavior Related to Employee Grievances and Turnover"; and D. E. Roach, "Dimensions of Employee Morale." The *Public Opinion Quarterly* for material from "Communication Processes among Immigrants in Israel," and "Conditions of Communication Receptivity," both by S. N. Eisenstadt. John Wiley and Sons for material from *The Social Psychology of Groups*, by J. W. Thibaut and H. H. Kelley. The American Sociological Association for material from R. F. Bales, F. L. Strodbeck, and T. M. Mills, "Channels of Communication in Small Groups"; B. H. Raven and J. R. P. French, Jr., "Legitimate Power, Coercive Power, and Observability in Social Influence"; and P. J. Runcel, "Cognitive Similarity in Facilitating Communication." The American Psychological Association for material from "A Note Concerning Homogeneity of Membership and Group Problem Solving," by M. E. Shaw. We also wish to thank Charles and Margaret Hermon for making available their unpublished manuscripts on power.

HAROLD GUETZKOW

Evanston, Illinois
March, 1964

Contents

CHAPTER ONE

Building a social psychology of

group processes for decision-making

The reader is invited to join with us as we develop a social psychology of group processes for decision-making. The printed word is seldom final for long, and the margins of each page invite your personal comments and contributions to our common effort.

In a developing science, readers inevitably possess resources not utilized by their authors. Experimental and field evidence may have been unavailable, unnoticed, or unpublished as the writers went through their own decision-making. A group of readers will have access to a variety of perspectives that generate differing generalizations from the present bibliography. But an ideal science is cumulative; each worker should be able to build on the contributions of his predecessors, and we extend this challenge to our readers.

Hopefully, new data on group processes will suggest only refinements or extensions to the propositions of this book. But if the history of the field is any indication, some of our generalizations will prove to be false starts; future workers certainly will have to begin their thinking anew on some of the topics developed in this book. It is the nature of empirical theory—which is constrained by data—that it proceed step by step with an occasional retreat and new beginning.

Our motivation for writing this book was grounded in an optimism about the unrealized potential in the scattered *empirical* studies of the group process. We made an effort to focus on that segment of the social psychology of group processes for decision-making which is founded on empirical data—quantified data that were gathered under controlled methods of observation. Many of the findings were gathered in laboratory situations in which an experimenter directly manipulated one factor or variable, such as the amount of agreement expressed by other group members, and drastically simplified the total setting in order to reduce the interplay of other background variables. The experimenter might, for example, isolate each subject in a separate booth and restrict communication to written notes. Or the experimenter might simulate an environment of group interaction for single subjects with a tape recording (Blake and Brehm, 1954). Although these techniques may decrease the similarity between the experimental setting and "real life," such simplification increases control and potential for quantification and manipulation. Furthermore, many of the investigators whose work we used relied extensively on a population of college students who can easily be recruited to serve in laboratory settings. There can be no doubt that a test on a single population of subjects has its limitations. Any single source of knowledge has limitations. We were fortunate to be able to support many of our conceptions with studies in both field and laboratory settings as well as with data obtained from many different kinds of subjects. These generalizations are greatly strengthened by this breadth. On the other hand, some findings are more limited in the scope of the supporting data. Although still useful, these latter generalizations are weaker for their narrowness.

In our attempt to systematize the findings in social psychology which have relevance to the group processes involved in decision-making, we endeavored to build eclectically and cumulatively upon the thinking and empirical work of our predecessors and colleagues. This book presents an inductive theory of face-to-face groups. As we built on these findings, however, we tried to recognize that they might ultimately have implications for practice. In 1947 Herring posited the need for a "social science technician," using the term broadly to mean "an individual who has

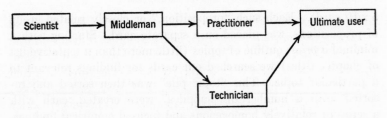

FIGURE 1.1.

been professionally trained to apply to practical situations the facts, generalizations, principles, rules, laws, or formulae uncovered by social science research" (Herring, 1947, p. 5). Schramm further elaborated the "anatomy" of utilization with a three-link chain (see Figure 1.1) between scientist and final consumer (Schramm, 1954, p. 39).

Guetzkow (1959) has argued that the role of the "middleman" should be extended:

Among practitioners whose life work is concerned with individual and social behavior, such as social workers, educators, lawyers, administrators (in business and in government), and politician statesmen, there is much reliance upon intuitive knowledge, applied with skill and art derived from long experience. As information in the social sciences increases, there is more need to differentiate the expert in social science knowledge from both the social scientist and the practitioner. The social engineer is the broad-gauged "middleman" who knows how to transform basic knowledge from the various social science disciplines into usable forms. He differs, too, from the technician (the pollster in business and industry, for example) whose competence is restricted and who may be only slightly familiar with the fund of basic knowledge underlying his specialization (Guetzkow, 1959, p. 77).

Hopefully, the state of our science—as represented in the chapters which follow—has reached the stage where it will be of some use to the growing class of "middlemen."

AN INDUCTIVE SUMMARY AND THEORY OF SMALL GROUPS

Let us explain the procedures we used to create the successive drafts of the book. We began by abstracting each empirically tested hypothesis in the studies in our initial bibliography onto

5 x 10 cards. Each such "proposition," or closely related group of propositions, was placed on a separate card. Starting with a minimal *a priori* outline of topics (little more than a tentative list of chapter titles) we searched our cards for findings relevant to a particular topic. This "topic pile" was then sorted and re-sorted until a number of "subpiles" were created, each with a series of relatively homogenous and focused empirical findings. Next, the "subpiles" were studied for common themes. In some cases several studies appeared to be testing the same general phenomenon. If the findings were consistent, or *almost* consistent, then a proposition might be formulated to subsume the separate findings. If the findings were apparently inconsistent, then reasons for the contradictions were sought. In some cases, such as the impact of heterogeneous personality (Chapter Five) and the communication to a deviant (Chapter Nine), a plausible explanation for divergent findings was found. In other cases, our efforts were not rewarded. Often we did not feel that the different cards in a "subpile" tested essentially the same proposition. In these cases the studies are still presented under the same conceptual heading, even if we could not formulate a specific proposition which plausibly subsumed all of the data.

Our heavy debt on previous workers is detailed with the frequent citations throughout the text. But we were surprised that standard review articles seldom allowed us to borrow directly from their summary statements. Campbell's (1958) propositions concerning errors induced by human links in communication systems is a notable exception. This is not because the quality of these reviews is not excellent; rather, we found that other reviewers either had not worded their conclusions in proposition form or else the propositions were not at a level of abstraction appropriate to the context of our other propositions. Lorge, Fox, Davitz, and Brenner (1958), Bass (1960), and Hare (1962) were frequently used for summaries and bibliography, but they did not use a propositional format. Also, Homans (1961) worked at a higher level of abstraction than most of the propositions in this work.

After a series of such propositions were found, they were examined for logical interdependence. Traditional philosophies of science (Cohen and Nagel, 1934, for instance) have placed heavy emphasis on the logical eloquence of the interrelationship between verbal or mathematical statements. Although our propositions were reorganized, reworded, and the data examined anew in service of a logical framework, our first concern remained with the inductive (descriptive and predictive) value of each individual proposition.

This book, then, is inductive in its origin. This is not to say that judgment and bias are absent. In many cases the actual operational definitions of the variables involved in a single proposition are quite different, but we postulated that a single, more fundamental process underlies divergent operational definitions. Even though we began with data, the very process of grouping several empirical tests under one conceptual proposition is a rudimentary kind of theorizing, and is bound to arouse our implicit theoretical biases.

In summary, our goal has been to present a special blend of theorizing and empirical review which we have called an "inductive summary and theory" of face-to-face group processes. We have restricted ourselves to empirical and quantitative data. Like any inductive process, the result has been strongly influenced by the selection of data from which the inductions were made. Since the selection of studies has played an important role in developing the following chapters, criteria for selection are reviewed.

Criteria for selecting the bibliography. (1) The first criterion was methodological. No study that did not report a relatively rigorous and formal collection and analysis of empirical data was included. Purely descriptive and insightfully speculative works were left for writers of other books. Furthermore, many studies were excluded if, in the judgment of the present authors, the experimental design did not allow a relatively unambiguous interpretation of the results. No attempt has been made to footnote the omissions; studies rejected because of fundamental weaknesses in design or other methodology are simply not included in the bibliography.

There are, however, a number of studies included whose interpretation seemed less than clear. Here again judgment entered. Depending on the seriousness of the ambiguity, such studies are discussed in the main text, in an optional section, or in a footnote. Although they did not completely invalidate the research findings, these methodological problems imposed an extra barrier to reliable induction. These studies were included for various reasons, to fill conceptual gaps, and, in the case of a few widely known studies, to point out their shortcomings so that their conclusions can be regarded with more caution.

(2) The second criterion concerns our substantive interest. Throughout the preparation of our bibliography, we worked toward a social psychology of group processes for decision-making. Only a minority of the studies reviewed actually deal with a "group" which is "making a decision." But this book was written in the faith that insight into group processes in general will be helpful in understanding group processes for decision-making in particular. Nonetheless, our original bibliography was considerably trimmed as articles were eliminated whose bearing on our subject matter seemed too remote.

(3) As the book progressed into later drafts, a third criterion emerged. The usefulness of a study was evaluated in the context of other research on similar topics. If an isolated hypothesis was barely confirmed statistically and further weakened by design flaws, it was probably omitted. But had this same finding been surrounded by other research on the same topic, then the more marginal item was included as evidence of additional support. Several ambiguous confirmations certainly do not equal one straightforward validation, but they are stronger than a single isolated ambiguous finding, especially if the source of ambiguity differs from study to study. We faced a happier dilemma when several studies seemed to make the same point. Although such studies were included, they were sometimes discussed in a footnote so as not to impede the progress of readers not interested in total documentation.

Contradictory evidence. We made a special effort to avoid omitting evidence merely because it seemed to go against the main theme of our generalizations and interpretations. There are a number of approaches to the problems of contradictory evidence. In the first place, a contributor believes that his generalizations and propositions—by and large—are true. He usually thinks his interpretation is the best available abstraction of the data. Some readers are interested in the best generalization that a writer can make and are not interested in exceptions which mar a fit between a practical proposition and empirical evidence. This approach is particularly tempting when working with statistically supported hypotheses which undoubtedly contain "confirmations" due to random error (i.e., inappropriate rejections of the null hypothesis). To include these supposed exceptions in the text, some say, adds only confusion and ignores the fact that few generalizations in social science will completely subsume all the published findings.

On the other hand, scholars frequently criticize those who ignore contradictory evidence. The omission of "exceptions to the rule," they say, gives the less-than-sophisticated reader a false impression about the tenuousness of all theory in general and the author's generalizations in particular. Perhaps the most central reason for including the contradictions is their potential in sparking new and better formulations by others.

Our position is as follows. First, we stand behind the propositions we present as the best abstraction we can make from the data available to us. Secondly, we try to report the experimental designs and specific measurements in enough detail so that the reader can evaluate our generalizations. Third, we try to find reasons for contradictions. In a few cases we feel that we may have found the "other thing" which violates the ceribus paribus qualification implicit in any generalization. Finally, we demote to footnotes specific discussion of data we do not understand. For example, in discussing the relation of interaction to attraction in Chapter 6, a relatively well-founded generalization is qualified by a footnote. This supplementary evidence aids both authors and reader to recognize that the glibness of our more general conclusion should be viewed with circumspection. The practitioner and cursory readers can skip these footnotes and optional sections without losing the main argument. The more skeptical and the sophisticated professionals, however, are assured that we tried to include all data which, at this stage of the science, did not seem to fit our inductions.

FORMAT

The following section on "Elementary Technical Concepts" illustrates the format that will be used to set the optional sections off from the main text. Each optional section will begin with a symbol identical to the one immediately below, and the entire optional section will be set in a slightly smaller type. The reader who is interested mainly in our tentative generalizations can skip to the end of the material set in the special type. The student of group processes who requires a more complete statement of the foundations of our assertions can pick and choose among the material in footnotes and optional sections. The material in the main text should stand as a complete unit, however, without recourse to a single footnote or special section.

The reader who is not familiar with the conventions of psychological journals will note that "subjects" is often abbreviated as S (singular) or Ss (plural) and "Experimenter" as E or Es.

❧   ❧   ❧

SOME ELEMENTARY TECHNICAL CONCEPTS

Variable. The social scientist often uses the term *variable* to designate factors or elements in the situation he is describing. For example, Altman and McGinnies (1960) were interested in the effect of (*a*) varied personality composition on (*b*) spontaneity of behavior, (*c*) rate of response, (*d*) spread of participation, (*e*) direction of communication flow, (*f*) attitude change, and participant ratings of (*g*) attraction to the group, (*h*) relevance to the discussion topic, and (*i*) friendship choices. Each of these factors is considered a variable. Of all the things the experimenter could have paid attention to, these are the aspects of the group and its environment he chose to record. Note that each variable can vary in amount or strength—and these variations can be quantified by assigning numbers to different degrees of magnitude.

Sometimes a variable is described as being *independent* or *dependent*.

This means merely that the factor is considered by the experimenter as having a special relationship to other variables in the situation. *Independent variables* are those elements taken as given, factors which initiate the causal sequence which ends in the measured *dependent variables*. Frequently independent variables are some aspect of the group's environment, the task, the group's composition, etc., which the experimenter deliberately changed or manipulated. He then records the impact which these manipulations have on the dependent variables. In the above example, Altman and McGinnies manipulated the personality composition of the group (the independent variable), and then studied the ways in which the dependent variables changed as a result of these manipulations.

Phenomenon. Whenever two variables are consistently related to each other, we call the relationship a phenomenon. Altman and McGinnies found that when the group was composed of two subgroups of equal size, group performance was inhibited. Many similar findings are reviewed in Chapter Five. Since groups with two antagonistic subgroups are reliably ineffective, the relationship between incompatible subgroups and group performance is a social psychological phenomenon. The verbal statement of a phenomenon in a general form is a *proposition*.

Correlation coefficient. It is often useful when comparing two measurements on the same person or group to be able to indicate by a single number or index the extent to which the two different aspects are associated with each other. Statistical devices used for this purpose are called correlation coefficients and are often symbolized by an r. There are many kinds that are used depending upon the particular situation. The ones used in this volume range from -1.00 through zero to $+1.00$. When the coefficient is relatively high, in the .60's, .70's, or .80's, concomitance in the two measures is considerable. When the correlation is low, in the .10's, .20's, or .30's, there is little consistent relationship between the measures. When the r is prefixed with a negative sign, as in $-.75$, the relationship between the two measures is "negative" or inverted, that is, high values of the one variable tend to correspond to low values on the other. When the coefficient stands alone or is prefixed by a plus sign, as .75 or $+.75$, the correlation is positive or direct, that is, high values on the one measure tend to correspond to high values on the other.

Statistical significance. When a researcher discovers a finding which interests him, there are inevitably a host of rival alternative explanations for the finding. One of the most plausible of the rival hypotheses is that the finding might have occurred by chance. For example, an experimenter might divide his subjects (Ss) into two groups and tell one group that they are going to like each other and tell the other group that they are not going to like each other. If he finds that the "liking" group members have more influence over each other than the "disliking" group members, he may want to believe that this extra influence was due to his verbal instructions. It would be possible, however, that he would have found a difference between the two groups even if he had told them nothing. Perhaps he "just happened" to have assigned the most gullible people to one group and the most independent to the other.

Fortunately, we have a set of mathematical models which predict the probability (p) that a given difference could have occurred by chance. One of the most widely accepted conventions (and the one used in this book) is to reject chance as a rival alternative hypothesis whenever a given difference would have occurred by chance only 5 times out of 100 (i.e., $p < .05$). The reader will find references to p values and "levels of significance" throughout the book. It is our recommendation that the reader seriously consider hypotheses supported at the .05 level or smaller (the smaller the p value, the less often the difference would occur by chance). However interesting and suggestive they may be, hypotheses not confirmed at the .05 level seem to us to be not acceptable as a part of scientifically verified results.

Some of the tests which can be used to evaluate the level of significance are the F test (Analysis of Variance), t test, and Chi Square. More details are available in any introductory statistics book such as Guilford (1950) or Underwood, Duncan, Taylor, and Cotton (1954).

OVERVIEW

In Chapter Two, the data contrasting individual and group productivity are reviewed, and the reader is introduced to theoretical issues and concepts which will be important in later chapters. Most of the investigators represented in Chapter Two were interested in a definitive and final answer to the question "Which is better—the individual or the group?" For a variety of reasons, these investigators were disappointed in their original aspirations. But the extensive data contrasting an individual working alone with the same individual working in a group give us insight into the unique properties of group processes. Chapter Three documents the notion that variables important in contrasting individual and group productivity are also important in contrasting one group with another group. In Chapter Four, some of the definitions, classifications, and distinctions are made explicit and a simple, working model of interpersonal behavior and task performance is presented.

Participants in most groups tend to focus on the task before them, just as they would do if they were working on the same task in isolation. Commendable as this task focus may sound, readers of Chapter Five will discover that interpersonal obstacles can also inhibit productivity. Chapter Five documents the extensive list of interpersonal obstacles that scientific experiments have discovered blocking the path to effective group action. Even more important than this specific list of potential trouble spots, however, is the generalization that group members face two sets of obstacles in their groups, task-environmental obstacles and interpersonal obstacles.

Chapters Six and Seven uncover the bases and sources of the high power group member's extra influence. These "sources of power" turn out to be closely related to the same variables which facilitated productivity. Chapter Six discusses the way in which a group member can build his power on the physical possession of resources important to other group members. Chapter Seven reports the many ways in which a group member can gain indirect control over the commodities valued by his peers.

Chapter Eight examines the behavioral implications of power. Since power was defined in Chapter Six as the ability to influence the behavior of others, Chapter Eight begins with a review of the empirical measures which have been used to reflect this heightened influence. The remaining propositions list other differences in the mannerisms of the "haves" and the "have nots."

Some of the best replicated findings in this book are reported in Chapter Nine. In the first part of the chapter, the variables channeling communication and interaction are exhibited. The second half of the chapter is devoted to a number of generalizations about the ways in which communications are understood.

Since early studies failed to reveal a positive correlation between satisfaction and productivity, satisfaction appears to have lost its place as one of the central variables in social psychology. But, in Chapter Ten, we examine the variables which have been related to satisfaction. Satisfaction is a judgment of the amount of rewards which the participant has received, and a list of the variables related to judgments of satisfaction gives us a "participant's eye view" of the experiences he has found rewarding.

We did not choose to utilize "leadership" as an organizational or conceptual theme throughout the book. Rather, empirical studies with "leadership" in their titles were discussed under what we considered more fundamental social psychological processes. But two interesting streams of research remained when we finished the early drafts of the first ten chapters; so Chapter Eleven concludes the book with two topics from leadership: the study of leadership traits and the conceptual-empirical distinctions that have been made between the "task leader" and the "social-emotional leader."

Now, will you join us? Your own efforts to use social psychology to understand group processes may well reveal weak spots in our presentation. But we hope our errors of omission and commission are not too serious, and that you will publicly record our mistakes in the hope that they will not be made a second time.

CHAPTER TWO

Group and individual performance

W hat happens to Mr. C. Member when he leaves the comfort and privacy of his office or home and ventures out to participate in a face-to-face decision-making conference? According to the popular paperbacks, such as *The Organization Man* and *The Lonely Crowd,* C. Member faces a mortal battle between the sacred forces of individualism and the dread army of creeping conformity. Perhaps the title of this chapter should be The Group *versus* Its Individual Participants. Perhaps David Riesman is on the right track when he argues that the organization and conference so smother individual creativity in our times that the individual must retreat to the inner recess of his den if he wants to assert his individual initiative.

On the other hand, perhaps the democratic philosophy involved in Elton Mayo and Kurt Lewin's research, as expressed by the "human relations" industrial psychologist, is sound. The organization and conference may provide the common man with a most effective expression of his individual worth. The conference and committee may be an answer to the authoritarian hierarchy where each individual must blindly follow instructions which he neither understands nor questions.

Neither of these views of the decision-making group may be suitable. Perhaps the decision-making conference has no impact of any kind except to waste the time of the participants. In some organizations the standard greeting among frustrated

13

junior executives goes: "Are you coming from or are you going to a conference!" We shall soon review evidence which suggests that committees frequently take more time to accomplish *some* tasks than an individual working alone. Is it true that the decision-making conference will only waste C. Member's time while the chairman dodges responsibility for his difficult decision?

It is certain that we cannot find a final answer to the difficult questions raised by these extreme views. But the data gathered from the scientific study of small groups do have a lot to say about what happens to an individual when he begins to work with others in face-to-face groups for purposes of decision-making. Many researchers have compared the productivity of single individuals with the productivity of a collection of individuals working together in a group. Following the results of these studies closely, we shall discuss the ways in which groups and individuals compare in what they produce.

Comparisons of the group and its individual members are a good place to begin this book on the group processes in decision-making. In the first place, the relatively large amount of experimental works allows us to illustrate the way in which the *findings* from experimental social psychology form the foundation for a model about group process. Second, the contrast between the individual working alone and individuals working together introduces us to many of the central problems of social psychology which will be discussed further in later chapters. Third, these experiments emphasize the close relationship between individual psychology and group psychology. Both individual and group psychologies are important in the decision-making group. Finally, the studies to be reported have immediate practical implications. The administrator must frequently decide whether a matter for decision should be assigned to a conference, to an individual, or to some combination of both. The results of these studies may help him with these decisions.

AN EMPHASIS ON THE CONDITIONS UNDER WHICH GROUPS ARE SUPERIOR TO INDIVIDUALS

Lorge and his colleagues made an extensive and critical review of the literature of individual and group comparisons up to 1958:

"In general, in the evaluation of the relative quality of the products produced by groups in contrast to the products produced by individuals, the group is superior. The superiority of the group, however, all too frequently, is not as great as would be expected from an interactional theory. In many studies, the product of the 'best' individual is superior to that of the 'best' group" (Lorge, Fox, Davitz, and Brenner, 1958, p. 369). It is not possible to state simply that group productivity is or is not superior to the productivity of individuals working in isolation. "It depends—!" Thus, our major task for this chapter is to specify the conditions under which groups will and will not be superior to individuals. For purposes of both theory and application, it is necessary to understand *why* the group is not always superior, which usually means that we must specify the conditions under which groups are superior and the conditions under which individuals are superior.

Observers of group interaction are impressed with the great differences among groups and among the individuals in each group. One group may be successful while another is not. For the moment, however, let us set aside these important differences among groups and individuals. Rather, let us contrast the performance of individuals working in a group with the performance of these *same* individuals working in isolation. Because this chapter is devoted to over-all differences between groups and individuals, considerations of different personalities and different patterns of interpersonal relations will be postponed for later chapters.

THE NATURE OF THE TASK

The world is complex. We cannot discuss comparisons between individuals and groups without also discussing the task on which they are working. For this reason, we must find ways to characterize different group tasks before we turn to the data from group versus individual comparisons. Hopefully, we work toward a method of identifying (*a*) those tasks on which groups will excel, and (*b*) those tasks on which the individuals will excel face-to-face groups.

Roby and Lanzetta (1958) suggest that we analyze a task in

terms of its *critical demands:* "We may expect that the most useful method of classifying group tasks will be with reference to those aspects of group behavior or procedures which these tasks bring to the foreground. In other words, we would expect that the distinctive features of particular tasks will be the degree to which they require certain group behaviors for adequate performance. Such behavioral requirements will be referred to as 'critical demands' " (1958, p. 95).

For example, groups are likely to perform particularly well when they are able to divide the labor of the task among the group members. For this reason we would expect that "division of labor" will be an important critical demand for tasks which are used to compare individuals and groups. There is little reason, for example, to assume that a group of individuals would do a better job than would a single individual of plotting the geographical locations of branch units with pins on a map. It is true that a group of kibitzers might catch an occasional oversight, but there is little that the extra "members of the group" can contribute to a single member's map work. All 25 members of a group might see that a pin representing a branch should be placed in Cleveland; but since there is only one pin and one map, the 25 individual efforts can appear but once in the group product. Since the task is simple and routine, 25 members would redundantly replicate each other's efforts with little gained by the multiple checks.

Even in group interactions on complex tasks where the group is most likely to excel, only one person can speak at a time; and while one member is speaking, the others must listen. One listener may be stimulated to make a valuable criticism or modification later; but, for the time being, the other members are partially "idle" in the sense that they are not *overtly* producing information, alternatives, or conclusions for the benefit of the other group members.

Much the same argument will apply to less extreme examples. If a problem is so simple that the major difficulty is the time it takes to fill in the correct responses to an agency questionnaire, a group hardly could be expected to improve on the effort of one of its members. If the major portion of the task is "writing

words," and only one person will write at a time, there is little
that the extra members can do to help. On the other hand, if
the problem required a wide range of backgrounds in order to
discover all the answers, a group of individuals might do a better job than its most capable member.

Although some divisions of labor may allow a group to utilize
its full resources, other divisions might limit the group to the
ability of its poorest member. If the decision requires unanimous
agreement, as is the case in some boards of directors or government commissions, the inability of one member to understand
a technical solution could seriously delay the group decision.
We must recognize that the task or problem on which the group
is working influences the extent to which a group is—or is not—
superior to its individual members working in isolation.

Propositions about Individual and Group Productivity: Division of Labor and Consolidation of Information

We shall focus on three general ways in which the output of a
group of individuals differs from the output of single individuals
working separately. In this first section propositions concerning
the "group's" utilization of its potentially greater resources are
presented. In the next section we consider the changes in motivation which are produced when one individual begins to work
with others. The final section examines the way that persuasion
and conformity contribute to the group product. The chapter
ends with an optional section on some of the global research
which has been done on group discussion as a democratic process
and/or technique for persuasion.

In many senses the topics of this chapter comprise a varied and
heterogeneous list; but—in at least three senses—these topics are
appropriate for an early chapter in a book on the social psychology of group processes. First, these topics introduce the reader
to most of the broader issues which are developed more fully in
later chapters. Second, each proposition gives us insight into the
way in which the "group" differs from the "individual." Finally
a list which contrasts individuals and groups provides insight

into group processes. If we remain alert to the processes which distinguish individuals from a group, we are likely to discover those variables which will help us distinguish one group from another.

It should be understood throughout this book that the phrase "other things being equal" is implicit in each proposition.

PROPOSITION 2.1. When several individuals work collectively on a single task their activities will (a) overlap and/or (b) make a division of labor possible.

The experimental and field data to be used in building our propositions in this part of Chapter Two encompass a wide variety of problems—from the almost trivial (estimating the number of beans in a bottle) to the more serious (finding satisfactory ways to increase significantly the output of an assembly line). Whether overlap and division of labor increase the adequacy of the group will depend on the critical demands of these tasks and on the effectiveness of the group's pattern of internal relations.

PROPOSITION 2.1-A. For tasks involving random error, combining several individual estimates or solutions into a single group product will increase accuracy.

Many tasks (working arithmetic problems, guessing weights and room temperature, estimating branch office sales, forecasting clientele reactions, etc.) involve many sources of error. It is a statistical axiom that, for problems which involve random errors, the average of several judgments will be more accurate than a single judgment. The greater the number of separate judgments included in the final answer, the more accurate will be the final average. The errors tend to cancel out each other.

In her unpublished master's thesis, Hazel Knight (1921) had college students estimate room temperature. According to Lorge et al. (1958), "The judgments of the individuals ranged from 60° to 85°; the 'statisticized' group judgment was 72.4°, approximating the actual room temperature of 72°. The 'statisticized' group judgment was better than that of 80% of the individual judgments . . ." (p. 344).

This increase in the accuracy results from the arithmetical combination of individual hypotheses and does not depend on the criticism and evaluation of group members. It has been demonstrated that such individual judgments do not need to be made in the presence of the other individuals (Farnsworth and Williams, 1936). All that is required is that a number of separate hypotheses which contain a random error be combined in some manner. Stroop (1932) reports that accuracy was increased by combining five separate judgments of the same individual. The responses of single individuals are, of course, more likely to contain a constant bias which will not be canceled out by combination.

On the other hand, a series of hypotheses taken from different individuals often contains a constant bias that may be accentuated by the grouping of answers. Error cancellation requires that the errors be random. The individuals whose judgments are pooled must have been subjected to varying and heterogeneous background experiences. Farnsworth and Williams (1936) used a task which required the subjects (Ss) to estimate the weight of three objects. One object was lighter than the others, but also larger in size. In this case the individual errors were not random; since all individuals had experienced larger objects as heavier, they made mistakes in the same direction. The average of the pooled judgments was not superior to individual performance on this task.

Gordon (1924) had students rank objects by weight and then correlated these rankings with the rankings obtained by physical measurement. The average correlation of individual rankings with the true ranking was only .41. But, then she averaged several individual estimates together and correlated this "group" estimate with the true scores. These "group" correlations were considerably higher; the average rank order correlation between "groups" of 50 averaged individual judgments and the true order was .93.

Stroop (1932) was the first to indicate that the increased size of the correlations was a "mathematical" rather than a "social" phenomenon. He replicated Gordon's findings, and also executed several additional variations in the design. He demonstrated that the increased accuracy was almost exactly that which would be predicted from a statistical formula (the Spearman-Brown Prophecy Formula), and then showed that grouping increased the correlation size even with data generated randomly from card sorting. Similar results have been reported by other experimenters.[1]

In summary, the combined estimate of several group members is likely to be more accurate than the estimate of any single member. This is true only when each individual estimate contains random sources of error so that the errors tend to cancel out. Combination does not eliminate a constant bias.

PROPOSITION 2.1-B. For tasks which involve creating ideas or remembering information, there is a greater probability that one of several persons will produce the information than that a single individual will produce it by himself.

In 1955 Lorge and Solomon published a detailed mathematical model which predicts the degree to which a group will surpass its individual members on a problem where the answer is "obvious" to everyone as soon as it occurs to anyone in the group. It seems reasonable that when one person has a certain probability of discovering the answer by himself, then there is an even greater probability that at least one of several group members will discover it. By the same reasoning, the group is likely to stumble on the answer faster than a single person working alone. After having individuals solve a relatively complicated problem individually and then resolve it in groups, Tuckman and Lorge (1962) conclude: "The evidence in this study suggests that groups are superior to individuals, not so much on account of the greater

[1] Smith (1931) applied the Knight technique (see above) to groups of 5, 10, 20, and 50 undergraduates who worked individually judging personality and behavior traits of children from written reports of their behavior. The correlations with the criterion increased with the size of the group.

Bruce (1935) had subjects judge the weight and number of buckshot in a sample. The correlation for the statisticized group was higher than the average individual correlation.

Klugman (1945) obtained similar results when high school students judged the number of unfamiliar objects in a bottle, although there was no significant difference for familiar objects. Schonbar (1945) found that interacting pairs were more accurate than individuals in estimating the length of lines.

effectiveness of groups in solving problems, but rather on account of the greater probability of getting a good solution from a group of five than from any one individual" (p. 51). Hoppe (1962) finds that the Lorge and Solomon model accurately predicts the degree to which groups will exceed individuals in recalling nonsense syllables. Although they suggest qualifications to be discussed in Proposition 2.3, Davis and Restle (1963) report that a greater proportion of groups reached a correct solution within the time limit than did individual members working alone. Yuker (1955) reports an experiment in which individuals tried to reproduce three times a story which had been read to them. First they worked separately, then groups were formed to prepare a common story and finally the same Ss again attempted to reproduce the story individually. "The group recall was superior to the average initial individual recall, the initial individual recall of the persons with the best memories, and to the average final individual recall" (Yuker, 1955, p. 22). In summary, the data confirm our proposition. Several individuals are more likely than a single person to hit on an improbable but obviously correct idea.

The argument to this point can be extended to situations where the group seeks more than one alternative. For instance, several individuals would be more likely to stumble on five separate alternatives than a single individual would be. Gibb (1951) [2] found that the number of different solutions suggested by a group increased with the size of the group in a negatively accelerated function. In other words, the number of extra solutions increases rapidly as the first few members are added, and then the gain per individual begins to drop off.

PROPOSITION 2.1-C. Groups will be efficient when the critical demands of the task emphasize the gain (a) from a duplication of effort and/or (b) from the division of labor.

[2] "1,152 college students [were] drawn at random from a group of students in elementary psychology classes. . . . Groups of varying sizes were given a set [of instructions] to produce as many solutions as possible to a series of problems permitting multiple solutions. The groups varied in size, containing 1, 2, 3, 6, 12, 24, 48, or 96 members. Each group session lasted

So far in Proposition 2, we have seen how the group can eliminate random errors and has access to a greater pool of alternatives. Now we see that these facts can be either strengths or weaknesses—depending on the task environment. A larger number of available solutions, for instance, would increase the productivity of larger groups only when a larger number of solution alternatives are necessary for optimal output. For many problems the surplus of alternatives may lead merely to conflict and would not increase the quality of the final product. Of course, multiple estimates of the same judgment can increase the accuracy of the group product, but this effect may be more than canceled by the time spent sorting out twenty alternatives when four would have been enough for a particular task. Furthermore, both the number of alternatives added per person and the increased accuracy per person drop off as the group becomes larger.

In 1938 Thorndike conducted an experiment to test the hypothesis that the superiority of the group over the individual will be highest for tasks which afford a wide range of possible solutions.[3] In general, the hypothesis was confirmed. It appeared, however, that composing a crossword puzzle was so complex a problem that Thorndike's newly formed groups were unable to organize themselves adequately for the task. This limitation to the superiority of groups will be considered in Chapters Four and Five. Husband (1940) found that pairs were superior to individuals when working on problems requiring some originality or insight, but not on the more routine arithmetic problems. Perhaps the

exactly 30 minutes after the instructions containing the set were read" (Gibb, 1951, p. 324).

[3] Thorndike (1938) had college subjects meet for four sessions, each of which was one week apart. Each subject worked as an individual twice and in a group twice. All tasks were completed within a session. All tasks were designed in two forms, one form with a wide range of alternatives and another with a narrow range.

Groups were superior when working on "fill in blank" vocabulary tests (versus multiple choice) and when filling in three lines of a limerick (versus one line). The fact that the individuals had a greater superiority over groups when composing a puzzle (versus completing a crossword puzzle) suggests that extremely complex tasks may require so much interpersonal organization within the group that group superiority is thereby lessened, at least for newly formed groups.

arithmetic problems were so easy that no random errors were involved.

Implications of proposition 2.1. These propositions have important implications for the utilization of groups for decision-making in government and industry. When quantitative judgments must be made, it is well to increase the size of the group and to include persons with widely varying experiences relevant to the matter at hand. It would seem wise, for example, for the Internal Revenue Service to assemble personnel with a large variety of experiences in assessment of tax write offs when the impact of new regulations is being estimated. When a large variety of information must be brought to bear and unusual solution alternatives must be produced, it again would seem that increasing the size of the group would improve the quality of productivity. These considerations might well prompt an industrial firm to bring its foremen together and have them suggest alternative proposals for a new plant which the architects then would work over before completing their final drawings. But remember—the improvement with increasing size yields diminishing returns. Finally, the superiority of the group may be washed out in organizational confusion if the task requires a high degree of patterning of the internal relations.

PROPOSITION 2.2. When several individuals are limited to a single product, it will be selected from available ideas and information.

In other words, the final *group* product will not contain all of the information which each group member might have used in his *individual* product. Up to this point, we have stressed the fact that the group has access to more information than a single individual. But, more often than not, the group must select from the information which it has available. Few solutions are so obvious that the group does not have to choose among several alternatives in order to make its final decision.

PROPOSITION 2.2-A. The final group product will exclude some of the ideas and information potentially available to each member.

In the first place, each individual is aware of only a few of the events in his environment and can "bring to mind" only a small fraction of his total knowledge. Second, each individual will report only a small fraction of the events in his awareness to the group. The total information available in the group is still further pruned when the other group members fail to assimilate everything reported by their fellow members. Furthermore, the other group members will reject as "false" or "not up to par" many of the individual contributions which are assimilated. For that matter, the group interaction may lead an individual to reconsider an idea which he himself proposed.

It has been possible to isolate a portion of this selective process in a series of experiments which compare an interacting group with a nominal or synthetic group. Lorge et al. (1958) use the term "concocted," but we shall use "synthetic" because it connotes both the artificial nature of the "groups" and the fact that they are constructed from separate and independent parts. In experiments on synthetic groups, the researcher has individuals work out a common decision in face-to-face group interaction; then he has an equivalent set of individuals work on the problem independently. The *experimenter* then combines the results of the individual efforts into a single group product; he eliminates ideas which overlap and credits the entire "group" with all solutions achieved by any single individual. Note that the synthetic group *does not complete the process of problem solving.* Members of synthetic groups only can generate a wide number of alternative solutions; it remains for someone else to select one or edit out the overlapping alternatives.

Proposition 2.2-A argues that the solutions of the face-to-face group usually contain fewer alternatives than those of the synthetic group because the contributions of the interacting group have undergone the entire selective process of face-to-face group interaction. Furthermore, the superiority of the synthetic groups should be most evident on tasks (such as those described in Proposition 2.1-B) where little is to be gained from the criticism and selectivity uniquely present in face-to-face group deliberation.

An experiment by Faust (1959) serves to illustrate the reliable superiority of synthesized groups over interacting groups for problems which require little sophistication and otherwise do not allow for division of labor or criticism. Faust had his subjects work for an hour on two tasks: (a) one set of tasks in which the problem was presented in a diagram and a verbal description, Ss were to "draw" the answer; (b) the second set of tasks was three anagrams. The anagrams were placed in envelopes within envelopes in such a way that Ss were forced to work jointly on each step of a multiple step problem. Note how this latter limitation makes the problem relatively routine and prevents the members from dividing the work.

Groups of four working together performed better than a single individual working alone, but a group synthesized from the products of four individuals (who had actually worked separately) was superior to the product of four interacting group members (who had actually worked together). Similar results have been found by Watson (1928)[4] and in a study by Taylor, Berry, and Block (1958).

Taylor, Berry, and Block (1958) formed twelve groups of four men each and compared the productivity of these groups with the

[4] Watson (1928) divided 108 graduate students in education into 20 newly created experimental groups of three to ten members. Subjects were given a set of envelopes containing jumbled letters and were asked to form a word from the letters. "The first ten-minute period was spent by each person making as many words as he could by himself. . . . After a brief intermission, the group came together for a group-thinking process. The group secretary kept the list of words, and each person called his contribution aloud. Ideas, just in the process of becoming suitable words, were expressed in the group and others helped to supply the desired term or modification. This continued for exactly ten minutes" (Watson, 1928, pp. 329–331).

In other words there were four sessions separated by a brief intermission: (1) 10 minutes alone, (2) 10 minutes in group, (3) 10 minutes in group, and finally (4) 10 minutes working alone. Scores were compiled for the sessions each individual worked separately, the time spent in the cooperative face-to-face group, and for a synthetic group based on the sum of individual member scores during the individual sessions.

Taking the average individual production as 100 per cent, "the poorest person had an efficiency of 55 per cent, the best of 150 per cent, the cooperative group of 231 per cent, and the compiled [synthetic] group . . . would average 268 per cent. In every group the group thinking [face-to-face interaction] produced more words than the best individual of the group. In [only] five of the twenty groups the cooperative group work produced more words than did" the synthetic group (Watson, 1928, p. 332).

results of 48 individuals working separately. The researchers gave both groups and individuals a set of instructions designed to increase creativity (i.e., no criticism, wild ideas encouraged, quantity emphasized, etc.). The groups and individuals were then given three problems: how to increase tourist travel in the United States, difficulties of having two thumbs, and steps to meet the teacher shortage. Group members were then asked to list as many suggestions as they could. Note that group members did not have to choose a correct solution or evaluate the proposals in any way.

Under these conditions, the four-man groups produced *more* unique suggestions than a *single individual*, but the interacting groups produced significantly *fewer* suggestions than a group synthesized from four individuals who had worked separately. There was some evidence to indicate that the suggestions from the interacting group were superior in quality to those from the synthetic group.

In a brief overview of their research, Parnes and Meadow (1959) reported that they failed to replicate the basic Taylor et al. study. Parnes and Meadow also reported that brainstorming groups (groups with instructions stressing creativity) are superior to synthetic groups without the instructions. Furthermore, brainstorming groups are superior to nonbrainstorming groups.

Implications. We should emphasize that these particular studies do *not* offer evidence that the group of interacting individuals is inferior to a group of individuals working separately. The products of the two types of groups are not comparable directly. In the first place, the *experimenter* combines the products of the synthetic group. Thus the comparison in the Faust experiment should be: four individuals working together with no help from Faust versus a group of four individuals working separately from each other *plus* Faust's (or his research assistant's) clerical aid in combining the lists and omitting duplicate ideas.

Data from studies on group and individual problem solving frequently reveal that one or two of the group members could have solved the problem without the aid of the rest of the group. These skilled members even may have been slowed down by the necessity of listening to the inferior contributions of other group members and of demonstrating the worth of their own ideas. Why, then, do we not assign the problem to these superior group members in the first place?

We frequently do not know which individual has the correct answer *before* the group conference. The experimenter may well know the "correct" answer to a problem before he assigns it to a group of laboratory subjects. But, if the executive knows the correct answer to a problem, then he would not need to assign it to anyone, much less a decision-making group. And, if he knows that a single expert can solve the problem, the problem often is delegated directly to the expert. It may turn out *after* the decision-making conference that a certain individual or a group of individuals (specified by hindsight) working separately could have done the job more efficiently. In order to utilize an individual or synthetic group we must know *at the start* of the decision-making process which individual(s) to choose, how the work is to be divided, and how solutions are to be recombined as a synthetic solution of separate individuals.

If the task is relatively routine, if emphasis is on quantity rather than quality, and if an administrative aide is available to combine the individual efforts, then an executive might well turn a problem over to a roster of separate individuals and an administrative assistant rather than forming them into a committee. Such an administrator would still have the task of communicating the final list of solutions to the individuals who had contributed them and then might have to persuade them that the additions from the other participants were worthwhile; but these obstacles may not be serious considerations in many situations, especially if the practice had become routine. In any event, the final group product of face-to-face groups will exclude some of the ideas and information available to each member.

PROPOSITION 2.2-B. The accuracy and quality of the final group product will be increased through the elimination of inferior individual contributions.

Dashiell (1935) staged an incident in a classroom and then had two of the students present serve as "witnesses" before a class in legal psychology. Shorthand accounts of the "testimony" were taken and each member of the class prepared a written report. Then the "jurors" from the legal class met in a group conference and produced a single unanimous report. This unanimous report was "less complete [Proposition 2.2-A] than that of any individual witness or individual juror since everyone had to agree on each fact, but clearly *more accurate* [Proposition 2.2-B] than that of any individual witness or juror" (Dashiell, 1935, pp. 1135–1136).

Omissions do not always improve the final group product. For example, Lorge, Aikman, Gilda, Spiegle, and Tuckman (1955) reported that untrained, newly formed discussion groups lost almost 80 per cent of the ideas contributed by individual members; and, as a result, 75 per cent of the individual decisions were superior to the best group decisions. Although training in staff techniques significantly improved group performance, these newly formed groups continued to omit important individual contributions from their group product.

Of course, it may be to the group's advantage to omit certain individual contributions, especially if these contributions are in error. In later propositions we shall see how this selective process in interaction works to improve the quality of the final group product. A group decision which finds a place for every individual contribution may turn out to be an unworkable conglomeration.

Utilization of information in the decision-making group. In these early propositions we made much of the differences in the amount of information available to the individual and to the group. We saw how access to an increased range of information increases the probability that the group will hit on an "obvious" solution (Proposition 2.1-B); and we shall see how this same increased range of information will increase the total man-hours of time which the group members spend working toward the solution (Proposition 2.3). Even with the extra time, groups still do not use all of the information at their disposal, and these omissions sometimes can increase the quality of the group product (Proposition 2.2).

These propositions have examined group decision-making from a rational or statistical perspective; little attention has been given to the psychology of group members as they listen to the presentation of information. Shaw (1963) examined the behavior of group members who were given access (by the experimenter) to different numbers of alternative solutions to the problem being discussed by the group. The groups were discussing human relations problems which demanded that the group reach agreement on one of several plausible solutions. These problems differ from the "eureka" problems cited earlier in which the answers are "obvious." On these problems other group members usually do not agree as soon as one member hits on the correct solution.

When compared to other group members who were given no extra solutions, Shaw found that (a) the task relevant contributions and (b) the participant ratings of contributions to the decision by the "informed members" was higher. This difference, however, *decreased* as they were given more information. The difference between the informed members and the other group members was greatest when the informed member was given two possible solutions, next greatest when given access to four solutions, and least great when given access to six alternative solutions. Are these results caused by the fact that the informed members did not make use of the information available because they were less persuasive in their presentation of the information? Although Shaw reports no quantitative data, he suggests, "from observing group processes," that the informed member "does not make use of six units of information in the same way that he does two units. With two units, he tended to mention both suggested solutions, but selected one of these to try to sell to the group. With six units, he tended to mention all six suggested solutions, but did not give the impression of being committed to one in particular" (Shaw, 1963, p. 77). It is possible that possession of the extra information caused the individual to change his role from an advocator to a provider of information. Whether or not this role change improves group productivity will depend on the critical demands of the task.

Extending the work on the behavior of an informed group member, Shaw and Penrod (1962) used a similar technique to study the impact of varying amounts of information on the quality of group solutions. The experimenters gave all participants the first paragraph of a human relations case. In some experimental conditions, a certain participant (the informed member) was given one or two additional paragraphs of the problem. Although this procedure manipulates the amount of information, it also changes the definition of the problem. Perhaps because of the fundamental nature of the information, it appears that the other group members were reluctant to accept the information presented by the informed member. Two separate experiments fail to demonstrate a significant improvement in the group solutions when a single member is given extra information. It is not enough that the information be present; it must also be presented persuasively and legitimately documented before the other group members are likely to accept it.

We shall have more to say about the influence process in later chapters. For the time being, it is sufficient to stress the fact that the availability of information does not mean it will be effectively used. The contributor may fail to support his ideas, and listeners may be skeptical. For that matter, we must not assume that increased information *always* improves the quality of the group product. We cited many studies which seem to demonstrate that the increased range of information available in a group makes the interacting group superior to the individuals working alone. These studies, however, utilized tasks which did not require extensive evaluation of the alternatives. The answers were usually "obvious" in the sense that other members are likely to agree as soon as one member hits on the correct answer. But what about the problems without a single "correct" answer? Is it not likely that group members could get so bogged down in alternatives that they never would choose a single "best" answer? There are, of course, times when no answer is better than a wrong answer. There are other times when the important task is to reach agreement or consensus on any one of a large number of equally "correct" alternative solutions. In the latter case, extra information, in the form of too many alternatives, could decrease productivity.

PROPOSITION 2.3. A group of individuals working together will usually consume more man-hours when compared to (a) an equal number of individuals working separately, and (b) a group with fewer members.

Since this proposition compares the productivity of individuals and groups, it is relevant only in cases where both individuals and groups can complete the task. If the individual is unable to solve the problem at all, then a comparison between a group and an individual is meaningless. But, for those tasks which both individuals and groups can complete, we generalize that man-hours (number of hours spent times the number of members working) will be greater for interacting groups than for synthetic groups and greater for large groups than for small groups. It should be stressed that we do not know *in advance* what problems can be solved only by groups because individuals are unable to complete the task.

Davis and Restle (1963) make this same prediction—that groups take longer than individuals—from a mathematical model which assumes that the group product results from a combination of both the correct *and incorrect* contributions of each individual member. For the experimental data they collected, their model more closely predicts group solution times than does a modified Lorge-Solomon model which assumes that the group combines only the correct individual contributions.

It should be noted that Davis and Restle used an experimental procedure in gathering their empirical data which limited the superiority of the group over its individual participants. Davis and Restle did not specify any method by which the group was to reach a group agreement: "any member was allowed to record the answer." Furthermore, group members were instructed to talk "freely among themselves" and out loud as much as possible. The first procedure means that the group must devote time getting organized; and the second may increase the tendency of a member to contribute an idea, even if he does not think the idea is particularly good. Both of these instructions may have placed the group at a disadvantage with respect to individuals.

Taylor and Faust (1952) used a modified version of the 20 questions parlor game in which the subjects had 30 questions to guess the name of an object which the experimenter (E) had in mind. E found that groups of two and four members required fewer questions and less time than single individuals to discover the correct answer. But when the experimenter multiplied the time taken to reach the solution by the number of members in each group, groups of two took significantly more *man*-hours than individuals; and groups of four took significantly more *man*-hours than groups of two to reach the correct solution.

In this case, the group considered as a whole produced solutions superior to individuals working alone (Propositions 2.1-B and 2.2-B), but the superiority was bought at the price of extra man-hours (Proposition 2.3). Although it may be true that the best group member could have solved the problem in fewer man-hours, we cannot always know which member is the "best" until after all the members have tried to develop the solution.

Implications. When the solution must be closely coordinated and a few proposals must be carefully integrated into a single answer, the decision-making group should be small in size, perhaps of four or five persons. This kind of problem is least likely to benefit from a wide range of alternatives, the elimination of random error, and the elimination of inferior proposals. The small size minimizes the problems of interpersonal organization and the lost man-hours of duplicated effort. On the other hand, should the problem require a quantitative estimate where individual errors are likely to be random (Proposition 2.1-A), the generation of an unlikely association or "obvious" solution (Proposition 2.1-B), increasing the number of members should improve the group's potential. This increased potential, however, is bought at the cost of greater man-hours (Proposition 2.3). The advantages of the group deliberation are particularly costly when the problem requires the group members to develop an elaborate pattern of interpersonal relations (Chapters Three and Five). Finally, it may be cheaper to tap the resources of many men by having them work in isolation and then delegating an administrative assistant to pool the individual efforts.

Propositions about Individual and Group Productivity:
Motivational Impacts of Working with Others

Be forewarned, the data on social motivation, social influence, and the global value of groups are ambiguous. In comparison with the propositions which follow, the earlier propositions seem well documented, relatively rigorous, and specific. In fact, it may seem at times that the evidence is too sparse to warrant a summary proposition. But, let us not forget our second purpose in this chapter—in addition to summarizing the data on individual and group comparisons, we seek to introduce the reader to some of the central social psychological issues in the process of group decision-making. We now turn, then, to a consideration of social motivation.

To this point, we have examined how a group combines individual products into a single group product. We have discovered many facts about this combination and seen how these facts can result in group products which are either superior or inferior. Now we shall turn to the ways in which an individual's motivations change as he leaves the privacy of isolation and begins to work in the presence of other individuals. The presence of other individuals will modify the means by which an individual seeks his goal *and* the reason *why* he seeks it. In fact, the presence of other individuals may modify the goal itself.

PROPOSITION 2.4.   When an individual works in the presence of other persons, a variety of social motives becomes relevant which are not evoked when an individual works alone.

Many motives important to C. Member concern his relationship to the other people who surround him. He likes to appear in a favorable light before other people, have friends, "get ahead" in the world, impress the boss, etc. When C. Member works alone, the influence of the people who ordinarily surround him is at a minimum; so the influence of the social motives is also at a minimum. Of course, many activities completed in private do have relevance to his social interaction, but the generalization probably holds that the presence of other people *increases* the relevance of social motives.

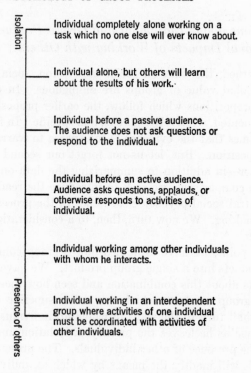

FIGURE 2.1.

Thus, when C. Member is working in a group, much more of his behavior is influenced by social motives. He may work harder to improve his prestige, or he may be more careful of his answers in order to avoid embarrassment. In other words, the presence of other persons creates *new implications* for an individual. The effect of these new implications on performance will depend on the individual's expectations of what he must do in order to receive social rewards from other participants.

As it turns out, "the presence of other individuals" is not a simple either-or variable. A junior executive, for instance, may be profoundly influenced by his *expectations* of approval from his boss even though he works behind locked doors. The continuum in Figure 2.1 suggests some possible steps in a social continuum.

The steps in Figure 2.1 are only a few of the many possible; it may be that even the order will have to be rearranged as more data come in. Figure 2.1 does illustrate, however, the fact that "the presence of other individuals" varies in degree rather than qualitatively in an either-or fashion.

PROPOSITION 2.4-A. The presence of other individuals will frequently increase individual productivity, although the effect may be temporary.

Several investigators have observed the productivity of individuals working alone and in the presence of other individuals. Subjects are not required to interact; they merely work in each other's presence. The results of these studies [5] are not entirely consistent, but the general sense of the data seems to be that the presence of other individuals will increase productivity, at least temporarily, for the simple repetitive tasks which are employed in these social facilitation studies. Proposition 2.4-A assumes that the individual believes that increased productivity will earn him social approval or otherwise satisfy social motivations. Groups in which the members have set quotas and reward new group members for lowering productivity would constitute a major exception to this proposition. Proposition 2.4-A implies the generalization: High productivity is socially rewarded in decision-making groups more often than not. This generalization may be the best we can make at the present time; but there seems little doubt that, as further data come in, the problem will turn out to be more complex.[6]

[5] Allport, 1920; Sims, 1928; Sengupta and Sinka, 1926; Mukerji, 1940. These studies are reviewed briefly in Lorge et al., 1958, pp. 352–353.
[6] For instance, Shaw (1958b) had three groups of subjects work on the same task. In one experimental condition individuals worked separately; other individuals were led to believe that they were cooperating with another subject; and the final set of individuals were led to believe that they were competing with another subject. The experiment was repeated for two kinds of tasks. Since the procedural requirements of the task were

PROPOSITION 2.4-B.   The presence of other individuals may increase the defensiveness of the individual, although the effect
may be temporary.

To be specific, C. Member may tell fewer stories related to definite personal experiences (Allport, 1924) or take longer to choose
the word which best fits a phrase (Wapner and Alper, 1952).

Wapner and Alper (1952) conducted an experiment in which
they varied, among other things, the type of audience and the
nature of the task.

*The experiment was conducted in a one-way vision observation room.
Three audience situations were used: (1) No audience. The curtains
were drawn across the one-way mirror and only the E was present in the
room with the S. (2) Unseen audience. The one-way mirror was exposed. Ss were informed of the nature of the mirror and were told that
there were people behind it who could both hear and see what was going
on in the experimental room. (3) Seen audience. The one-way vision
mirror was exposed. The illumination was equalized between the experimental and observation rooms so that the audience could see the S and
the S could see the audience (p. 222).*

*The S was required to choose which of the two words fitted the given
phrase more closely . . . Personality-oriented items were designed to
emphasize characteristics or traits of people. Neutral-oriented items,
however, had an impersonal reference, emphasizing concrete or abstract
qualities of things (p. 223).*

*Time to make a choice was longest in the presence of an unseen audience,
next in the presence of a seen audience, and shortest when there was
no audience other than the experimenter. The significant differential
effects of the audience variable occur only for the first half of the experimental session . . . Items with personality reference yielded longer
times than neutral items (p. 228).*[7]

identical for the three groups, differences in performance probably reflect
differences in social motivation. On both tasks the cooperative individuals
evidenced the greatest productivity. But the isolation condition was
superior to the competitive condition on the motor task only. There were
no differences between the isolation and competitive motivations for the
memory and reasoning task. The interpretation of these results is not
clear, but they do serve to illustrate the modifications in Proposition 4-A
which additional data will probably require.

[7] One finding was at odds with both our predictions and those of the
original authors. Some subjects were given instructions which stressed the

PROPOSITION 2.4-C. The presence of other individuals can constitute a distraction and lower productivity.

Individuals may believe that their social motives are best served by increasing their productivity, but there is no reason to argue that social motives never inhibit productivity. The presence of other individuals is likely to be particularly detrimental for tasks which require sustained attention of the individuals. The other individuals constitute stimuli which compete with the task for attention. Allport (1924) reports some decrease in productivity resulting from distraction.

In summary, we see that individuals do not have the same motivations while working in groups that they have while working alone. The presence of these motives will be important as we build a model of the decision-making conference; but few simple generalizations can be made about the impact of motivation *in general* on productivity. Social motives frequently increase productivity and defensiveness of group members; they can also produce a distraction. We shall have more to say about the impact of specific kinds of motivations in later chapters.

Propositions about Individual and Group Productivity: Social Influence

From the very first proposition in this chapter it has been implied that division of labor is possible in a group working on a common task, and now is the time to analyze the social prerequisites to such an economy. Advantageous division of labor implies that all of the members of the group (i.e., the group as a whole) can benefit from the activities and experiences of a single individual; so now we turn to an examination of social mechanisms which make such collaborative action possible.

In another context, Donald T. Campbell (1961, 1963) suggested that there are three major ways in which an individual

importance of the task and other subjects were given ego-oriented instructions. "Contrary to expectations there was some indication that time to make choice is longer for task-oriented than for ego-oriented instructions" (Wapner and Alper, 1952, p. 228).

can acquire information or learn a habit. Perhaps the most primitive way an individual can learn is through direct experience with the environment—either through physical movement or visual exploration. Second, an individual can observe other persons as they explore the environment and can learn without active investigation on his own. Finally, an individual could acquire the same information through the verbal instructions of another person. Again he learns without active investigation of his own.

If we translate Campbell's theory into the language of this chapter, we would say that there are three sources of information about the problem available to each member of the group: (1) direct personal investigation, (2) observation of another member's investigation, and (3) verbal reports of other members. In terms of the final information (or acquired behavioral disposition as Campbell would call it), *knowledge and habits gained through any of the three sources can contribute to the group product.* Here we discover the mechanism which makes intellectual division of labor possible. Although one group member must first "learn" or observe on his own, the rest of the group can assimilate the same knowledge with less effort than was involved in the original learning. In short, the verbal statements of a single group member are an important and efficient source of knowledge for other group members.

In Propositions 2.5-A, B, and C, we examine the manner in which the group utilizes the verbal reports of its members as sources of information. In separating Propositions 2.5-A from 2.5-B and 2.5-C, we are following a distinction made by Aristotle in his *Rhetoric* (Cooper, 1932) and since amply supported by experimental evidence. Proposition 2.5-A argues that individuals believe what other group members tell them because it seems to make "good sense." Proposition 2.5-A is thus concerned with content or task-centered influence. Propositions 2.5-B and 2.5-C indicate that individuals will also tend to believe what they are told because of the way in which it is said or because some particular person said it; these propositions deal with social or personal-centered influence.

PROPOSITION 2.5. The quality of the group product frequently increases when group members utilize social sources of knowledge.

PROPOSITION 2.5-A. The group is most likely to accept a member's contribution (a) when it is well supported by evidence, (b) when it is logically sound or internally consistent, and (c) when it is consistent with past experience.

With all the current publicity about the persuasibility of the "organization man" and the common man's susceptibility to propaganda and advertising, we tend to lose sight of the "logical" or factual determinants of behavior. The housewife may buy a box of soap because of an advertising campaign; but, if the soap is clearly inferior to another brand she has used recently, she is not likely to buy it again. The fact that soaps are *not* clearly different, and that there is no factual evidence or "logic" to support either soap, obscures the operation of Proposition 2.5-A in this particular illustration.

Cathcart (1953) found that when arguments were backed up with specific evidence, they produced more attitude change or "conformity" than the same arguments without the evidence. Furthermore, according to Shaw's (1963) summary, Shevitz (1955) has shown "that a group member who exclusively possesses task-related information attempts to lead more than others and has more status than other group members" (Shaw, 1963, p. 71). In summary, there is evidence that the group members with good ideas are more likely to make a contribution and that other group members are more likely to listen to them.

PROPOSITION 2.5-B. Social (or personal-centered) influence frequently causes the better alternatives to be chosen.

People are often mistaken in what they tell us; they also lie or distort facts to their own advantage. Nevertheless, we are dependent on other people for much of the information vital to our everyday life. Therefore, we must frequently choose between belief in and rejection of what people tell us. The details of the way that people decide to believe or not to believe a message have been extensively investigated by social psychologists. The literature on attitude change or persuasion is already impressive and is rapidly growing.

Campbell (1961) prepared a review of much of this literature which he organizes about the "multiple modes of knowing" scheme cited earlier. Clearly C. Member cannot learn from observation or verbal description unless he places some faith in the person he observes. An executive is frequently faced with conflicts among these different modes of knowing: personal experience, vicarious observation of another's exploration, and verbal reports from others. For instance, he knows from past experience that a product similar to a proposed new line did not sell. However, his advisers assure him that the market is now ready for the new commodity. *When he weighs the advice of his advisers and forms his decision on the basis of this social mode of learning, we say he has conformed.* Note that we do *not* use the word conformity in a way that implies conformity is necessarily undesirable. Any individual who has heeded the wise advice of an expert consultant or has taken his subordinate's word for production figures without personally checking has—to that extent —conformed.

It is a good decision-maker who "recognizes the fallibility of each mode of knowing and the gain in predictive certainty achieved through triangulation through separate modes" (Campbell, 1959, p. 108). In other words, the wise conference participant will recognize that even he can be wrong and will weigh the opinions and experiences of others as he makes his decision. On the other hand, C. Member may make an even greater mistake when he ignores his individual experience completely, conforms totally, and bases his decision *entirely* on social sources of information. It is our general theme, however, that many of the processes in conformity make for more "rational" decisions than could be made by the individual alone. We shall sample a few of Campbell's (1961) propositions (omitting the evidence) to illustrate the kind of data which would support Proposition 2.5-B.

"The more competent the person has been in learning, problem solving, generating valid" (p. 115) solutions individually, the less he will weigh social sources of knowledge. In other words, competent people are least dependent on social sources of knowledge. "Intelligent, strong, successful, high status persons will induce more conformity than low status ones . . ." (p. 119). Persons who have demonstrated their capability in the past will have the most influence. "The clearer and more distinct the perceptual situation . . . the less conformity is likely to occur . . ." (p. 117) —that is, the more obvious the facts and the stronger the knowledge learned individually, the less the importance of social sources of knowledge. "The prestige generalization is greater the more similar to the present situation were the past rewarded acts of the model . . ." (p. 119). In other words, an expert will be most persuasive in his special area of competence.

PROPOSITION 2.5-C. The social weighting given to the majority opinion (i.e., conformity) frequently causes the better alternatives to be chosen.

There are many situations in which the majority is more likely to be correct than the minority, and the decision-making conference is frequently such a case. When men of approximately equal ability gather together to solve a problem, the majority opinion has the greatest probability of success. The general tendency to weigh the majority opinion heavily (Asch, 1956), then, will frequently lead to the selection of the best alternative.

Qualifications for proposition 2.5. We have asserted that, for the most part, conformity and social learning improve the quality of the group decision; but this is a weak generalization. Overdependence on the thinking of the "other guy" can be worse than conferences where no one listens to anyone else. Proposition 2.5 clearly implies that social sources are useful origins of information. Although the assumption is generally true, it is not at all difficult to think of exceptions (e.g., the Asch, 1956, experiments in which the other group members were hired by the experimenter to "lie").

There are a number of circumstances where social influence is likely to lower the quality of a group product. (1) An expert may continue to receive the respect of an authority even though the topic is outside his own area of specialization. (2) A group member may conform merely for social approval.   (3) Conformity and agreement can set in so soon so that all opinions are not considered.   (4) Finally, group members can become so much in the habit of depending on other persons for knowledge and information that they cannot make contributions on their own.

Useful as social knowledge may be, it must be used intelligently. It may be that we place too much emphasis on getting along with others and not enough on the content of communication in our culture.   A training program for conference participants should probably stress the "what is said" rather than the "who said it" in decision-making; but we must not let the possible misuse of social influence obscure the constructive possibilities in social learning.

INTERACTION IN THE FACE-TO-FACE GROUP AND "RISK-TAKING" BEHAVIOR

One of the central issues in the debate between the devout defenders of group decision-making and the equally religious critics concerns the impact of group experience on the "conservatism" or "risk-taking" behavior of group members.   Whyte's (1956) *The Organization Man* argues that the conformity pressures in committees produce overly conservative and mediocre decisions. Osborne (1957), on the other hand, asserts that the application of his "brain storming" techniques in groups stimulates bold and radical innovations.

There are several experiments which bear on this controversy. A series of experiments (Stonner, 1961; Marquis, 1962; Wallach, Kogan, and Bem, 1962) have attacked the problem by means of a set of pencil and paper problems developed by Wallach and Kogan (1959) to measure propensities for risk taking.   These studies, which are reviewed below, report that both unanimous group decisions and the final private responses following group interaction indicate more risk taking than the initial private answers.   Unfortunately, the impressive regularity of these results is restricted to studies which use the Wallach-Kogan test as a measure of risk taking.   Several studies, using other measures, contradict this generalization; Wallach et al. (1962) report two studies (Lonegran and McClintock, 1961; Hunt and Rowe, 1960) that failed to find any difference between group and individual conditions and one study (Atthowe, 1961) that found that groups of two manifested *less* risk taking than single individuals. Lonegran and McClintock used a betting situation involving monetary gain or loss as a measure of risk taking, and Hunt and Rowe studied riskiness of investment decisions. Atthowe's experiment is examined in more detail:

The experimental task required subjects to choose the better of two alternative wagers. Each wager contained two possible monetary outcomes; the probability of each outcome was .5 and was assumed to be dependent upon the roll of an "unbiased" die. To reduce the immediate effects of reinforcement, no money was dispensed during the game. Furthermore, subjects were never told whether their choices were correct or not. The instruction emphasized the reasoning nature of the task. The wagers were said to be problems taken from the mathematical reasoning section of an advanced intelligence test and arranged as wagers. Partners were required to reach agreement before the dyadic decision could be specified. . . . The typical strategy employed by the dyads in making decisions was one of minimizing their maximum possible loss. Dyadic decisions were significantly more conservative than extravagant ($p \leqq .05$) (Atthowe, 1961, pp. 115–117).

In contrast to the "no difference" findings from the first two studies and the conservative strategies of Atthowe's two-man groups, studies using the Wallach-Kogan pencil and paper test report an array of replications over a wide range of subject populations. In the general procedure, individuals first answer the questions in private. Two typical items are summarized by Wallach et al.:

"1. An electrical engineer may stick with his present job at a modest but adequate salary, or may take a new job offering considerably more money but no long term security.

"2. A man with a severe heart ailment must seriously curtail his customary way of life if he does not undergo a delicate medical operation which might cure him completely or might prove fatal" (Wallach et al., p. 77). After answering these questions individually, subjects are then formed into groups and make a "group decision" for each problem. Finally, the participants again indicate their personal opinions privately. Both group decisions and the private opinions following group interaction reflect more

44 SOCIAL PSYCHOLOGY OF GROUP PROCESSES

"risk taking" than the initial private questionnaire. This phenomenon has been demonstrated for graduate students in industrial administration at M.I.T. (Stonner), summer school undergraduates at the University of Colorado (Wallach et al.), and mature executives in an executive training program (Marquis). Wallach et al. further find that a control group did not change scores from the first to the second administration when the second testing did not follow group discussion.

Marquis discusses a number of mechanisms which might account for the increased risk taking as a result of group interaction. One interpretation suggests that the individual members shift responsibility to the group. "In real life situations problems are often referred to committees for decision when the responsible person is unwilling to assume the risks involved in making the decision himself. Following this line of thought one might expect that people would be willing to agree to a group decision that was more risky than they would personally be willing to make. The group process would be a diffusion or spreading of the responsibility, resulting in an increased tendency to risk taking" (Marquis, 1962). In order to test this hypothesis, Marquis made one change in the general procedure described above. The member whose risk-taking score was closest to the middle of each group was chosen as a leader. "Instructions emphasized the authority and the responsibility of the designated leader, who was told that he should conduct the discussion however he desired; that he should make his own personal decision on each problem; and that he should return to the class prepared to defend his decision against leaders of other groups and in front of the class and the instructor" (Marquis, 1962). Both (a) the leaders and (b) the other group participants indicated a greater propensity for risk taking on the questionnaire administered after the group session. Since the responsibility was clearly placed on the leader and not on the group, these findings led us to reject the notion that the increased risk taking is produced by a shift in responsibility to the group.

Although the mechanisms are as yet unclear, several findings led us to include this material under social influence. In the first place, Wallach et al. report a significant correlation between initial risk-taking scores and participant ratings of influence.

This may mean that persons with initially high risk-taking scores were more influential in the group discussion than conservative members, either because risk-taking positions are easier to defend or because risk takers are a persuasive kind of people. Although leaders in Marquis' experiment were chosen to be in the middle of the group *on the average*, there were some particular items in the test where the other members of the group scored somewhat higher or somewhat lower than the leader. Marquis constructed a score which represented the difference between the initial position of the leader and the average initial position of the other group members. The correlation between this measure and the leader's change in risk taking was .73, which was just about as high as could be expected considering the nature of the measures. As Marquis points out, this correlation does not explain why the leaders manifested a general increase in risk taking; the rest of the members were more conservative than the leader half of the time and less conservative the other half. If this influence process were the only factor operating, the changes in the two directions should cancel out and leave no *average* change over all items. But, this high correlation does demonstrate that group members and designated leaders are strongly influenced by the opinions of their fellows. This influence, coupled with the persuasiveness of high risk takers, would provide one possible explanation for the increase in average propensity for risk taking.

In summary, the studies working with the Wallach-Kogan opinion scales report an impressive regularity in the tendency for group decisions and post-discussion individual decisions to move in the direction of more risk taking. This result is not confirmed, however, by at least three other experimenters using other measures of risk taking. For this reason, the evidence was reviewed, but no formal proposition has been offered.

A Summary Proposition

PROPOSITION 2.6. Group members may collectively achieve more than the most superior members are capable of achieving alone.

This proposition summarizes the factors involved in the first five. The increased production of a face-to-face decision-making conference may be due to division of labor and constructive overlap

(Proposition 2.1), the selectivity (Proposition 2.2), the investment of extra man-hours (Proposition 2.3), social motivation (Proposition 2.4), or social influence (Proposition 2.5). For many tasks the superiority of teamwork is immediately apparent. For example, it would be impossible for a single individual to open a vault door which requires two persons to simultaneously turn two keys sixty feet apart.

Barnlund (1959) has demonstrated that the group can surpass its most capable member in a less obvious case. On the first day of a college course in group discussion, Barnlund administered the "Recognition of Valid Conclusions" test to the freshmen students. The problem is to select the conclusion which follows logically from the premises. According to Barnlund, "The arguments cover a wide range of subjects and are phrased deliberately to complicate the decision for the reader; that is, statements involve atheists, Communists, Republicans, college professors, and other terms likely to prejudice judgment" (p. 56).

Eight or nine weeks later, the students were formed into groups of approximately equal ability on the first test score. Experimental groups were then given an alternate form of the same test and told to reach a group decision on each of the 30 problems. Control students took the test individually as before. *The interacting groups performed significantly better than their superior members had performed on the previous form of the test* ($p < .01$). The interacting group also performed better than a synthetic group which was formed by combining individual scores.[8]

Barnlund thus demonstrates that groups can achieve efficiency

---

[8] Although the discussion course undoubtedly contained some instruction on reasoning, the fact that the control students did not score significantly better on the second administration of the test suggests that it was the group versus individual difference and not the early-in course versus late-in course difference which caused the increase in final scores.

The synthetic group was created by crediting the group with the correct decision if a majority of the "members" were correct. Barnlund does not report scores for groups synthesized by crediting the group with the correct answer if *any* "member" was correct—the procedure used to create the synthetic groups discussed under Proposition 2.2-A.

beyond the ability of their most capable member on a complex task. Other experimenters have also found that not all of the group superiority could be attributed to the pooling of individual products (Thorndike, 1938b; Timmons, 1939, 1942).

It will be useful to review the previous propositions by comparing them with the reasons for group superiority listed by Barnlund.

1. "Membership in the experimental groups produced a higher level of interest in the successful completion of the task" (p. 58). This translates immediately to the more general proposition on social motivation (2.4-A).

2. "Membership in the experimental groups had an inhibiting as well as facilitating effect. Knowledge that one's opinions were to be shared publicly made group members more cautious and deliberate in their own thinking" (p. 58). This is a point similar to Proposition 2.4-B which suggests that the presence of other individuals may increase the defensiveness of the individual, and 2.2-B which describes the selectivity of group interaction. On Barnlund's task the greater hesitation found by Wapner and Alper (1952) apparently increased the accuracy (Proposition 2.2-B) of the individual contribution although it also may have decreased the total number of suggestions (Proposition 2.2-A).

3. "Groups had greater critical resources than did individuals working alone. In spite of the uniform level of ability, group members saw different issues and a larger number of issues than a single person working alone" (p. 58). The critical demands of Barnlund's task apparently increase the gain from a duplication of effort and division of labor (Proposition 2.1-B) and a greater accuracy from selection (2.2-B).

4. "A more objective view of the problem resulted from competition between the private prejudices of group members" (p. 58). From the perspective of our propositions, this fourth point is quite similar to Barnlund's third. Both stress the greater accuracy which results from selection (2.2-B).

❧ ❧ ❧

INTERACTION IN FACE-TO-FACE CONFERENCES AND CHANGES IN (1) THE MOTIVATION, (2) THE KNOWLEDGE, AND (3) THE PERSONALITY OF THE GROUP MEMBERS

It is not the purpose of this particular book to evaluate the place of group interaction in democracy, democratic education, therapy, or the day-to-day life of the common man. Although we have limited ourselves to the use of the small group decision-making process, the implications of group deliberation extend far beyond the particular task or problem at hand.

The methodology of most global studies which portend to demonstrate the general superiority—or inferiority—of group interaction can be legitimately criticized, and, for this reason, we do not offer a formal proposition. Nevertheless, the value of group interaction for persuasion and information transmission has received appreciable empirical support. Early studies by Lewin (summarized in Lewin, 1953) suggested that group discussion was an effective method of social change. An example by Coch and French (1948) will serve to illustrate the dramatic effects which can be produced in "real-life" situations.

The experiment took place in a pajama factory in Marion, Virginia. Workers were paid by an incentive plan which was based on standard production rates determined by time and motion studies. Even though the company relations in the community were generally good, workers seemed to react strongly against a shift from one job to another within the factory. Productivity seldom reached the same level on the new job that had been achieved on the old one; and new employees adapted to job changes much faster than experienced employees in spite of the fact that time and motion studies found little evidence of direct physical conflict between the two jobs. Finally, a shift of jobs was associated with a great deal of antagonism toward management and a high rate of resignations.

Within this context, the experimenters instituted three methods of shifting jobs: (1) no participation, (2) participation through representation, and (3) total participation.

The [no-participation] control groups of hand pressers went through the usual factory routine when they were changed. The production department modified the job, and the new piece rate was set. A group meeting was then held in which the control group was told that the change was necessary because of competitive conditions, and that a new piece rate had been set . . . (p. 521).

[For the "participation-through-representation" group the need for change was presented as dramatically as possible. A general plan for improving the job methods was presented which would involve the participation of a selected few of the group members. The representatives then remained and worked out the details for the new job.] The new job and piece rates were presented at a second group meeting to all the operators involved. The "special" operators served to train the other operators on the new job (p. 521).

[The total participation] . . . groups went through much the same kind of meetings. The groups were smaller . . . , and a more intimate atmosphere was established. The need for a change was once again made dramatically clear. The same general plan was presented by management. However, since the groups were small, all operators were chosen as "special" operators; that is, all operators were to participate directly in the designing of the new jobs, and all operators would be studied by the time-study man (Coch and French, 1948, p. 521).

Even though none of the groups came to any formal decision, the results were dramatic. Participation groups learned at significantly higher rates, expressed much less antagonism to management, and had lower rates of resignation. The total participation group was highest, the "participation-through-representation" next, and the no-participation group lowest. Some time later the group which had been changed by the no-participation method was again changed to a third job by the total participation method. The results were similar to those of the original total participation group; total participation increased ease of job changes.

It is difficult to state analytically the reasons for these results. Coch and French present some evidence to suggest that the group set informal standards to regulate production after the job shift. Presumably the increased rate of production might be caused by higher standards set by the participation group. The results could have been caused by the "Hawthorne" effect (Roethlisberger and Dickson, 1939), which suggests that any sort of attention or special study will increase productivity. Whatever the cause, something associated with group interaction apparently produced profound effects.

Two replications of the Coch and French study are in the literature. French, Ross, Kirby, Nelson, and Smyth (1958) report that the participation techniques were successfully applied to a series of much more extensive changes within the same company.

A study quite similar to the original one by Coch and French (1948) was conducted in a Norwegian factory by French, Israel, and Ås (1960); and several factors are suggested by this study which limit the generality of the original study. French et al. suggest that:

Increased participation (and the opportunity to participate) would affect production, labor relations, and job satisfaction only to the extent that four conditioning variables were present: (a) the decisions were important, (b) the content of the decisions was relevant to the dependent variable (production, labor relations, or job satisfaction), (c) the participation was considered legitimate, (d) there was no resistance to change (i.e., no negative reaction to the methods of managing the change) (French et al., p. 17).

French et al. report that there was no difference between the experimental and control groups on production, perhaps because these conditions were not met. The data from the second study do reveal, however, that—within the limitations listed above—participation did increase job satisfaction and improve labor relations. Our science is not yet at the stage where we can be very specific about the values of group interaction and the conditions where these values are most likely to be realized. Nevertheless, studies similar to Coch and French's alert us to the fact that group interaction can have implications far beyond that of the immediate group task.

Intervening mechanisms. It may be that group discussion in the Coch and French study increased productivity by influencing the goals which an individual sets for himself. Horwitz (1954) designed an experiment in which the experimenter announced a "decision." Although the decision actually was made and announced by the experimenter, each group member thought it had been made through a group vote. The evidence suggests that individuals accepted these "group decisions" as personal goals.

Maier (1955) reports an unpublished study by Bavelas on goal setting in a field situation:

A coordinating group of workers held three brief weekly meetings with the psychologist in the plant for the purpose of deciding on a definite production which they could attain within a certain time. The goal decided on in the first meeting was to get production up to 84 units per hour within five days. Up to this time, 60 units were standard and 75 was supposed to be the ceiling. Nevertheless, the goal was reached.
. . .

In order to determine whether the increase in production was caused by the group decision or some other factors associated with the group meeting, two other working teams held interviews with the psychologist. They received the same attention and friendly encouragement, but no production goal was decided on. . . . There is no evidence to indicate that production was favorably influenced by holding meetings when no group decision was made (Maier, 1955, p. 151).

Pro and con evidence from other studies. It should be stressed that the evidence does not unequivocally imply that group discussion produces more attitude change or superior learning. In fact the results are quite ambiguous and may depend entirely on the task and the nature of the group (see Lorge et al., 1958, especially pp. 348–352, pp. 366–377; and Barnlund and Haiman, 1960, especially pp. 323–345). Furthermore, even when "group discussion" does prove to be superior on a particular task, it is not clear what aspect of the discussion is responsible for the effect. These studies have been cited merely to illustrate some of the far-reaching effects which group discussion *can* have for the participants.

Robinson (1941) found that students who had studied material relevant to social issues *and* participated in various forms of group discussion changed their attitudes significantly more than individuals who had studied the material without the discussion.

Radke and Klisurich (1947) compared group discussion and individual conferences as a means of increasing the use mothers made of orange juice and cod-liver oil in their baby's diets. Members of the discussion groups indicated a greater use of cod-liver oil on the follow-up tests two and four weeks later.

After some introductory work, Thie (1925) divided her elective English class into sections approximately equal in ability. Both sections were given the same assignments, but the methods of recitation differed. In the "group" condition, the students sat in small groups to read their homework. The other members of each group criticized the recitation and then "each group had the privilege of selecting its star, or best story teller. The one honored in this way was assigned a new and very interesting story which he might tell . . . to the entire class" (p. 135).

"In the class using the regular method . . . instead of telling the stories in groups, each child came to the front of the room, told his story to the entire class, and received the criticism and help of the entire class" (p. 136). Note that the regular recitation is quite similar to the group condition; it differs only in that (*a*) the size of the group was larger, and (*b*) there were no "star" rewards. The students in the group conditions learned appreciably more, but the ambiguity of the manipulations makes interpretation difficult.

On the other hand, several studies fail to find a superiority for the "group" methods. Spence (1928) and Asch (1951) found that the group discussion conditions were significantly *lower* than control groups when learning factual materials. Guetzkow, Kelley, and McKeachie (1954) found no difference in group versus individual tutorial teaching methods. Gurnee (1937) found that individuals were unable to perform a task they had mastered as a group. Tomeković (1962) reports that a persuasive speech explaining work instructions to school children increased performance on an arithmetic task; but a less competitive speech combined with group discussion and group decisions on the value of the same issues covered in the persuasive speech did *not* increase performance.

CHAPTER SUMMARY

There are three major factors which differentiate the productivity of an individual working alone from the productivity of that same individual working in a face-to-face decision-making group; resources, social motivation, and social influence.

Resources. The group will have access to more extensive resources than an individual member. Depending on the nature of the task and the effectiveness of the group's interpersonal relations, these extra resources will either inhibit productivity or be utilized to produce an assembly effect bonus. The most crucial feature of the task is the extent to which it lends itself to a division of labor. A task so structured that divisions of labor are impossible makes it difficult for the group to utilize its potentially greater resources.

Group products will frequently be superior because the pooling of individual judgments eliminates random error. This aspect of group productivity is purely statistical and is not dependent on group interacton in a face-to-face conference, although it does occur in group deliberation. The greater potential resources of a collection of individuals mean that the group is more likely to discover an alternative than a single individual. In other words, there is a greater probability that one of several individuals will "come up" with the alternative than that any given individual would "come up" with it working alone. But, the group does not utilize all the information at its command. The process of group deliberation is selective, and the final group product will contain fewer alternatives than would have been generated by all the group members working separately. As a generalization, this selectivity often improves the quality of the group product. These advantages of group deliberation are bought at a price; a group of individuals working together will consume more man-hours when compared to (a) an equal number of individuals working separately, and (b) a group with fewer members.

Social motivation. The presence of other people in the face-to-face decision-making conference creates new motivational implications for each group member. Many of the goals and rewards which an individual values are available only when he is in the presence of other people. An individual working in the presence of other people will be striving for goals and rewards which are irrelevant when he works in isolation. If we generalize that, more often than not, high productivity is rewarded by other group members, then we can generalize that the presence of other persons will increase productivity. However, these same fellow members can also increase defensiveness and create a distraction.

Social influence. Once one group member has gone to the effort to learn information or acquire a skill through individual trial and error, other group members can benefit from the efforts of their fellow. Several generalizations can be made about the way in which group members utilize their fellows as sources of information. A contribution is most likely to be accepted if it is (a) well supported by evidence, (b) logically sound and internally consistent, (c) and consistent with past experience. A group member is most likely to accept social influence in areas of his own ignorance, and he is most likely to be influenced by an expert on the subject at hand. Generally speaking, this kind of social influence improves the quality of the group product. Similarly, a weighting of the majority opinion will increase the quality of the group product in many circumstances. The processes of social influence may *decrease* the quality of the group product if used unintelligently. In particular, social influence may decrease effectiveness when: (1) an expert continues to be influential outside his own areas of expert knowledge; (2) a group member conforms in order to buy social approval; (3) conformity and agreement set in so quickly that the full resources of the group are not brought to bear; and (4) group members become accustomed to depending on others and do not think and learn on their own.

Conclusion. The end result of all these processes is that the group members may achieve collectively more than the most superior members could achieve alone. Furthermore, while the evidence is not methodologically sophisticated enough to identify the specific mechanisms, the data strongly indicate that face-to-face groups have profound impacts on the motivations, knowledge, and personalities of the participants.

LIST OF PROPOSITIONS

PROPOSITION 2.1. When several individuals work collectively on a single task their activities will (a) overlap and/or (b) make a division of labor possible.

PROPOSITION 2.1-A. For tasks involving random error, combining several individual estimates or solutions into a single group product will increase accuracy.

PROPOSITION 2.1-B. For tasks which involve creating ideas or remembering information, there is a greater probability that one of several persons will produce the information than that a single individual will produce it by himself.

PROPOSITION 2.1-C. Groups will be efficient when the critical demands of the task emphasize the gain (a) from a duplication of effort and/or (b) from the division of labor.

PROPOSITION 2.2. When several individuals are limited to a single product, it will be selected from available ideas and information.

PROPOSITION 2.2-A. The final group product will exclude some of the ideas and information potentially available to each member.

PROPOSITION 2.2-B. The accuracy and quality of the final group product will be increased through the elimination of inferior individual contributions.

PROPOSITION 2.3. A group of individuals working together will usually consume more man-hours when compared to (a) an equal number of individuals working separately, and (b) a group with fewer members.

PROPOSITION 2.4. When an individual works in the presence of other persons, a variety of social motives becomes relevant which are not evoked when an individual works alone.

PROPOSITION 2.4-A. The presence of other individuals will frequently increase individual productivity, although the effect may be temporary.

PROPOSITION 2.4-B. The presence of other individuals may increase the defensiveness of the individual, although the effect may be temporary.

PROPOSITION 2.4-C. The presence of other individuals can constitute a distraction and lower productivity.

PROPOSITION 2.5. The quality of the group product frequently increases when group members utilize social sources of knowledge.

PROPOSITION 2.5-A. The group is most likely to accept a member's contribution (a) when it is well supported by evidence, (b) when it is logically sound or internally consistent, and (c) when it is consistent with past experience.

PROPOSITION 2.5-B. Social (or personal-centered) influence frequently causes the better alternatives to be chosen.

PROPOSITION 2.5-C. The social weighting given to the majority opinion (i.e., conformity) frequently causes the better alternatives to be chosen.

PROPOSITION 2.6. Group members may collectively achieve more than the most superior members are capable of achieving alone.

CHAPTER THREE

Group productivity: Interpersonal relations and the task

We have tried to let the empirical "facts" determine both the over-all organization and the specific propositions of this book. A primary purpose of the propositions of Chapter Two was to summarize and organize the experimental comparisons of the group and its individual members.

But we aspire to more than a mere collection of isolated experimental findings; hopefully, it will be possible to develop some more general notions which stress consistencies among the isolated findings and help extend each insight to situations different from those which were specifically investigated. To this end, we shall work toward a more general model of group interaction in the next two chapters. It is a model which has seemed to increase the meaningfulness of the data already reported and the data yet to come in later chapters.

The reader must be constantly aware of the way in which our model builds on the myriad of separate insights provided by each scientific investigation of the small group. Our model is only one step in the cumulative wisdom of science in which each scientist can build on the work of his predecessors. The reader is invited to participate with us in the construction of this model and to constantly evaluate it as a summary and integration of the empirical data which are reviewed in this volume and to revise it in the light of the flow of scientific evidence which will continue after this work goes to press.

Chapter Two introduced us to some of the bare facts of social interaction. But at least four more or less fundamental insights into the nature of social interaction emerged from the morass of fact and detail. In Chapter Two we focused on comparisons between the group and a single individual; so these insights were not conceptualized in a way most useful for comparisons between two different groups. It will be useful to reorganize the material as it will be used throughout the rest of the book—from a perspective which contrasts two different groups rather than the group and a single individual in it.

1. In the first place, the performance of a group is highly dependent on its task environment. Social philosophers have traditionally asked, "Is the group superior to its individual members?," but the data have compelled us to reformulate that question. It seems more profitable to ask, "On what kinds of tasks and in what environments will the group perform better than its individual members working separately?" The group differs from a collection of individuals working separately in several ways. For instance, the interacting group will have a wider range of information and a greater critical facility. These factors can produce either the efficiency of division of labor or the wasted effort of duplication. The outcome depends on the nature of the task on which the group is working.

2. In the second place, an individual participant is profoundly influenced by the other individuals in the group (i.e., his interpersonal environment). The experience of interacting with (or merely being in the presence of) other human beings strongly affects the behavior of each individual. As we have seen, the presence of other individuals may either increase task motivation or increase defensiveness. These findings only illustrate the impact of the interpersonal environment on an individual. Furthermore, the experiences in an interpersonal environment appear capable of producing relatively permanent changes in personality and behavior.

3. A third insight derived from the data reported in Chapter Two is that the performance of an interacting group depends on its ability to pattern and integrate the potential skills of its physically segmented group members. The relationship among the

group members may allow the group to accomplish tasks beyond the ability of the most capable group member. The productivity of a group is frequently determined by the ability of each individual member to relate himself to the other group members as well as by his task abilities. The way in which group members relate to each other (organize or structure the group) can produce either the efficiency of division of labor or the wasted effort of distraction.

4. A fourth important insight gained from the data in Chapter Two is that group productivity can be divided into many separate components. The final group product will be partly produced by the segmented efforts of the separate group members. Many "group" products could have been produced by a single individual working alone. Other parts of the final group product could be generated if some clerical worker combines the products of the individuals who had worked in separate offices. It is also possible that the group product may contain parts that even the best group member could never have achieved working alone and which could not have been created by a simple combination of individual efforts. This latter part of group productivity is called the "assembly effect." *An assembly effect occurs when the group is able to achieve collectively something which could not have been achieved by any member working alone or by a combination of individual efforts.* The assembly effect bonus is productivity which exceeds the potential of the most capable member and also exceeds the sum of the efforts of the group members working separately.[1] When we compare the productivity of two groups we shall continue to distinguish between (a) the goals which are reached through the sum of individual efforts and (b) the assem-

---

[1] Rosenberg, Erlick, and Berkowitz (1955) use the term "assembly effect" in a similar, but more restricted sense. We use assembly effect to mean an increase in productivity when individuals form *any* group. Rosenberg et al. use the term to mean differences in productivity due to the particular patterns of individual skills, traits, etc., in a specific group. In other words, we compare the productivity of individuals and groups, while Rosenberg et al. compare the contribution which the same individual might make in several different groups.

bly effect—the goals which the group can achieve only through cooperative and interdependent effort.

Previously, we inquired into the nature of the group by analyzing the contributions of each separate individual. Now we focus on the group as a whole, and we shall compare one group with another. We shall see that many of the factors which can make the *group* more effective than its *individual participants* are the same factors which will make one *group* more effective than another *group*.

Figure 3.1 is the first building block in our working model of group structure and productivity, and it incorporates the four insights gained in Chapter Two. The task environment and the social environment are included as two of the major variables influencing group productivity. Group productivity depends on (*a*) individual task efforts and (*b*) the way in which group members respond to each other. The fourth point is incorporated in Dia-

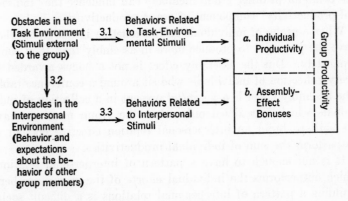

FIGURE 3.1. Task environment and interpersonal stimuli as factors in group productivity.

Summary of Propositions

3.1 Obstacles originating in the task environment directly inhibit the productivity of individual members.

3.2 The task environment creates interpersonal obstacles which inhibit both (*a*) individual productivity and (*b*) assembly effect bonuses.

3.3 Interpersonal obstacles originating in the behavior of other group members inhibit (*a*) individual productivity and (*b*) assembly effects.

gram 3.1 since group productivity is split into two parts: (*a*) the sum of individual productivities, and (*b*) the assembly effect bonus.

When each group member focuses only on the immediate requirements of the task at hand, the group is nothing more than a collection of individuals. So long as they focus only on the task environment, it makes no difference if they are seated around a conference table or seated in individual offices in separate towns. Even though the group is located physically in one place, the "group" productivity is composed of the sum of the individual efforts. In Figure 3.1, this fact is represented by the single arrow from the behaviors stimulated by the task environment. Behaviors which are stimulated *only* by the task environment cannot generate an assembly effect bonus.

The presence of other group members can influence the productivity of a single individual even though he is working independently. This fact is represented by arrow *a* which indicates that the behavior of other group members can influence the "individual productivity" component of group productivity.

When a group of individuals gather together into a group, they have the potential to produce more in assembly than they could separately. But the assembly effect is not a bonus awarded to every collection of individuals who sit around a conference table. The assembly effect is a *potential* present in a collection of individuals which is realized only when the group members have the skill to build an interpersonal relation effective enough to outperform the sum of individual productivities.

It is not enough to have a pattern of interpersonal relations which outperforms the individual efforts of the group members. Building a pattern of interpersonal relations is a difficult social task. Members must spend time developing interpersonal relationships which they could have spent working in the task. The resultant interpersonal pattern must be so good that it exceeds the sum of individual efforts *and also* makes up for the lost time it takes to build and maintain the interpersonal organization. It is not enough for the new techniques to do the job better than the "old way"; the savings must be great enough to offset the cost of developing the new techniques.

Figure 3.1 illustrates one of the "costs of conversion." According to Proposition 3.2, obstacles in the task environment make demands which create interpersonal obstacles. Certain restrictions in the channels of communication among group members, for instance, may demand that certain patterns of communication among the group members be developed. An individual can no longer attend only to the task environment; now he must concern himself with the communication behavior of other group members. Building and maintaining these interpersonal relations will be one of the "costs of conversion" from a collection of individual efforts to an organized group effort.

Proposition 3.3 indicates another "cost of conversion" in the development of interpersonal organization. While group members are responding only to stimuli in the task environment, there are no competing responses evoked by the behavior of other group members. The behavior of other group members may be irrelevant because the members are physically separated or because group members ignore each other. Although the group members may be passing up a potential assembly effect bonus, they are not distracted from their individual work. Proposition 3.3 and the whole of Chapter Five discuss distractions and obstacles in the social environment which can inhibit individual productivity.

In summary, we are separating two aspects of the "cost of conversion" from task-environmental behaviors (which are stimulated by the environment external to the group) to interpersonal behaviors (which are stimulated by the other group members). First, we stress how the group must build and maintain interpersonal relations effective enough to outproduce individual workers (Proposition 3.2). Secondly, we stress problems which are created because a group member must divide his attention between the task environment and the social environment (Proposition 3.3).

PROPOSITION 3.1. Obstacles originating in the task environment directly inhibit the productivity of individual members.

By and large, difficult tasks lower the productivity. "Obvious" as this statement may seem, it does need qualification. Although an easy task may be easy to perform, the group members may have little motivation to complete it. For example, Pepinsky, Pepinsky, and Pavlik (1960) found higher productivity with a complex task. They state, "An increase in task complexity does have a positive motivational effect through maintaining interest in the performance of repetitive operations. This interpertation is supported by the statements of the Ss independent of their measured team performance" (p. 37).

PROPOSITION 3.2. The task environment creates interpersonal obstacles which inhibit both (a) individual productivity and (b) assembly effect bonuses.

The potential ability of individuals to organize into an interacting group with division of labor is both an asset and a liability. Organization can produce a group which is more efficient than its most capable member, but the problems of interpersonal relations can also absorb so much time and effort that the assembled group members accomplish less together than they would working alone.

There is some evidence that group participants can develop effective interpersonal relations even within relatively short laboratory sessions. Bales and Strodtbeck (1951) report relatively stable "phases in group problem solving" for laboratory discussions of human relations problems. This suggests that the conference participants achieved an implicit agreement on the patterning of their interaction.

Pryer and Bass (1959) report an intriguing experiment which probably represents the development of interpersonal relations among the group members. Participants were asked to rank sets of ten cities with respect to population, first privately and then as a group after three minutes of group discussion. Thirteen of the groups were given the correct ranking of the cities following each trial and thirteen groups were given no feedback. The feedback conditions were significantly more accurate in their group rankings, but *not* more accurate in the initial private rankings of individual group members. This latter finding suggests that the authors were successful in their efforts to find a task where the feedback would not improve the task skills of the individual group members, but the group was able to develop interpersonal relations which produced an assembly effect bonus. Although it is possible that the superior decisions in the feedback condition reflect a higher motivation, it seems likely that the feedback allowed the group to develop more effective interpersonal relations, even though feedback on one trial was not of use for the specific problem on the next trial. Pryer and Bass suggest that the feedback groups may have learned one attack on the problem which was more effective than another approach for working on the task. Or the group may have learned that one or two members were more accurate and these members then had more influence on the group rankings (using social sources of knowledge, Proposition 2.5 in Chapter Two).

Interpersonal relations in communication nets. One way in which the critical demands of the task or environment have been used to vary the difficulty of interpersonal obstacles to group productivity is the modification of the Bavelas (1950) communication net reported by Guetzkow and his associates (Guetzkow and Simon, 1955; Guetzkow and Dill, 1957; Guetzkow, 1960). In these experiments, the Ss are isolated in separate, but adjoining, stalls so that it is possible to control the potential channels of communication by opening or closing the slots between the stalls. All the communications are written and coded as to sender and receiver; so the experimenter has an independent measure of the patterns of communication among the group members and the task performance. The three nets used by Guetzkow are diagrammed below:

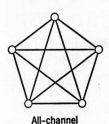
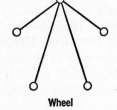
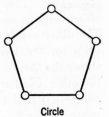

All-channel   Wheel   Circle

The task was identical to that used by Leavitt (1951): each of the five Ss had five out of six standard pieces of information;

their task on a given trial was to determine which piece was held in common by all five Ss and then to identify this common piece for the experimenter. We can call this task a *task-environmental obstacle* since the stimulus for the problem is a physical event external to the group (the five pieces) and not another group member. In order to solve the problem, however, it is necessary to make some arrangements for transmitting information; we can call this an *interpersonal obstacle* because the immediate stimuli of the difficulty are events in the behavior of other group members.

Efforts to solve these two problems are separated in the Guetzkow experiments because task and interpersonal communications were separated. During the operating trials, the Ss exchanged messages on precoded cards which contained places for information and answers. The communication in these operating trials was restricted to task communication only. During the intertrials the Ss were free to write each other uncoded messages on blank cards about their organizational arrangements.

Through a Methods-Time Measurement (Maynard, Stegmerten, and Schwab, 1948) it was determined that the task was most efficiently completed through the use of a two- or three-level "Hierarchy."

Consider first the Wheel net: If the task is divided so that the "spokes" send their information to the "hub," the latter can make the decision and in turn return answers to the spokes. We will call this pattern a "two-level hierarchy." Next consider the Circle net: If two neighbors send their information to their opposite neighbors, who in turn relay this information with their own to the fifth member of the circle, this "keyman" can make the decision and relay the answer back through the "relayers" to the "endmen." We will call this pattern a "three-level hierarchy." In the All-Channel nets, either one of these procedures—or others—may be used (Guetzkow and Simon, 1955, p. 237).

The difference between the Methods-Time Measurement predictions for the two- and three-level hierarchy "(which actually shows the three-level hierarchy to be slightly more efficient than the other!) is not consequential" (p. 338). It follows from this analysis that the difficulty of the external task does not significantly differ for the three communication nets. *If a two- or three-level interpersonal organization is adopted*, the performance scores should not differ from net to net. Differences in performance scores should reflect differences in interpersonal relations and not differences in task accomplishment.

According to this analysis, the "All-Channel" net has a difficult organizational problem. "The lack of communication restrictions means an open field with almost too many opportunities . . . [it] has the difficult job of developing its own restrictions—deciding that certain available channels will *not* be used" (p. 239). The symmetry of the net positions does not help solve the problem of which group member is to be the keyman. The "Wheel" net, on the other hand, has the easiest organizational problem. All of the "unnecessary" channels have been blocked, and there is no necessity to "relay" through a second party. Furthermore, the structure of the net almost designates which of the group members will be the "keyman" of the team.

The "Circle" net has the most difficult problem. The symmetry of the net makes no recommendations for the "keyman," and it is necessary to set up a "three-level hierarchy." Although the three-level hierarchy should be as efficient as the two-level *once organized,* it presents a more formidable problem of interpersonal organization.

The results strongly support the analysis. The Circle groups clearly take longer per trial than the Wheel groups after the first trial and the All-Channel groups are intermediate. Analysis of the inter-trial message patterns reflect the differences in productivity. None of the Wheel groups failed to develop a stable information and answer exchange while the Circle and All-Channel groups were about equal in this respect. A later analysis (Guetzkow and Dill, 1957) demonstrates that, considering only those groups which organized into stable interpersonal relationships, the differences among the nets largely disappear. A group with a stable interpersonal organization performs comparably in all three nets.[2] Furthermore, performance increases significantly from before to after the development of a stable interpersonal organization.

[2] This analysis would seem to predict that a Circle group which had all channels open during the organizational periods (but only Circle during task interaction) would perform comparably with the Wheel net. The Guetzkow and Dill experiments fail to confirm this prediction.

In short, even if two groups are faced with a task of potentially equivalent difficulty, productivity may be lowered if the task environment demands that one group develop complex interpersonal relations.

PROPOSITION 3.3. Obstacles originating in the behavior of other group members inhibit (a) individual productivity and (b) assembly effect bonuses.

Ewart Smith's (1956) carefully conducted experiment provides an example of problems in interpersonal relations which originate in the behavior of other group members. In order to establish a base line of comparison, Smith ran control groups of three and five subjects working on a "40 questions" type problem. After the group had interacted for 15 minutes, Smith kept track of the number of problems solved in the next 10 minutes.

In his first experimental condition (A) Smith merely introduced two plants into the group who, unknown to the subjects, were instructed to remain silent throughout the experiment. The second experimental condition (B) was quite similar with one exception. Just before the experiment began Smith passed around a check list of various roles which it would be possible for a member to take—arbitrator, attentive supporter, listener, etc. The plants always checked the "listener" category, and, since Smith announced the results from the check list, the subjects had some explanation of the silent roles which the plants were to play. The three basic conditions are compared with respect to the internal and external problems in Table 3.1.

The groups with the silent plants, then, are faced with a serious problem of *interpersonal* relations; the silent plants do not directly increase the difficulty of the task. In fact, the presence of two "silent plants" decreased productivity; and the loss of effectiveness was greatest in Experimental group A where the obstacles originating in the behavior of other group members were the most severe.

Table 3.1

Condition	Task-environmental obstacle	Interpersonal obstacle
Control	Solve difficult "40 question" problem	Minimum degree of cooperation and communication necessary to solve problem
Experimental (*B*)	Same	Same *plus* adjust to fact that 2 members of group are completely silent but have identified themselves as "listeners"
Experimental (*A*)	Same	Same *except* no possible explanation for the silent behavior of plants is offered

CHAPTER SUMMARY AND LIST OF PROPOSITIONS

This chapter constituted a transition from the data of Chapter Two (individual alone *versus* individual in group) to the data reported in the rest of the book (one kind of group *versus* another kind of group). Four variables emerged as we traced the path of a conference participant from privacy into face-to-face group deliberation: (1) the importance of the task-environment, (2) the impact of the presence of other people, (3) the manner in which patterns of interpersonal relations contribute to group productivity, and (4) a division of group productivity into individual contributions and an assembly effect.

The first stage of a working model of group processes, which incorporates these four points, was presented in Figure 3.1, and three propositions were presented.

PROPOSITION 3.1. Obstacles originating in the task environment directly inhibit the productivity of individual members.

PROPOSITION 3.2. The task environment creates interpersonal obstacles which inhibit both (*a*) individual productivity and (*b*) assembly effects.

Proposition 3.2 was illustrated by experiments in communication nets. Groups with different communication nets differed in productivity, not because the task was directly more difficult, but because some nets placed heavy demands on the interpersonal relations of the group. For those groups which developed an adequate pattern of interpersonal relations, there was no difference in productivity among the various communication nets. Group members, unlike individuals working alone, cannot focus their attention on the task solely; the greater problem-solving potential available in the face-to-face group is not to be realized without a cost. For the group member, the task implies two sets of problems: (1) the problems which stem directly from the task, and (2) the problems which stem from the necessity to build the interpersonal relations with other group members which fulfill the unique problem-solving potential of an interacting group.

PROPOSITION 3.3. Interpersonal obstacles originating in the behavior of other group members inhibit (a) individual productivity and (b) assembly effects.

Many of the problems created by the presence of other people have no relationship to the task or external environment of the group. The introduction of two silent group members into the discussion significantly impaired group productivity. This is true even though there is no reason why the presence of silent members should make the task more difficult (some control groups had the same number of active participants). These silent members posed an obstacle in and of themselves irrespective of the task environment. The list of experimentally demonstrated interpersonal obstacles which could be used to illustrate these last two propositions is so long that a special chapter, Chapter Five, is devoted to the interpersonal obstacles which inhibit effective group action.

CHAPTER FOUR

A simple working model of factors molding

interpersonal behavior and task performance

It may now be useful to bring more sharply into focus some of the thoughts that developed implicitly in earlier chapters. In this chapter, we shall distinguish between the task environment of the group as a whole and the interpersonal environment of each individual group member. Two important kinds of stimuli are found in each environment: (*a*) obstacle stimuli which define the problems of the group and its members, and (*b*) reward stimuli which serve to mold and maintain group behaviors. We shall further distinguish between behavior instigated by task-environmental obstacles and behavior which arises in response to interpersonal obstacles.

TASK ENVIRONMENT AND INTERPERSONAL RELATIONS

The task environment is made up of all stimuli which are external to the group. It is the configuration of environmental stimuli which impinges on the group. For example, the task environment of a board of directors is composed of its stockholders, the financial community which must be tapped for resources, the executives within the company itself, etc. For a production planning committee the environment is composed of the production capabilities of the firm, the market surveys used for predicting sales, the capital available for revamping factory layouts, etc. In short, the task environment is made up of all stimuli, obstacles, rewards, and "things" except the behavior of other group members. Interpersonal stimuli are presented by the behavior of other members of the group—including expectations about what should be and what will be done by other group members.

The distinction between task-environmental stimuli and an interpersonal stimuli creates a boundary which separates the stimuli which are outside the group from the stimuli which are inside the group. Note the environment of the group is different from the environment of an individual member. The task-environment is external to both the group and its individual members. The behavior of other group members, however, is a part of the internal workings of the group; but it is part of the environment of a single individual. In order to reduce this source of confusion, we have tried to use the word "environment" to mean that which surrounds the entire group. When reference is to the external world of an individual, we shall use a more specific term such as interpersonal stimuli, obstacles, or rewards. The analysis, then, is at the group level; task-environmental obstacles and rewards are in the group's environment while interpersonal obstacles and rewards are a part of the internal workings of the group.

Task-environmental and interpersonal obstacles. A task-environmental obstacle is a particular aspect of the total task environment which blocks, inhibits, or limits group productivity. A summary statement of task-environmental and interpersonal obstacles which have been involved in several experimental studies is presented in the upper portion of Table 4.1. Examples from decision-making conferences have been included in the lower part of Table 4.1.

The problems in the Guetzkow (1960) and Smith (1956) studies were discussed in detail in the previous chapter. Altman and McGinnies (1960) asked the subjects to discuss a movie on prejudice; so this was the problem specified by the task environment. Among the many problems of interpersonal relations which had to be solved in order to achieve a coherent discussion, one was particularly difficult. Altman and McGinnies constructed some groups in such a way that the members strongly disagreed about

Table 4.1   Chart of task-environmental and interpersonal obstacles

EXPERIMENTAL STUDIES	TASK-ENVIRONMENTAL PROBLEMS	INTERPERSONAL PROBLEMS
1. Guetzkow (1960)	Determine which piece of information was held in common by all five *Ss*	Determine who would be keyman, endman, and relayers; interlock these roles into "organization"
2. Smith (1956)	Solve "40 questions" problem	Adjust to two silent "plants" in group
3. Altman and McGinnies (1960)	Discuss a movie on prejudice	Adjust to fact that other *Ss* differed on Ethnocentrism Scale
4. Pryer and Bass (1959)	Rank cities in order of population size	Utilize feedback to better organize—even though feedback may not improve task skill
5. Deutsch (1949)	Cooperative group—get group rated as best *group* in course	Develop division of labor; coordinate efforts; establish communications
	Competitive groups—get self rated as best *individual* in own group	None necessary
6. Lanzetta and Roby (1956)	Set switches to match information on gauges	Obtain needed information from other subjects

FIELD STUDIES [a]	TASK-ENVIRONMENTAL PROBLEMS	INTERPERSONAL PROBLEMS
1. Shop Committee in Manufacturing Company	Obtain coordination of two subassembly lines	Dominating behavior of foreman prevents others from talking
2. Safety Council in Operating Agency	Develop plans for Summer Safety campaign	Reduce apathy of participants
3. Bank Loan Group	Estimate risks involved in loans	Elicit information from submissive participants
4. Executive Council of Printing Firm	Reduce costs at component level	Secure participation to arouse motivation for execution of cost-reduction program
5. Editorial Conference in Newspaper	Choose priority among lead stories	Order discussion, so all don't talk simultaneously
6. Inter-Departmental Committee on Foreign Aid Program	Eliminate contradictions in program	Accord each agency its rightful status

[a] From unpublished data developed in connection with field observations of some 72 conferences from industry and government, as reported in Marquis, Guetzkow and Heyns (1951).

prejudice. The fact that each group participant had to adjust to the differing levels of prejudice expressed in the verbal behavior of other participants constitutes an interpersonal obstacle.

It will be remembered that Pryer and Bass (1959) asked their subjects to rank-order sets of ten cities with respect to population. The data supported the expectation that *individuals* would not be able to improve their task performance throughout the experiment even if they were given the correct rankings following each trial. This meant that the subjects could do nothing to improve their direct efforts in problem-solving. It is possible, however, that the group members could forge out a scheme of interpersonal organization which would increase their productivity; and the increased *group* productivity actually obtained provides some support for this interpretation.

Deutsch (1949) told the "cooperative" groups that they would be graded as a whole in comparison with other groups. In other words, the task environment (in this case, Deutsch and his assistants) would provide rewards if the group excelled as a whole. The task-environmental problem, then, was to get a good rating for the entire group. In order to solve this task-environmental problem, however, certain problems of interpersonal relations also had to be solved. Since problems of division of labor, coordination of effort, and establishing communication stem most immediately from the behavior of other group members, they are interpersonal obstacles.

The "competitive" groups, on the other hand, were told that each individual would be graded in comparison with the other individuals in the group. Within this task environment, an individual group member can gain his task rewards without building a relationship with the other group members; so there is no necessary interpersonal problem which must be solved in order to survive in the task environment.

Responses to task-environmental and interpersonal obstacles. Those responses stimulated by the task-environmental obstacles may be conceptually differentiated from those instigated by the interpersonal obstacles. However, in practice, group members may react to both environments simultaneously. The close interconnections between task and interpersonal responses are illustrated in an experiment developed by Lanzetta and Roby (1956, 1957, 1960; Roby and Lanzetta, 1957). Three Ss are seated in separate booths. By means of a projector, the experimenter projects instrument readings to each S separately. Also in each booth were two switches, each with one "off" and three "on" positions. Each S was provided with a table which specified the switch settings that were appropriate for each of the various instrument readings. The task of each S was to gather information from the instruments and set the switches accordingly. If an individual were working alone, it would be possible that all of his behavior might be stimulated by events in the task environment. But the subjects in the Lanzetta and Roby experiment worked in groups of three; so each S was influenced by the behavior of the other two individuals in the group. All of the behavior which has its *immediate* stimulus in another group member is part of the complex of interpersonal responses. If the task environment does not as yet *require* the group members to relate to each other, it would be possible for each member to ignore the others.

In fact, the task was not so simple. Each subject did not have all of the information he needed to set his controls because some of the information he needed was presented on instruments projected only to another group member. The individual subject cannot meet the demands of the task without consulting the other subjects. Each individual needed to work out interpersonal relationships which allowed him to receive the information he needed from the other group members and also to transmit to them the information they needed. Thus, it was necessary for him to devote some of his activity to an obstacle which stems directly from his relation to other group members.

The two sets of behavior are by no means entirely separate. Although some interaction may be entirely social (i.e., talk for the sake of talk), it is difficult to imagine any behavior which is completely unaffected by the task environment. In both of the examples given above, the interpersonal behavior was *immediately* concerned with interpersonal relationships, but it was soon reflected in task productivity. If a group member works hard to impress a fellow worker, his immediate concern may be interpersonal; but he also changes his rate of work on the task. Similarly, the external task required the Ss working with the instruments to establish interpersonal relationships to gather the necessary information, and the eventual consequences of that organization will be reflected in improved switch settings or task productivity. A further complication is introduced in that many problems of interpersonal organization are indirectly "caused" by events in the environment. The reason the Ss needed to form a group structure in the Guetzkow experiments reported in Proposition 2.2 was because such structuring of the interpersonal relations was required in order to overcome the task-environmental obstacle.

Homans (1950) made a somewhat similar distinction between the internal and external systems. Homans' distinction was made on the basis of the *purpose* or function of the behavior—not the instigating obstacle as we have done. While a focus on purpose and function has many advantages, it is hoped that the present focus on the stimulus or instigating obstacle of behavior produces distinctions that are more easily operationalizable and easier to apply in specific instances.

Task-environmental and interpersonal rewards. Where obstacles define the problems of the group and its individuals, *instigate* group behaviors, and limit productivity, it is a second class of stimuli—task-environmental and interpersonal rewards—which serve to *mold, maintain,* and *motivate* group behaviors. When applied, rewards increase the chances that the behavior with which they are associated will occur again. These stimuli may originate in the task environment, because of accomplishments by the group; or they may originate within the behavior of other group members. Group and individual goals are defined as those rewards which the group and group members seek. Also, when interviewed or filling out questionnaires, group members describe rewards as good and pleasurable.

A *task-environmental reward* is a stimulus or aspect of the task environment which will increase the probability of recurrence of the response which it follows. An *interpersonal reward* is a stimulus or aspect of the behavior of other group members which will increase the likelihood of repetition of behavior which it follows.

Subjects in Lanzetta and Roby's experiment were willing to work quite hard at setting switches in order to achieve the correct switch setting. This correct switch setting was an event in the environment which apparently was rewarding to the subjects; therefore, it qualifies as a task-environmental reward. Note that a task-environmental reward can support behaviors related both to the (a) task-environmental obstacles and the (b) interpersonal obstacles. That is, the participants were apparently willing to work on the problems directly imposed by the task and also to work on problems of interpersonal relationship because both kinds of behavior increased the rewards associated with successful task completion.

The behavior of fellow group members can also be rewarding. When the behavior of another group member increased the probability of a given behavior, then that behavior is serving as an interpersonal reward. Issues of primary or secondary rewards are not relevant here. It is not important in this discussion whether or not man has an innate instinct of "gregariousness" or whether his needs for social contact have been learned from more "basic" rewards. The fact is that the participants in any decision-making conference are profoundly and directly affected by the behavior of other group members. In many decision-making groups, a smile or other form of social approval is often more important than a successful task solution.

Several of the experiments in verbal conditioning (which have been reviewed by Krasner, 1958) will serve to illustrate how the behavior of other human beings acts as a reward. Two techniques have been popular. The first was reported by Greenspoon (1955). The experimenter asked the subject to "say words." In one condition plural words were followed with a "mmm-hum" (i.e., yes) by the experimenter, and in another condition plural words were followed by "huh-uh" (i.e., no). The positive reinforcement increased the probability of plural words and the negative reinforcement decreased the probability of that verbal class. Taffel (1955) asked subjects to make up sentences based on the verbs that he supplied. When sentences beginning with "I" or "We" were followed with the phrase "good," subjects produced more "I" and "We" sentences.

It is difficult to specify the full range of interpersonal rewards. Riecken and Homans (1954) speak of one social reward—social rank. But if they mean *all the privileges accorded social rank*, then there is wide variety in the kinds of rewards that could be included in the concept. Whatever the original source of the motivation, a good deal of the behavior of other group members qualifies as a reward. Just what kinds of behavior are rewarding is not easy to specify. Approval-disapproval appears to be an important dimension. Any behavior which implies that an activity is approved of by other group members is probably rewarding. For this reason, a smile, an overt compliment, or any of the behavior accorded the group member with high power-status (see Chapter Eight on the consequences of power) would act as a social reward. In Chapter Six (on the direct sources of power) we shall speak of the rewards intrinsic to interaction.

Interpersonal liking may be an aspect of the more general phenomenon of approval; considerable data suggesting that interpersonal attraction increases the rewardingness of interaction will be reviewed in Chapter Six. It is difficult to specify the overt behaviors which are used to indicate friendship and liking, but it is easy to believe that they are rewarding. If we may judge by the amount of purely social conversation we observe, individuals apparently are rewarded when others merely listen to them talk.

Interpersonal rewards, as was the case with task-environmental rewards, can be used to support the behaviors responding to both (a) task and (b) interpersonal obstacles. Early in Chapter Two we saw how the desire for approval increases task productivity. Interpersonal rewards also support interpersonal behavior. The leader who coordinates the activities of the other group members, group members who make helpful contributions, and persons who conform to the procedural norms in general can be rewarded through social approval or other interpersonal rewards. In this way the group can maintain an organizational system which will *eventually* lead to more environmental rewards even if the short-range functions of these behaviors are not sufficient to provoke an immediate task-environmental reward.

The experimental data on the timing of rewards suggest that they are most effective when they follow behavior within a few seconds. Although the ability of humans to verbalize and plan for the future increases the effectiveness of an environmental reward, many social systems would be impossible if events in the task environment were the sole source of reward. It may take a goodly time for the group to realize its goals, but social rewards may be applied immediately by verbal and gestural behaviors in the face-to-face group.

Rewards from the task environment, usually given to the group as a more or less reified entity, tend to be amorphous. This deficiency in task rewards is exhibited in two ways.

1. If a reward is given to the entire group, then each individual cannot know which of his own behaviors contributed and which detracted from group success. The task environment frequently does not make distinctions within a collection of individuals. The group as a whole is rewarded or punished without reference to the behaviors of particular individuals in the group. A group member who disrupts the conference with his self-oriented needs (Fouriezos, Hutt, and Guetzkow, 1950) for example, may not be individually punished even if these self-oriented needs cause the group as a whole to be less successful at some later time. An individual will not learn (alter his behavior) if the group as a whole is rewarded in such a way that the task-environmental rewards and punishments are not specifically coordinated to *his* behavior, as Rosenberg (1960) has demonstrated in a dyadic cooperative situation in which rewards were varied. "Each S was required to perform the simple motor response of turning a small concealed knob in a series of 50 trials. A reinforcing stimulus was delivered to each S separately after each trial . . ." (Rosenberg, 1960, p. 332). The reinforcement was a function of both the S's own behavior *and* the behavior of the other S, and the proportion of the reinforcement due to each S's own behavior was systematically varied. In general, at least 50 per cent of the reward must be determined by his own behavior before the subject can learn to make the correct knob adjustment. Zajonc

(1962) reports that the performance (reaction times) of seven-man teams was inhibited when individuals received only knowledge of the group success or failure and did not receive feedback on their own individual performance.

2. Rewarding the group as a whole not only makes it impossible for each individual to learn which of *his* behaviors contributed to the group success; rewarding the group as a whole also makes it difficult to reward some individuals within the group more than others. It frequently turns out that some individuals in a group work harder or have more ability than others. These individuals may feel that they deserve more than an equal portion of the reward; they may find that they can earn more rewards by working alone when they do not have to split the "take" with the other group members. Other group members are frequently willing to allocate extra rewards to these competent members, but it is often impossible to "pay off" the highly competent group members with a task-environmental reward.

Social rewards originating in the behavior of other individuals serve the group in a number of ways. Interpersonal rewards, such as liking and deference, can be used to provide differential rewards to group members. Since the rewards are directly under the control of the group members, interpersonal rewards can be tied intimately to the behavior of a single individual, different group members can be given different amounts of reward, and the rewards can immediately follow behavior. These interpersonal rewards are especially vital in freeing the group from the momentary fickleness of the task environment. Group behaviors which are known to be helpful can be maintained even when the group meets failure for some other reason. The group can take time off from its task activities for planning, even though this produces a momentary decrease in task-environmental productivity, as was demonstrated by Guetzkow and Dill (1957). Blau has noted how the respect earned by serving as informal consultant for others in a federal agency was found rewarding, especially when it was tied to deference behaviors on the part of those who received the help (Blau, 1955). Group behavior can be maintained by interpersonal rewards during momentary interruptions in the task environmental rewards.

The group may become so concerned with those task activities which are *immediately* associated with productivity that they ignore any vital long-range interpersonal planning which does not provoke *immediate* feedback (task rewards). Shure, Rogers, Larsen, and Tassone (1962) illustrate this principle in a communication net experiment. Shure et al. studied the effectiveness of newly formed groups in communication nets under three conditions: "(1) task performance periods are temporally separate from planning periods, (2) planning can occur only during performance periods, or (3) planning opportunities are not provided" (pp. 281–282). In the separate planning conditions, group members exchanged messages only during the time-periods between task trials. In the contemporary planning condition (number 2 above), group members could send extra task messages only during task periods. Furthermore, the extra task messages which were sent "predominantly concerned the modification of current trial behavior" (p. 282). Although all of the separate planning groups developed an effective pattern of interpersonal relations, only 20 per cent of the contemporary planning groups developed the efficient hierarchical organization; separate planning groups were much more effective. Shure et al. conclude: "It is apparent that group planning, even under conditions that are highly favorable for its emergence, is inhibited by task pressure" (p. 278). The authors go on to suggest mechanisms for this finding. They suggest that group members are seduced by the activities immediately associated with task rewards and forget the less immediately rewarding interpersonal planning, even though these interpersonal obstacles significantly inhibit task rewards in the long run. "Under conditions of task pressure, the reinforcing value of immediate action in a situation satisfying currently evoked goals was significantly greater than for cooperative planning. It is probably the case, as Bass (1960, p. 446) noted, that 'immediate rather than ultimate effectiveness is more significant for understanding interaction among individuals'" (pp. 278–279).

Groups members would be able to reward task and interpersonal planning immediately with *interpersonal* rewards. It may also be that high-status members and members who habitually assume interpersonal leadership roles are removed enough from concern with task rewards to maintain a more complete perspective. Nonetheless, the group must be responsive to the demands of the task environment in the long run, or it will fail to survive. Group members cannot live on love and status alone.

The distinction between task-environmental and interpersonal rewards is not always as clear as the previous sections imply. Sometimes there is an interdependence between the task reward and the interpersonal reward. In an experimental miniature warning center, Berkowitz, Levy, and Harvey (1957) found that airmen in basic training became attracted to their work partners only when they had high task motivation. This finding illustrates the interdependence between task-environmental and interpersonal behaviors.

A summary model. Perhaps it will be helpful to summarize the working model which has been made explicit in the preceding sections of this chapter, both in words and in diagram form (Figure 4.1).

First, we distinguished between events in the task environment external to the group and events in the behavior of other group members, as indicated by the two boxes on the left-hand side of the diagram. Some of the task-environmental events constitute problems or obstacles for the group, and these obstacles instigate some group behavior. Likewise, some of the behaviors (or at times absence of behavior) of other group members constitute problems or obstacles of an interpersonal sort; these interpersonal obstacles also instigate group behaviors. These relations are depicted in the diagram by the second series of boxes, reading from left to right, with arrows (1) and (3) connecting the obstacles to their corresponding behaviors. At times, obstacles in the task environment create problems in the interpersonal environment, as is illustrated by arrow (2). When asked about the problems they meet in their own decision-making groups, executives by and large mention only the task-environmental obstacles (Kriesberg, 1950). Yet leaders and members of groups must alert themselves to the interpersonal obstacles that are the immediate consequences of gathering individuals together in a

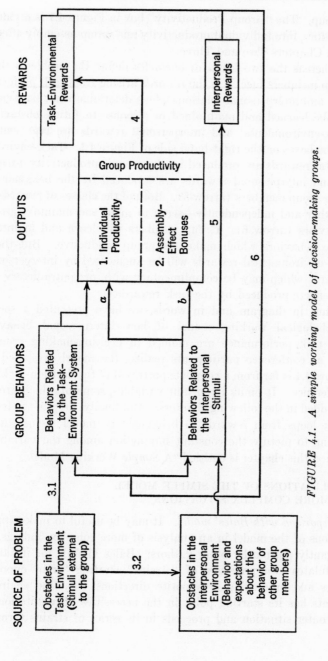

FIGURE 4.1. A simple working model of decision-making groups.

a group. The "Group Productivity" box in Figure 4.1 is divided, as before, into individual productivity and group assembly effects as in Chapters Two and Three.

Whereas the two kinds of *obstacles* define the problems that group members face, it is the *rewards* arising from task performance and interpersonal relations which determine what behaviors will be learned and maintained in response to future obstacles. Task-environmental and interpersonal rewards are represented by the boxes on the right-hand side of Figure 4.1. Task-environmental rewards are produced by the group's productivity (arrow 4) and interpersonal rewards are produced by the behavior of other group members (arrow 5). Both of the classes of rewards—together and independently—serve to mold and maintain group behaviors (arrow 6). Group members will learn and maintain those behaviors which make the group productive. But these task-environmental rewards will be augmented by interpersonal rewards which may be complimentary with, or contradictory to, the effects produced by the task rewards.

Thus in diagram and in words, we have presented a social psychological working model of how interpersonal behavior and task performance are molded in decision-making groups. But as conference participants realize, the model presented in Figure 4.1 is far from a complete portrayal of the decision-making conference. It omits important variables, some of which are to be added in the following chapters. And finally, despite the feedback loops from rewards to behavior, the model seems static, failing to picture the constant interaction among the variables. Hence, this chapter is entitled "A *Simple* Working Model."

APPLICATIONS OF THE SIMPLE MODEL
IN MORE COMPLEX SITUATIONS

Comparison with Bales' model. It may be useful to make applications of the model in an analysis of more complex findings, as elegantly posited by other authors. Bales (1955), for instance, postulates two processes of "strains" starting "from opposite poles and proceeding in opposite directions. . . . One chain of events has its starting point in the necessities of adaptation to the outer situation and proceeds in its series of strains through

changes in the division of labor, changes in the distribution of
. . . authority, and status . . ." (p. 127). Although this patterning of interpersonal relations originally arises in order to
cope with problems in the task environment, it has "malintegra-
tive terminal effects in the disturbance of the existing state of
solidarity" (Bales, 1955, p. 127). In the language of this chapter, we might say that interpersonal relations are developed in
order to increase task-environmental productivity, but the hierarchical differentiation sometimes associated with these interpersonal relations is less interpersonally rewarding than unstruc-
tural interaction. Some of the evidence supporting Bales' position is reviewed in Chapter Eleven.

Comparison with the Blau and Scott model. Extrapolation of
our working model also can be made for groups functioning within
the context of larger organizations. In their chapter on "Processes of Communication," Blau and Scott (1962) suggest: "There
is, then, some indication that differentiation of hierarchical status
in groups attenuates the very characteristics that have been hypothesized to be responsible for the superiority of groups over
individuals in problem solving" (p. 123). Blau and Scott postulate that a high degree of hierarchy in the group's pattern of
interpersonal relations inhibits *task* productivity, whereas Bales
suggested that differentiation facilitated task productivity but
inhibited interpersonal rewards.

Before turning to the insightful reasoning behind these conclusions, three ways in which the Blau and Scott model differs from
ours will be noted. (1) To begin with, Blau and Scott were
probably thinking about a much higher degree of differentiation
and structure than we have been considering. They were working within the context of the formal organization where groups
interact over long periods of time giving them ample opportunity
to develop an interpersonal organization. Furthermore, status
differences may be imposed by the legitimate structure of the firm
and the nature of the task. Even the newest foreman and crew
begin their interaction with more structure than a group of college students gathered together for the first time to discuss a
human relations case. In contrast, most decision-making groups

begin with less specified structure, and the task does not usually imply a specific interpersonal organization. (2) Blau and Scott placed their primary emphasis on the *dys*functions of hierarchical differentiation (although they did stress the value of differentiation for coordination) ; whereas we stressed the positive value of interpersonal organization. (3) Finally, Blau and Scott stressed the dysfunctional consequences of status differentiation for the task-environmental rewards while we have asserted that the primary loss occurs for interpersonal rewards.

After reviewing some of the same literature considered in Chapter Two, Blau and Scott state: "The superiority of groups over individuals in certain kinds of task performance has been attributed primarily to three factors: (1) the sifting of suggestions in social interaction serves as an error-correction mechanism [Propositions 2.1-A, 2.2] ; (2) the social support furnished in interaction facilitates thinking [we suggested that social support may increase criticism, but that it is likely to inhibit the production of alternatives, Proposition 2.2] ; and (3) the competition among members for respect mobilizes their energies for contributing to the task [Proposition 2.4-A]" (p. 121).

"Hierarchical differentiation of status, particularly when formally established, appears to curtail these three group processes. First, explicit status distinctions tend to reduce social interaction and social support" (p. 122). Blau and Scott then cited several studies in support of this contention. In Proposition 2.5 we stated that when status was correlated with worth in task performance, it might improve the group product; but the formally designated status may have little correlation with true worth on a specific problem. Differentiation does limit interaction and it will, therefore, limit the rewards associated with interaction (see Chapter Six on the sources of power). In the next chapter we shall consider the advantages and disadvantages of interaction with heterogeneous (other status) group members.

"Second, formally instituted status differences tend to undermine the process of competition for respect" (p. 122). "Third, status differences distort the error-correcting function of social interaction" (p. 123). Both of these points are well taken. Formally awarded status, if uncorrelated with true worth, may weaken task productivity. But a group faces both task and interpersonal obstacles which block the path to effective group action. It would be possible that some degree of structure would be required in order to overcome interpersonal obstacles and to coordinate and divide the labor. Formally awarded status might, for instance, give one group member the needed perspective necessary to prevent task pressure from driving out planning as it did in the Shure et al. experiment discussed earlier.

In both of these applications of our working model, its implicit complexity is revealed. In analyzing the work of others, we find that our simple model of the way in which task and interpersonal relations may interrelate makes it possible to obtain a somewhat more adequate understanding of more complex relationships.

CHAPTER SUMMARY AND CONCLUSIONS

These distinctions, which are again summarized in Table 4.2, are made for a number of reasons. Although both task-environmental and interpersonal rewards both follow the traditional learning theory laws, their application differs appreciably. Task-environmental rewards are events external to the group; they constitute feedback from the environment to the group. Task rewards may be delayed for long periods of time after group action. In contrast, interpersonal rewards are events in the behavior of group members and, therefore, internal to the group. Group

Table 4.2   Classification of stimuli

	OBSTACLES	REWARDS
External to group (Task environment)	Task-environmental Obstacles	Task-environmental Rewards
Internal to group (Behavior—and expectations about behavior—of group members)	Interpersonal Obstacles	Interpersonal Rewards

members will have much more control over their own behavior than they will over task-environmental feedback. For this reason, the group members can mold, maintain, and motivate behaviors through the use of interpersonal rewards which would not be supported if task-environmental rewards were the only motivating stimuli.

The task environment frequently treats the group as an entity and does not differentiate among the members of the group. This means that task-environmental rewards are usually not tied to the success and failure of individual group members, a fact which makes task-environmental rewards of little value for individual learning. Furthermore, the unitary nature of task-environmental rewards makes it difficult to allocate extra rewards to deserving group members. Interpersonal rewards, however, can be tied to the success and failure of individual group members, can follow the behavior immediately, and extra rewards can be allocated to the competent members.

Some authors seem to separate completely task-environmental and interpersonal activities. Bales (1958, see Chapter Eleven), for instance, apparently argues that the "social-emotional" specialist ignores task activities in his attention to interpersonal issues and that the "task specialist" ignores interpersonal considerations. In contrast to these positions, we stressed that *interpersonal* rewards can be used to support *task* activities and that *task-environmental* rewards can mold and maintain certain patterns of *interpersonal* relationship. Both kinds of rewards can support either or both classes of behavior.

The distinction between task-environmental and interpersonal obstacles is primarily made to emphasize the importance of interpersonal obstacles. There are certain problems, such as distraction and increased defensiveness, which are created whenever one individual works in the presence of another. These interpersonal obstacles are just as likely to provoke a group failure as are task obstacles. In fact, since group members are more likely to identify the task obstacles and are more willing to work toward the solution of task problems, interpersonal obstacles may be the major barrier to effective group action in most actual and experimental settings. Some of the interpersonal obstacles which have been experimentally demonstrated are discussed in the next chapter.

We have seen how the group has the potential to exceed the productivity of the best group member and/or the sum of the efforts of all individual members working separately. This assembly effect bonus, however, does not automatically occur whenever a collection of individuals meet in a face-to-face conference. In order to actualize the potential assembly effect, group members must focus on the set of task-related obstacles *and also* the set of interpersonal obstacles, such as the needed divisions of labor, which bar the way to effective interdependent group activity.

If an individual works alone, then he can focus his entire attention on the task obstacles. When he works in the presence of other people, however, he must also attend to the interpersonal obstacles (*a*) which are dictated by the necessities of the task (Proposition 3.2) and (*b*) which are inevitably presented by the presence of other people (Proposition 3.3). Ignoring these interpersonal obstacles is not the answer. If they pose serious enough problems, then the task should not be assigned to that particular group. If the advantages of group interaction outweigh the disadvantages of the interpersonal obstacles, then the group members should give the interpersonal obstacles an equal priority with task obstacles.

CHAPTER FIVE

Obstacles to effective interpersonal relations in a group

Task obstacles are often defined in the memo stating the purpose of the conference, in the constitution of the organization, or in the title of the group. In general, group members usually have a much better understanding of the task obstacles than they do of the interpersonal obstacles which inhibit group effectiveness. In this chapter we present evidence on a number of interpersonal obstacles which have inhibited the effectiveness of groups everywhere. This entire chapter is devoted to a full documentation of Propositions 3.2 and 3.3 which dealt with interpersonal obstacles inhibiting individual and group productivity. These specific obstacles, which range from individual personalities to uncomfortable status relationships, are important in their own right as specific areas of potential trouble in any group. Equally important, however, is the generalization which can be drawn from the specific list detailed in this chapter. Meeting interpersonal obstacles contributes as much toward group productivity as meeting the problems posed by task-environmental obstacles; in fact, because group members have a tendency to ignore the interpersonal issues, interpersonal obstacles may be the major barrier to task effectiveness in many groups.

THE DISRUPTION OF INTERPERSONAL RELATIONS
THROUGH INDIVIDUALISTIC MOTIVATION

When participants in conferences are motivated by their personal, self-centered needs, their group's effectiveness is often reduced. Evidence clarifying and substantiating this contention is found in a number of studies. Two of these emphasize the disruptive character of competitive, individualistic motivation. Mintz (1951) created an experimental task which demanded a high degree of interpersonal organization. A large glass bottle was fitted with a bushing to narrow its neck. Aluminum cones with strings attached were placed in the bottle. The size of the bushing and cones was such that only one cone could be taken out of the bottle at a time. If the participants in the experiment tried to remove more than one cone at a time, the cones would jam at the neck. Each participant was given a string the other end of which was tied to a cone; the group's task was to get the cones out as fast as possible. Rewards and punishments were given to each individual on the basis of the time taken to get his cone out of the bottle. In general, Mintz found that this individualistic reward structure lowered productivity, i.e., created traffic jams at the bottle neck. Group members under competitive reward structures did not establish interpersonal relationships such as turn taking which would allow them to increase productivity.

The findings in the Michigan study of 72 decision-making conferences in business and industry suggest that the results of the foregoing laboratory study apply in the field (Fouriezos, Hutt, and Guetzkow, 1950). These researchers studied the role of "self-oriented needs." One of the three observers of each conference kept a record of the instances in which the behavior of each participant in a conference seemed to be dominated more by strong ego needs than by the demands of the immediate situation. This observer noted particularly behavior which showed a strong need for dominance, a need for status in the group, a need for the support of others, or a need to express aggression or emotional feelings which appeared inappropriate to the situation. From these records, the observer made a final rating of each conference group on the extent to which such self-oriented need behavior dominated the meeting.

This self-oriented need behavior was associated with inadequate interpersonal relations; self-oriented need ratings correlated significantly with participant ratings of high group conflict ($r = .73$), low participant satisfaction ($r = -.37$), and low group solidarity ($r = -.55$). In light of these correlations, it is not surprising that self-oriented need behavior was found in conferences with low task productivity ($r = -.32$). (Productivity was measured through an index of the number of items completed over the number undertaken and by observer rating.)

$\$ \qquad \$ \qquad \$$

Morton Deutsch and his associates (Deutsch, 1958) have worked with a task which creates certain interpersonal obstacles. Each of the two experimental subjects could make a choice between two alternatives from a "game theory matrix" which is described more fully by Deutsch (p. 269). In general, we can say that it was to the long-run advantage of both subjects to choose cooperatively a certain set of alternatives.

Deutsch varied the motivational sets of his participants through verbal instructions "to the subjects which characterized for them the objectives they were to have in playing the game and the objectives they could assume their co-player to have" (Deutsch, 1958, p. 270). (Note that expectations of others as well as personal motivation has been manipulated.) Three different motivational orientations were used:

(a) *cooperative—each subject was led to feel that the welfare of the other person as well as his own welfare was of concern to him and that the other person felt the same way;* (b) *individualistic—each subject was led to feel that his only interest was in doing as well for himself as he could without regard to how well the other person did and that the other person felt the same way;* (c) *competitive—each subject was led to feel that he wanted to do as well as he could for himself and he also wanted to do better than the other person and that the other person felt the same way* (Deutsch, 1958, p. 270).

The objective reward structure of the task was not changed; the only difference among the groups was the instructions to the Ss and their expectations about the motivation of the other player.

Generally speaking, the cooperative instructions produced greater task-environmental rewards, i.e., the cooperative Ss achieved the best task scores. Competitive instructions resulted in the poorest performance, and individualistic instructions produced generally intermediate results. In summary, both types of self-oriented motivations lowered task output for Deutsch's task.

Shaw (1959b) found that group productivity was low in *unstructured* groups which scored high on a specially constructed scale called "Individual Prominence." The scale includes such items as "In meetings of groups to which I belong I often find myself trying to get things organized," "In group situations I am quick to take the lead when an opportunity presents itself," and "If I disagree with someone, I rarely let them know that I disagree." (Agreement with this last item is scored as low prominence.)

Unstructured groups were told to take two minutes to discuss each choice and then make a group decision. Structured groups, in which a leader had been designated by the experimenter, were told to discuss for two minutes, but the final choice was assigned to the appointed leader. Groups with high average scores on the prominence scale were less productive only in the unstructured condition. Does this mean that the individually prominent behavior did not create a serious interpersonal obstacle in groups where the experimenter prearranged the interpersonal organization? Perhaps it was not necessary to build an interpersonal organization because a leader had been designated by the experimenter.

Bernard Bass has recently developed an "Orientation Inventory" which contains a "self-orientation" scale. "On a battery of personality inventories and attitude questionnaires, the highly self-oriented subject described himself . . . as disagreeable, dogmatic, aggressive-competitive, sensitive-effeminate, introvertive, suspicious, jealous, tense-excitable, manifestly anxious, lacking in control, immature-unstable, needing aggression, needing heterosexuality, lacking in need for change, fearing failure, and feeling insecure" (Bass and Dunteman, 1963, p. 420). Groups of supervisors who had been meeting "sensitivity training groups" (groups with no leader and agenda) were recomposed so that some groups were made up of members who were all high on the self-orientation scale. These self-oriented members themselves indicated that they thought the quality of their recomposed group was of significantly lower quality than that of the previous randomly composed groups.

It is possible that this decrease in evaluation is due to a general dissatisfaction with the procedures involved in arbitrarily breaking up the old groups and reconstituting new groups. Three of the four classes of reconstituted groups rated the reconstituted group lower in quality. However, this decrease in the quality rating was significant only for the self-oriented groups, and one of the four groups evidenced a substantial (but not statistically significant) *increase* in the quality ratings.

These findings indicate a number of practical suggestions for the operation of decision-making conferences with greater effectiveness:

1. If possible, select conference participants whose self-centered needs are of a less intense variety; as a minimum, include among participants some whose motivation is less individualistic in its orientation.

2. Attempt to strengthen motivations of a cooperative nature by the initial instructions given to the conference participants and by constant reminders of the cooperative nature of the task as the group proceeds from one phase to the next. Emphasis on the cooperative aspects of the task would seem to facilitate the solution of interpersonal problems once the conference is underway.

CONFLICTING PATTERNS OF INTER-PERSONAL PERSONALITY TRAITS

That self-centered motivation or behavior inhibits group effectiveness was demonstrated in the previous section. Now we turn our attention to the different personality styles which people exhibit in their relations with others. In this section we examine groups which agree to cooperate, but disagree on *how* to cooperate. In this case it is not the absolute amount of a trait which inhibits productivity—it is disagreement and differences among group members. For instance, both a quiet and a noisy group could solve many tasks with equal effectiveness. But, if a group spends all its time trying to decide how much talking is appropriate, little time is left for the task. If this were the case, we would not want to measure the *average* amount of talkativeness among the group members; groups high and low on talkativeness could perform equally well. What would be needed in this hypothetical situation is a measure of the *differences* among the members in talkativeness.

The following sections present evidence from studies which have found that differences among members in styles of interpersonal behavior decreased effectiveness. Schutz distinguished persons with power orientation from persons with personal orientations. Groups with members of mixed orientations are shown to be ineffective. Altman and McGinnies (1960) and Haythorn et al. (1956) demonstrated that the effectiveness of groups is inhibited when the members hold different amounts of prejudice. Ghiselli and Lodahl (1958) focused on the relationship between the leader and the rest of the group. Finally, Exline (1957) presented data demonstrating that productivity can be inhibited by instructions which suggest that the group members will be incompatible.

Different patterns of "Fundamental Interpersonal Relations Orientations." William Schutz (1955, 1958) defined and measured orientations which might be compatible and incompatible. In his early article Schutz (1955) distinguished between two general criteria for making interpersonal decisions. These two sets of criteria should result in fundamentally different styles of interpersonal relationships—a *power orientation* and a *personal orientation.*

The first class of criteria emphasizes authority symbols. The orientation of people who behave in terms of this class is dominated by the assumption that the way a person gains his end is by working within a power framework. This is done by following rules, following the leader. . . .
The second class of criteria emphasizes interpersonal considerations. The orientation of people who behave in terms of this class is dominated by the assumption that the way a person gains his end is by working within a framework of close personal relations. This is done by getting people to like him, by being a "good guy," by liking others . . . (Schutz, 1955, p. 431).

By means of attitude scales Schutz was able to compose groups of subjects who were either compatible or incompatible with respect to these fundamental interpersonal orientations. The compatible groups were either power orientated or personal orientated. Incompatible groups were formed with two subgroups, each of which was centered about a "focal person." Both focal persons were relatively high in dominance, but one subgroup leader and his supporting member were *low* on personalness and the other subgroup members were *high* in personalness.

In general, Schutz (1955, 1958, pp. 128–135) found that incompatible groups perform less effectively. As we would expect from our discussion concerning the importance of the task environment, this decrement is most severe for tasks which require the most interaction and agreement and under conditions of high time pressure.

Differences in amounts of prejudice of group members. Several other studies lend support to the notion that personality dispositions may conflict and thus lower group effectiveness. Altman and McGinnies (1960) used a slightly modified version of the California E scale. The E scale is designed to measure generalized intolerance or prejudice. On the basis of the E-scale scores, groups of 6 were formed with various combinations of low and high E-score members (groups had either 0, 2, 3, 4, or 6 low E members). The participants then discussed a movie dealing with the problem of minority groups—a task particularly likely to bring out the differences in prejudice. Although some differences were found between homogeneously high E groups and homogeneously low E groups (see, also, McGinnies and Altman, 1959), the most interesting findings concern the groups with 3 high E Ss and 3 low E Ss. The sort of subgroup formation (the three prejudiced versus the three nonprejudiced) built into Schutz's groups would most likely be in these balanced groups. When compared to all other combinations, members of balanced groups were less attracted to their groups, less accurate in judgments of each other's attitudes, and less likely to feel compatible with the individuals who held opinions similar to their own. Evidence for subgroup formation in these groups is found in the tendency for little *intergroup* communication, i.e., little communication from prejudiced members to nonprejudiced members or vice versa.

Haythorn, Couch, Haefner, Langham, and Carter (1956) experimented with Ss who were either high or low on the F scale of authoritarianism.[1] For the experimental session one S was appointed leader by telling him "he was to take charge of group

---

[1] Ss were (1) 32 male undergraduate students who were high on the F scale, "conservative" as judged by the Cattell Q_1 scale, and relatively normal as estimated by the MMPI; and (2) 32 male undergraduate students who had low F-scale scores, were liberal as determined by the Q_1 scale, and who were "normal" as judged by the MMPI.

activities that day and would be responsible for getting the job done." Half of the groups were constructed with leaders who had F-scale scores similar to the rest of the participants, and half were constructed with contrasting F-scale scores for leaders and followers. For the next session, the conditions were reversed so that all groups had experience with both similar and contrasting leader personalities.

Again differences emerge from the contrasting behavioral dispositions of leaders and group members; groups with contrasting leaders were less secure (second session only) and demonstrated more conflict as measured by observer ratings.[2]

Patterns of managerial traits and group effectiveness. Ghiselli and Lodahl (1958) reported an experimental study on the way in which patterns of managerial traits influence interpersonal relations in groups. Their college student subjects were given personality measures which had been developed to measure managerial traits. One scale, called the *Decision-Making Approach,* was made up of items which distinguished top and middle management along the following dimension:

. . . *people holding top management positions tended to perceive themselves as being active and self-reliant, and willing to take action on the basis of confidence in themselves and their own abilities. . . . People holding middle management positions tend to see themselves as careful in planning and thoughtful in actions, seldom making rash decisions. They seem to wish to avoid giving the appearance of being controversial personalities and of exhibiting self-centered behavior* (Ghiselli and Lodahl, 1958, p. 63).

A second scale, which was also made up of items from an adjective check list, is called the *Supervisory Ability* scale. This scale of self-descriptions had previously been found to correlate with supervisor's ratings of effectiveness. The two scales correlate .365 and the same person was highest scorer in 20 of the 30 groups.

Groups of subjects were put to work on a model railroad problem which had several different sets of controls. Ss were instructed to run two trains in opposite directions around the track as many times as possible in a three-minute trial. Neither the

[2] Participant ratings of conflict did not differ significantly.

mean score of an entire group nor the score of the highest scoring member on the Decision-Making Approach or the Supervisory Ability scales was related to productivity (number of trips around the track). This suggests that neither the absolute level of attitude in the entire group nor the level of the highest scorer in the group influenced group productivity.

The relative scores, however, were strongly correlated with productivity. Groups with a large difference between the highest scorer and the next highest scorer were more productive than groups where the top two scorers earned about equal scores on either of the two scales. This suggests that a group is most productive when it has a member who is uncontested in supervisory ability and/or decision-making approach. Groups who have only one member whose personality qualifies him as a leader do not have to spend time selecting a leader and building an interpersonal organization. This interpretation is supported by data on the number of changes in the interpersonal organization and the number of changes in methods for working on the task which the group members made during the experiment. As might be expected, productivity was negatively correlated with the number of organization changes ($-.64$) and with the number of methods changes ($-.55$). Furthermore, groups which contained one uncontested leader and homogeneous followers (as measured by the Decision-Making scale) made significantly fewer organization changes and fewer method changes.

There is a convergence of findings between the Guetzkow communication net studies reviewed earlier and the Ghiselli and Lodahl experiments reported here. Both experiments work with tasks which require an elaborate interpersonal organization to coordinate the efforts of the group members. Guetzkow simplified the interpersonal obstacles by manipulating the task environment so that one group member was almost automatically nominated as the leader or "keyman." The problem of selecting a leader in the study reported above was simplified if the personality of only one group member qualified him to be a supervisor.[3]

[3] This interpretation would be strengthened if we had evidence from the Ghiselli and Lodahl study which demonstrated that the groups' members who

Perceived compatibility. The effects of incompatible personality dispositions on interpersonal relations need not be grounded in reality. Exline (1957) was able to induce interpersonal disruption merely through instructions to group members. At the time of recruitment, he gave his *Ss* a standard personality test and questionnaire which purported to measure attitudes toward working in groups and told them that this information would be used to assign them to discussion groups. Although the *Ss* were actually assigned randomly, *congenial* groups were told that they stood very high on a scale of congeniality and that they should get on well together. *Noncongenial Ss* were told that they stood very low on the congeniality scale, that it was necessary to put people with opposing attitudes in the same group, that they were about as bad a matching as was possible, and they would probably not find the group very congenial.[4]

Although Exline did not have a measure of productivity, he found that congenial groups (versus noncongenial groups) demonstrated a higher liking of co-workers, a higher willingness to work with others in the group, and a greater satisfaction with the progress of the group. All of these measures might be taken as symptoms of superior interpersonal relations.

The congeniality inductions produced a greater accuracy in interpersonal perception of *task* issues (i.e., the *S*'s estimation of how he thinks other group members would rank potential solutions to the task discussed). This finding indicates that the interpersonal relations were such that adequate task communication was achieved. In contrast, the congenial groups were *not* more accurate in their perception of the patterns of interpersonal likes and dislikes among group members.

were unchallenged on their scale scores actually did assume supervisory functions and that challenged individuals were unable to assume the supervisory function.

[4] Although these inductions deal specifically with congeniality, it should be noted that they are quite similar to inductions which have been used to create high cohesiveness or high attractiveness of the group (see, for example, Back, 1951). Thus it is not demonstrated whether the results are due to the specific content of the inductions or to a more general stress on the attractiveness of the group.

The findings exhibited in our discussion of the effects of dispositional characteristics upon interpersonal organization within conference groups provide little leverage for improving the effectiveness of such groups, given the initial distribution of personal characteristics among participants. Inasmuch as any group usually contains some compatibilities, it may be possible to gain advantage by stressing these congenialities, as the findings from Exline (1957) intimate.

STATUS INCONGRUITY AS AN INTERPERSONAL OBSTACLE

Status is closely bound up with interpersonal rewards—people in our society value status in itself. Furthermore, the rights and privileges accorded to people of high status provide extra bonuses for high-status group members. Status is also closely related to other forms of interpersonal relations. Leaders use status as a base of power to implement their directions and groups reinforce diligent workers with interpersonal status rewards. The whole of Chapter Eight is devoted to differences in the behavior of high and low power persons, and status is closely related to power. These comments do not begin to describe the full role that status plays in interpersonal relations, but they do give us some insight into the reasons why disagreement on a person's status constitutes a serious interpersonal obstacle.

A person's status is determined by a multitude of factors such as education level, past performance in the group, and his status in other groups. Problems are created when the status which a person deserves on one dimension—educational level, for instance —differs from the status he deserves on the basis of his accomplishments on another dimension, e.g., official rank in the organization. Since the many sources of status seem to prescribe different statuses to the same persons, the group does not know the appropriate status for the group member. A person without clearly defined status presents an ambiguous stimulus; other group members do not know how to behave toward him. The effectiveness of the group is curtailed by this ambiguous stimulus in their midst, just as the "40 questions" productivity of Smith's (1956) groups was curtailed by the ambiguous silence of the paid experimental assistants. Task productivity can suffer while the group is absorbed in an interpersonal status conflict.

Adams (1953) measured the status positions of crew members in 52 eleven-man crews drawn from an Air Force training base on each of the following dimensions: age, military rank, amount of flying time, education, reputed ability, popularity, length of service, combat time, and position importance. Adams then compiled a measure of status *congruency* which is a comparison of an individual's rank on one dimension with his ranks on all other dimensions.

Adams found that group technical performance (measured by performance tests such as bombing scores, etc.) first increased and then decreased as group status congruence became greater. However, group "social performance" (morale, friendship, and confidence) increased continuously with higher group status congruency. These findings suggest that status congruence is interpersonally rewarding. Although higher and higher degrees of status congruency appear to continually produce increased *interpersonal* rewards, it appears that status differentiation and congruency can be carried to the point that *task environmental* rewards (performance) are curtailed.

Exline and Ziller (1959) demonstrate the liability of status incongruence in a different setting by using experimentally assigned status. The experimenter observed the interaction of groups of three women solving two problems. Four status conditions were created by varying both voting power (giving one S three votes, another two votes, and the third one vote versus giving each S one vote each) and presumed problem-solving ability. Ss were led to believe that there were, or were not, clear differences in the problem-solving ability among the three participants. The two congruent conditions were the one with no hierarchy in either voting or ability and the one with the same hierarchy with respect to both the power and problem-solving dimensions. The two status incongruent conditions were the one with a hierarchy in ability but not voting and the one with a hierarchy in voting but not ability.

The groups with incongruent status hierarchies manifested more interpersonal conflict than groups with congruent status hierarchies. Exline and Ziller found that status incongruence also led to poorer task performance (Ss erred more in estimation of number of dots in a figure and chose somewhat fewer numbers of correct criteria for evaluating movie-TV educational aids).

Not only does lack of agreement among the dimensions of status interfere with group effectiveness, but lack of consensus upon a single dimension of status within a group also interferes. In an experiment discussed in detail in Chapter Ten on participant satisfaction, Shelly (1960) found that low agreement among the group members in girls' clubs concerning who ranked first on a continuum of leadership was related to low participant satisfaction.

Heinicke and Bales (1953) studied five-man discussion groups over a period of six weekly sessions. At the end of each session, the group presented a written solution to the case which they had discussed. " 'Efficiency' was measured by the ratio of the productivity rating (average for the two raters) to the length of the discussion in seconds" (pp. 34–35). Groups with a high degree of consensus on leadership were more efficient than groups with disagreement on leadership ratings.

HOMOGENEOUS OR HETEROGENEOUS PERSONALITIES AND BACKGROUNDS IN EFFECTIVE GROUPS?

If we extrapolate the findings about personality to this point, we find that greater variations in personality increase the chance for incompatibility. It would seem to follow that heterogeneous groups should have lower productivity. Yet when we examine the empirical findings about the consequences of heterogeneity in personal characteristics, we discover disagreement among the researchers. Hoffman (1959) found that productivity increased with heterogeneity and, citing the findings of Pelz (1956) in his support, states ". . . the results reported in the present study are probably generalizable well beyond the limited population of college students who supplied the data" (Hoffman, 1959, p. 31). Shortly following the Hoffman article, however, Shaw (1960) published "a word of caution regarding the generalizability of the results . . ." (p. 448).

Two of the themes which were developed in earlier sections

can be used as a base for each of these opposite predictions. In Chapter Two we argued that much of the superiority of a group will lie in the larger number of alternatives and criteria available to it. Following the same logic, a group composed of members with heterogeneous personalities should have a larger number of alternatives and criteria than a homogeneous group; so a heterogeneous group should exhibit *higher* productivity. On the other hand, the data presented in this chapter illustrated the way in which heterogeneous personality composition can lead to disruption of the interpersonal organization and thus *lower* productivity.

It appears, then, that increasing the heterogeneity of personality and background can have at least two effects on group interaction.

1. *Increasing heterogeneity of personality will increase the difficulty of building interpersonal relations.* In other words, there will be more interpersonal conflict, less effective division of labor, lower rewards associated with social interaction, and lower group cohesiveness. We would expect such interpersonal disorganization to be greatest when (*a*) the dimensions of personality differences are directly relevant to the interpersonal relations of the group members; and (*b*) the task requires elaborate patterns of interpersonal relations.

2. *Increasing the heterogeneity of personality within a group will also increase the problem-solving potential of the group.* Random or sampling errors are more likely to be eliminated, constant biases are less likely, more alternatives are available for consideration, and a wider critical base is provided.

We would expect the *facilitating* task impact to be greatest when (*a*) the dimensions of personality differences are relevant to the critical demands of the task, and (*b*) the task is difficult, i.e., the advantages of heterogeneous perspectives can compensate for the time lost in ironing out interpersonal conflicts.

Hoffman, Harburg, and Maier (1962) reported evidence suggesting that conflict can increase the number of alternatives which group members generate. The experimenters asked college students to participate in a role playing session in which one student assumed the role of a foreman and the other group members played the role of workers. The instructions to the group members specified that the foreman was to introduce a change of work procedure which should increase productivity for the entire group, but which would probably increase boredom for the workers. The group could adopt the foreman's proposed change, retain the old system, or work out a creative or integrative solution which combined the better elements of both procedures. Previous research indicated that one main obstacle to developing integrative solutions was that the foreman would "railroad" his suggestion through without listening to the opinions of the workers.

By means of their instructions to the role players, the experimenters strengthened the position of the workers. The intention was to make the "workers" more likely to disagree with the foreman and thus force the group to seek out additional alternatives. Although Hoffman, Harberg, and Maier do not report any measures of disagreement, conflict, or alternatives presented, they do report that groups in which the "workers" had received the strong instructions reached significantly more integrative or creative solutions.

It is difficult to check the validity of this discussion because we have postulated two competing processes. Heterogeneity of group personality will either increase or decrease group productivity depending on whether task facilitation or interpersonal conflict is the stronger process. The postulated opposing processes will receive some verification, however, if we note examples of decreased productivity and find that conditions for task facilitation are absent, in the main, while conditions for interpersonal conflict are present. Similarly, experiments demonstrating an increased productivity should exhibit conditions for task facilitation while affording less opportunity for interpersonal conflict.

Studies where heterogeneity increased productivity. Hoffman (1959) and Ziller (1955) found that heterogeneity in personality was associated with high productivity. After administering the Guilford-Zimmerman Temperament Survey to students in a psychology of human relations course, Hoffman (1959) used an index of similarity among the profiles of the ten scores to construct homogeneous and heterogeneous groups. He deliberately chose one task which would stress the *advantages* and another which would stress the *disadvantages* of heterogeneous personality compositions.[5]

On the task with purely objective criteria (mined road problem), Hoffman found that heterogeneous groups produced solutions of significantly higher quality. The difference was not significant on the task primarily requiring consensus. Superiority of the heterogeneous groups has been further demonstrated in a second study which used a wider range of tasks (Hoffman and Maier, 1961). The interpersonal conflict does not appear to impair the *task* efforts of the heterogeneous groups on any of the tasks. The tasks are relatively complex and require intellectual effort for solution; it may be that all tasks were complex enough to benefit from the conflicts among alternatives and criteria.

Ziller (1955) asked members of Air Force crews to estimate the number of dots on a card 16 by 21 inches containing 3155 black dots. Individuals first made individual judgments and then reached a group decision. A "heterogeneous group scale of judgment" or high variability of the initial individual judgments

---

[5] The "mined road problem" was intended to be typical of problems which require "multiple perceptions and cognitive reorganizations for their solution" (p. 27), and thus its solution should reflect the increased alternatives and criteria available in a heterogeneous group. Group members must determine the best way to cross a mined road without leaving traces of crossing. Scattered around the area are some scrap materials, e.g., ropes, lumber, etc., that could be used to cross the road. Solutions to the problem are assigned a numerical score by a content analysis scheme developed by I. Lorge and his associates.

The "change of work procedure problem," however, was intended to be typical of problems which have "no objectively good solution—i.e., . . . the quality of the solution can be judged only in terms of the members' personal values and standards— . . . differences in affective structures in nonhomogeneous groups should . . . produce conflict" (p. 27). The task consisted of a role playing situation in which the group may maintain the status quo, accept the suggested new work procedures which involve some inconvenience, or invent a new solution. Although the problem can be quantified objectively into these three categories, the central criterion is agreement among the group members on the desirability of the solution since objective criteria are not obvious.

produced more accurate group judgments. Since variability of judgments does not seem to have any direct implications for the interpersonal organization of the crews and the heterogeneity is directly relevant to the task, this situation would seem to limit the disadvantages of heterogeneous group composition.

Studies where heterogeneity decreased productivity. Schutz's studies have already been discussed in earlier sections of this chapter; they will be mentioned again only briefly. It will be remembered that Schutz's FIRO scales are specifically designed to measure aspects of interpersonal behavior which are vital to interpersonal relationships, and that the decrement in productivity produced by heterogeneity was most pronounced for tasks which required a high degree of interaction and intersubjective agreement under time pressure.

Festinger and Thibaut (1951) present some evidence that perceptions of heterogeneity do lead to the kind of subgroup formation discussed by Schutz. They found that (with low pressure toward uniformity) a greater perception of heterogeneous group composition produced a decrease in the tendency to communicate to deviant group members.

Shaw (1960) has

conducted a series of experiments attempting to study the joint effects of group structure and composition upon group efficiency in problem solving situations. . . . The data were analyzed systematically to determine the relationship between various estimates of homogeneity and problem solving effectiveness under varying structural conditions. . . . The measure of homogeneity used in computing the correlations reported was the average deviation of scores earned by members of the group on measures of intelligence (the verbal scale of the Scholastic Aptitude Tests), acceptance of authority, and individual prominence (pp. 448–449).

The data reported by Shaw are presented in Table 5.1.

Although it is uncertain whether this exact pattern of results could have been specifically predicted from our theoretical formulation, the obtained data may be interpreted in such light. Attitudes toward authority would seem to be most important to interpersonal relations, and the conflict is more likely to inhibit productivity when power is decentralized. It is reasonable that

Table 5.1   The relation of member homogeneity to group performance and satisfaction

HOMO-GENEITY VARIABLES	STRUCTURAL CONDITIONS	N	GROUP PROCESS VARIABLES		
			Trials to target	Time scores	Ratings of satisfaction
Intelligence	Power:				
(Shaw,	centralized	20	+.07	+.38	−.49 [a]
1959a)	decentralized	20	−.07	+.08	+.21
	Communication:				
	centralized	24	—	.00	+.21
	decentralized	24	—	+.26	+.30
Acceptance of	Power:				
authority	centralized	20	−.11	−.17	−.08
(Shaw,	decentralized	20	+.48 [a]	+.53 [b]	−.59 [b]
1959a)	Communication:				
	centralized	24	—	.00	+.02
	decentralized	24	—	+.27	−.11
Individual	Power:				
prominence	centralized	22	−.22	+.06	−.18
(Shaw,	decentralized	22	−.08	−.26	+.20
1959b)					

Note: Signs of correlations have been adjusted so that a positive correlation indicates increasing efficiency or satisfaction with increasing homogeneity.

[a] p < .05.
[b] p < .01.

these two conditions should interact to produce inferior individual performance (two of the four significant correlations). It appears, however, that these task-environmental rewards (productivity) were achieved with few interpersonal rewards—and thus the low satisfaction.

The tasks used by Shaw are relatively routine, so little gain would be expected from heterogeneity. In light of the routine tasks and the dimensions of heterogeneity, the near zero correlations in the rest of the table are somewhat understandable.

Thus it seems that in some experiments involving hetereogeneity of personal characteristics it is possible to note the operation of opposing processes. When the task demands resources, hetereogeneity seems useful; when the interpersonal relations of the group are important, compatibility through homogeneity seems most helpful.

The Resolution of Task-Environmental (Substantive) and Interpersonal (Affective) Conflict [6]

In this section we shall describe, in some detail, the factors which were associated with success in overcoming interpersonal and task obstacles in the 72 conferences observed in the Michigan project.

DESCRIPTION OF STUDY

The process of conflict reduction has been studied in detail by Guetzkow and Gyr (1954) as a part of the University of Michigan study of 72 decision-making conferences on business and government. The general procedure of the study has been described elsewhere (Marquis, Guetzkow, and Heyns, 1951). After making their observations of the conferences, three observers estimated the extent to which the interactions of each meeting were characterized by important differences of opinion among the group members, intellectual or personal in origin. Each of the observers made this estimate in response to the question: "How much overt conflict was there in the group?"

Guetzkow and Gyr utilized two measures of conflict which parallel the distinction between the task-environmental versus interpersonal obstacles.

[6] This section is an abridged version of "An Analysis of Conflict in Decision Making Groups" by Harold Guetzkow and John Gyr (1954). The article was Publication No. 9 of the Conference Research project at the University of Michigan, sponsored by the Office of Naval Research (Contract N6 ONR-232, T.O. 7).

1. A measure of *substantive conflict* was based on a tally by the problem-solving observer. This tally contrasted the "opposing" and "supporting" comments made during the course of the meeting. An index of substantive conflict was constructed by determining the ratio of "opposing" contributions to the total of "opposing" and "supporting" comments made in the course of the meeting. We shall assume that substantive conflict as measured here is a measure of the difficulty of the task-environmental obstacles.

2. An index of *affective conflict* was an estimate made by the three conference observers on a more holistic basis in response to the question, "To what extent did the group seem to be frustrated?" The inter-observer reliability for this rating was .66, not as high as would be desirable. We assume that affective conflict as measured here is a measure of the difficulty of the interpersonal obstacles.

At first it seemed this measure would hardly be suitable for use as an indicator of affective conflict, for frustration may arise from many sources besides the person-to-person conflict which stems from interpersonal obstacles. However, this frustration measure was not related to nonpersonal frustration-inducing factors. For instance, there was no relation between frustration and insufficient information about agenda problems being considered, nor was there any relation between frustration and the group's having decision authority incommensurate with the problems being discussed. On the other hand, the group frustration measure was highly related to other indices of the affective atmosphere of the groups. For instance, group frustration correlated with the observer's estimate of how critical and punishing the group was to its members ($r = .81$). The frustration measure was inversely related to a global measure of the pleasantness of the group's emotional atmosphere ($r = -.76$). Thus, it seems justified to utilize the frustration measure as an index of affective conflict.

The correlation between the two specialized measures of conflict (.20 with .23 required for significance at the .05 level) indicate that they are relatively separate variables, quite independent of each other. Both measures correlate substantially with the observer's rating of overt conflict (.48 and .58).

Consensus was measured through the post-conference interview in which the participants were asked: "How much difference was there between your final opinion(s) on the questions discussed and the decision(s) which the group reached?"

Overview of analysis. The aim of this study was to find out the differences, if any, between groups which terminated their conflict in consensus and groups which did not. Thus, a comparison was made between groups in which conflict ended in consensus and groups in which conflict was never resolved. The comparison was made for groups which were characterized by substantive conflict as well as for groups in which affective conflict was predominant. A further breakdown was made for those groups which ranked high on either type of conflict and for those which ranked low on conflict. Table 5.2 presents the break-downs which were made and the number of conference groups in each break-down category.

Results

Readers not interested in a detailed discussion of the results are invited to skip this section and refer to the chapter summary.

The distribution of the cases among the eight classes, as presented in Table 5.2, is one of the most interesting results of the analysis. Groups in both types of conflict, substantive or affec-

Table 5.2   Number of conference groups within each class [a]

| | GROUP IN SUBSTANTIVE CONFLICT | | GROUP IN AFFECTIVE CONFLICT | |
	High consensus	Low consensus	High consensus	Low consensus
High conflict	13	16	9	14
Low conflict	19	9	20	7

[a] The mean of the population distribution on any particular dimension was used to make the separation into "High" and "Low" Conflict.

tive, tend not to terminate in consensus. And, more important, there was no differential tendency of either type of conflict in this regard. Groups in substantive conflict were as prone not to end in consensus as those in affective conflict.

There are a number of conditions under which both types of conflict, substantive and affective, result in consensus. There are also striking and significant differences between groups in the two kinds of conflict. A group in substantive conflict tends to achieve consensus by emphasizing those factors which positively promote consensus. A group in affective conflict tends to achieve consensus by reducing those forces which hinder the achievement of consensus. This reduction is largely achieved by withdrawing from a situation in which these forces are present.[7]

CONDITIONS UNDER WHICH BOTH TYPES OF
CONFLICT TEND TO END IN CONSENSUS

A number of conditions exist under which both substantive and affective conflict lead to consensus. The data supporting the following statements are presented in statistical form in Table 5.3. It is found that the expression of many self-oriented or personal needs by the conference participants is detrimental to the reaching of consensus. It is interesting to note that when self-needs are satisfied through rewarding personal interrelations within the conference itself (Code 85—see footnote a, Table 5.3) there is a significant tendency for the group to achieve consensus, especially when intense conflict prevails.

A positive affective atmosphere in a meeting is an important condition for bringing conferences in conflict toward agreement.

---

[7] In interpreting these findings, the limitations common to other observational studies apply also to this one. It is especially important to stress that when two phenomena are observed to occur concomitantly, it is impossible to determine which event is the cause and which is the effect. However, the results of this analysis will be more useful for further work if they are interpreted hypothetically as cause-and-effect relationships. They are then framed in such a way that the next two steps toward verification are more apparent. This paper presents no proof whatsoever that the relationships hypothesized as causal are actually such. Finally, a study of this kind makes no statement about any relationships which may exist between the causal variables themselves.

*Table 5.3   Measures differentiating between groups achieving
and not achieving consensus in both substantive and affective conflict*

| | HIGH-CONFLICT GROUPS | | LOW-CONFLICT GROUPS | |
| | Sub-stantive P^b | Af-fective P | Sub-stantive P | Af-fective P |
DESCRIPTION OF VARIABLES [a]				
Expression of self-oriented needs (Code 4-OR) [c]	.001	.01	.01	.01
Satisfaction with self-perform-ance (Code 85-PR) [d]	.001	.001	.001	N.S.
Pleasantness of atmosphere (Code 20-OR)	.001	.04	N.S.	N.S.
Unification of the group (Code 45-PR)	.001	.001	.001	N.S.
Orderliness of Topic Treat-ment (Code 76-OR)	.02	.04	.01	N.S.
Understandability of Dis-cussion (Code 67-OR)	.01	.01	N.S.	N.S.

[a] The code numbers following the description of each variable in this and the following two tables are keyed to information in the microfilms, as explained in Guetzkow and Gyr (1954).
[b] *P*—Probability level of significance of difference between the means.
[c] OR—Observer rating.
[d] PR—Participant rating.
N.S.—Means not significant, i.e., $P > .05$.

The over-all pleasantness of the meeting (Code 20), as seen by the observers, created a climate conducive to agreement when either substantive or affective conflict was present in large amounts. The pleasantness was not helpful, however, in producing consensus when there was little conflict in the meeting. The participants themselves were aware of this atmosphere (Code 45). They stated that they recognized the "necessity for unified action" and felt a "willingness to give and take."

The factors mentioned up to this point are concerned with motivational and emotional aspects of the meeting. Another area of importance is the intelligibility of the problem-solving activities of the meeting. Those meetings in which discussion is orderly in its treatment of topics (Code 76), and without backward references to previously discussed issues, tended to end in more consensus, despite large amounts of substantive or affective conflict. When participants discussed but one issue at a time, instead of simultaneously dabbling in two or three, it was more possible for the group to reach consensus. The ability of the members to understand what each said (Code 67) led to agreement. When participants knew the vocabulary the others were using and talked on a common conceptual level, high conflict tended to end in consensus.

Summary for affective and substantive conflict. Motivational, emotional, and intellective factors served in the conference to create conditions leading to consensus, even when the meeting was characterized by either substantive or affective conflict. The relative absence of strong self-oriented needs increased the likelihood for consensus to appear. The satisfaction of the self-needs, the positiveness of the meeting's affective atmosphere, and greater intelligibility in problem-solving were all found to operate toward consensus in groups permeated by either type of conflict.

CONDITIONS UNDER WHICH ONLY SUBSTANTIVE CONFLICT TENDS TO END IN CONSENSUS

Some conditions existing in the conference situation resulted in strengthening the tendency toward consensus only in those groups with high substantive conflict. These same factors were not significantly related to agreement for groups high in affective conflict (Table 5.4).

This is an age in which there is increasing recognition of the impact of nonrational or "unreasonable" forces in social affairs. And it is easy to overlook time-worn propositions stemming from other centuries. From the "rationalism" of the period of enlightenment comes the argument that agreement can often

Table 5.4   Measures differentiating between groups achieving and not achieving consensus in high substantive conflict
     (Differences not significant in almost all cases for affective conflict)

DESCRIPTION OF VARIABLES	HIGH CONFLICT GROUPS Substantive P [b]	LOW CONFLICT GROUPS Substantive P
Participants' expertise (Code 108-chairman's rating)	.04	N.S.
Factual background of participants (Code 74-OR) [a]	.001	N.S.
Amount of chairman's information seeking (Code IS-OT) [a]	.001	N.S.
Efficiency of problem-solving procedure (Code 70-OR)	.001	.01
Contributions directed to chairman (Code 60-OT)	.04	N.S.
Amount of chairman's solution proposing (Code SP-OT)	.02	N.S.
Personal liking among participants (Code 21-OR)	.05	.01
Amount group supports and accepts its members (Code 24-OR)	.01	N.S.

[a] OR—Observer rating.   OT—Observer tally.
[b] P—Probability level of significance of difference between the means.
N.S.—Is not significant, i.e., $P > .05$.

be obtained through examination of the facts. What happens in conflict when the facts are available and when they are used? Two measuring devices were used to appraise the role which factual information played in the conference. Before the meeting the group's chairman made an estimate of each participant's specialized knowledge of the problems considered at the meeting (Code 108). This gave an index to the amount of factual knowledge and background which was available in the group, through the particular persons included in it. During the course of the meeting itself the observers noted the extent to which the participants used the overtly factual background potentially available in their discussion (Code 74).

Comparison of the high consensus and low consensus groups reveals that facts resolve substantive conflict. Those groups that have more expertise available and that utilize this knowledge are those whose substantive conflict ends in more consensus. The utilization of expertise does not significantly influence affective conflict, however, except in low conflict groups (not included in Table 5.4).

These results (Table 5.4) are made more understandable by analyzing the behavior of the leader. Chairmen of groups in high substantive conflict which ended in consensus did three times more seeking for information of an objective factual nature from members of their groups than did chairmen in groups which did not end in consensus (Code IS). This type of difference in the chairman's behavior between high and low consensus groups was not statistically significant in the case of groups in high affective conflict.

Other more pervasive intellectual processes served as conditions under which substantive conflict led to consensus. When the give and take was thorough and efficient (Code 70), there was more agreement. The group at such times rapidly penetrated to the core of its agenda problems. Its chairman would help dissipate substantive conflict by proposing twice as many tentative solutions to the problem in hand (Code SP) than is customary. In such circumstances there was a significant tendency for the members to address their contributions to the chairman (Code 60) rather than to each other or to the group as a whole.

The intellectual forces serving to transform substantive conflict into consensus were reinforced by emotional factors. These special conditions operate only in the case of substantive conflict. When the members of the group seem to like each other personally (Code 21), substantive conflict tends to be more easily resolved. The attraction of the participants toward each other on the basis of personal characteristics helps to achieve consensus. This friendliness permeates their problem-solving activities. The participants are warm and supportive of each other (Code 24) and encourage the full expression of personal opinions, without restrictions.

Summary for substantive conflict. The special conditions which served to terminate substantive conflict in consensus were largely intellectual in nature: availability and utilization of facts and efficient problem-solving procedures. These intellectual techniques were given full opportunity to operate when the personal interrelationships existing among the participants were warm, friendly, and nonrestrictive. All of these conditions increased the factors making for consensus.

CONDITIONS UNDER WHICH ONLY AFFECTIVE CONFLICT TENDS TO END IN CONSENSUS

It has been seen that groups in affective conflict share with groups in substantive conflict some conditions making for consensus. As with groups in substantive conflict, however, there are also several conditions which influence uniquely the operation of groups in affective conflict (Table 5.5). But, instead of positively reinforcing the tendency toward consensus, these factors can be interpreted as reducing the forces hindering the achievement of consensus.

If groups having affective conflict included on the agenda problems which were independent of each other and needed no integration into a single, final decision (Code 77), then there was an increase in the tendency toward consensus.

Groups in affective conflict can be seen to employ yet another technique for reaching consensus. This is a device similar to the one mentioned above in causing withdrawal from the problem situation, but dissimilar in being concerned with the individual participant's, rather than the group's, relation to the problem. When the participants, as individuals, evince less interest in the discussions, and grow inattentive—as demonstrated by such withdrawal activities as doodling and private conversations with neighboring group members—the likelihood is greater of disagreement being lessened (Code 1).

Table 5.5 *Measures differentiating between groups achieving*
and not achieving consensus in high affective conflict
(Difference not significant in all cases for substantive conflict)

DESCRIPTION OF VARIABLES	HIGH CONFLICT GROUPS Affective P [b]	LOW CONFLICT GROUPS Affective P
Separability of agenda problems (Code 77-OR) [a]	.01	.05
General interest level of participants (Code 1-OR)	.02	N.S.
Spread of the participant's interactions (Code 113-OT) [a]	.06 near significant	N.S.
Members' functional differentiation (Code 50-OR)	.03	N.S.
Members' problem-solving interdependence (Code 75-OR)	.02	N.S.

[a] OR—Observer rating. OT—Observer tally.
[b] P—Probability level of significance of difference between the means.
N.S.—Is not significant, i.e., $P > .05$.

Because the members of groups with affective conflict are continuously in struggle, it is reasonable to find that a reduction in the sheer quantity of interpersonal relations reduces the opportunity for clashes to occur. It was discovered in this analysis that groups in which the participants tended to confine their interactions to fewer members of the group (Code 113) were more successful in reaching consensus. There are other group characteristics that reinforce this interpretation of the working of the tendency toward interpersonal isolation. When the members of the group perform like functions in the meeting (Code 50), little interdependence is seen among the participants, and hence, less tendency for interaction between them. Their similarity to each other in terms of activities performed in the course of discussion makes feasible the avoidance of interpersonal contact. In those aspects of group functioning involving problem-solving activities *per se,* considerably less interdependence exists in groups (Code 75) terminating in more consensus. Less tendency exists in groups in high affective conflict for members to perform specialized problem-solving roles. A participant becomes less often the "information giver" or the "solution-proposer."

At first it would seem feasible to interpret the findings presented in Table 5.5 more conservatively as follows: When the agenda consists of small, quasi-independent problems (Code 77), the agenda is easy and arouses little conflict. When no one cares (Code 1), any decisions go. In other words, when there are no issues, is it surprising that there is consensus? This type of interpretation neglects one essential factor: that the groups being considered were rated by the observers as having above average affective conflict (Code 52) in them throughout the meeting. They were undifferentiated in the amount of overt conflict exhibited (Code 53) from the groups in high substantive conflict. This overt conflict had to be handled in some way if the meeting were to end in consensus. According to Table 5.5, the conflict was reduced by withdrawal—the forces tending toward conflict being restrained by retreating. In the absence of such conflict-accentuating forces, whatever positive forces existed in the situation eventuated in consensus.

Summary for affective conflict. In groups in high affective conflict, there were no unique conditions reinforcing the tendencies within the group toward reaching consensus. Instead, the analysis disclosed only factors which could be interpreted as reducing the force of the tendencies hindering the achievement of consensus. There was a striking proclivity of the groups to withdraw from the problem itself, either by becoming less interested in it or by postponing its consideration. The participants also reduced their tendency to disagreement by developing forms of interpersonal isolation. This inclination toward a restricted range of person-to-person contact was reinforced by the participants tending to be much alike in the functions they performed in the meeting, so that little interdependence was necessary.

THE NEGATIVE FINDINGS: CONDITIONS WHICH DID NOT INFLUENCE THE TENDENCIES TOWARD CONSENSUS

Up to this point all the findings mentioned have concerned factors that "make a difference" in determining whether substantive or affective conflict will or will not eventuate in consensus. Out of the fifty-four factors examined, approximately half were significantly associated with differences in consensus. Some of the factors that failed to show a relationship were examined only on the basis of vague hunches. However, there were two sets of conditions whose failure to accompany differences in consensus were surprising.

It was thought originally that the group's formal procedures should increase the tendency to consensus. Historically, parliamentary procedures have evolved as machinery to bring consensus out of conflict. The hypothesis was stated that the degree to which a group used formal procedure (Code 73) (e.g., the use of formal votes, motions, etc.) would reduce the impact of interpersonal clash occurring in groups in affective conflict. Although interpersonal isolation was helpful in increasing consensus, it was surprising to find that a procedure expected to "guard" the participant in the discussion was not related to the eventual extent of consensus. Even protective, formal, interpersonal devices (e.g., the use of "Mr. Smith," etc.), did not increase consensus in either the substantive or affective conflict groups.

The other set of factors unexpectedly having no association with consensus was related to characteristics of the agenda being considered by the groups in conflict. The hypothesis was stated that groups with problems needing *urgent* solution would tend to come to consensus (Code 13). Such was not the case, even though on theoretical grounds it might be supposed that the forces opposed to consensus might be restrained by strong needs to come to decision for given deadlines. Although there was a marked tendency for meetings with urgent items on their agenda to complete more of the items they considered, the participants did not reach any more or any less consensus in such meetings than in those having less urgent items on the agenda. The *importance* of the agenda problem to the welfare of the organization (Code 16) also had no bearing upon the way in which the conflict was handled. The hypothesis was stated that the groups with more important problems would tend to have more difficulty in reaching consensus. Such groups would tend to do a more thorough job of exploring all facets of the problem and would need information often not available. It was also thought that members of such groups, inasmuch as their careers were at stake, would tend toward less consensus by unconsciously interjecting their self-needs in the discussion. Thus participants would emotionally invest their substantive arguments and become more stubborn and persistent in maintaining contrary positions. The results of the analysis show that these suppositions were, in the context of this study, unfounded.

CHAPTER SUMMARY

The obstacles involving interpersonal relations among participants pose serious problems for those wanting to use conferences for decision-making. Disruption may be induced by the individualistic, competitive motivations of the participants. The conference's effectiveness may be hindered by incompatibilities among the underlying personal characteristics of the conference. Or, it may be that the status incongruities operating within the conference disturb its outcomes. Yet these heterogeneities sometimes bring constructive end products, as when the differences in personality contribute to the problem-solving abilities of the group.

At times the incompatibilities may be eliminated by the preselection of the conference participants, should one possess latitude for such choice. Once under way, however, disruptions in the conference due to such incompatibilities can be reduced in intensity by playing them down, as was demonstrated by Exline.

Certain conditions existing within conferences in either substantive or affective conflicts are associated with successful conflict reduction and consensus.

CONDITIONS ASSOCIATED WITH HIGH CONSENSUS IN GROUPS IN EITHER SUBSTANTIVE OR AFFECTIVE CONFLICT

1. When there is little expression of personal, self-oriented needs.

2. When whatever self-needs are expressed tend to be satisfied during the course of the meeting.

3. When there is a generally pleasant atmosphere and the participants recognized the need for unified action.

4. When the group's problem-solving activity is understandable, orderly, and focused on one issue at a time.

CONDITIONS ASSOCIATED WITH HIGH CONSENSUS IN GROUPS IN SUBSTANTIVE CONFLICT

(These conditions do not hold for groups in affective conflict.)

1. When facts are available and used.

2. When chairman, through much solution proposing, aids the group in penetrating its agenda problems.

3. When the participants feel warm and friendly toward each other in a personal way.

CONDITIONS ASSOCIATED WITH HIGH CONSENSUS IN GROUPS IN AFFECTIVE CONFLICT

(These conditions do not hold for groups in substantive conflict.)

1. When the group withdraws from its problem-solving activities by tackling only discrete, simpler agenda items.

2. When the participants withdraw from the problem situation and have little interest in what is being discussed.

3. When the participants withdraw from interpersonal contact with each other.

CHAPTER SIX

Direct sources of power and interpersonal influence

POWER AND REWARD

The emphasis in the first five chapters has been on variables which influence the productivity or output of the group. Now we shift our attention to the process of group interaction with the next three chapters on power, a chapter on communication and interaction, and a chapter on satisfaction. Throughout these chapters and especially in the power and satisfaction sections, the concept of reward will appear repeatedly. In Figure 4.1, two kinds of rewards were identified—task-environmental rewards which are found in environmental task feedback and interpersonal rewards which are found in the behavior of other group members. Both kinds of rewards can be used to mold, maintain, and motivate both task-related and interpersonal behaviors. Now we examine additional functions of these rewards. In the next two chapters, rewards are shown to be the source of power for individual group members and for the group as a whole. In the satisfaction chapter, the way in which rewards produce satisfaction is detailed. The reader is reminded that the rewards discussed in the following chapters in relationship to power and satisfaction are the same rewards which reinforce behavior.

OVERVIEW AND DEFINITIONS

Power was a favorite concept of the 19th century social scientists who attempted "to select and develop one simple and sovereign formula that seemed . . . to hold the key to social behavior" (Allport, 1954, p. 9). In the 20th century, Cartwright (1959, pp. 1–14) entitled his presidential address to the Society for the Psychological Study of Social Issues: "Power: A Neglected Variable in Social Psychology." In spite of the difficulties connected with the concept of power, we found it useful in organizing the empirical relationships reviewed in the next three chapters. We present our definition as a starting point in this chapter.

When the acts of an agent can (actually or potentially) modify the behavior of a person, or group of persons, the agent has power over that person or group of persons.

Agent. The agent is any part of the environment or that world outside the individual himself. The agent could be a leader who has power over the group, a friend who has power over an individual, a traffic light which has power over the drivers at an intersection, or a social norm which has power over all who accept it. In this and subsequent chapters, we are largely interested in the power of one group member over other group members; so the agent usually will be the powerful group member. But, it seems desirable to follow Cartwright (1959, pp. 183–219) and define an agent as any entity which can produce effects.

Act. By act we mean any stimulus a person can discriminate, which serves as the medium through which an agent exerts its power. For nonhuman agents, the act might be the flashing red light of the stop light or the pleading whine of the pet dog. For human agents, the act could be a verbal statement, a facial expression, a gesture, or a written command.

Behavior. We will call a tendency to *think* or act in a certain way a *behavioral disposition*. It is helpful to talk about a disposition to behave rather than overt behavior, because the effects of power may not be immediately evident in the overt behavior of the influenced person. For example, a group member's comment might make the leader less certain in his efforts to change the topic of discussion; so we would say that the comment has modified the leader's behavioral *disposition* to change the topic, even though his overt behavior did not change. In this way, we meet March's criticism that many definitions of power "Ignore changes in the individual's latent readiness to act" (1955, p. 433).

Potential. Power does not have to be overtly exercised in order to exist. The agent does not try to exert his power; he may be ignorant that he has the power; he may have values against being "bossy"; or he may decide that this is not the proper time to exert his power.

Modify. We say that an agent has modified a person's behavioral disposition if, following the action of the agent, there is a change in the person's disposition to behave which would not have occurred otherwise. (We should remember that this change in the person's behavioral disposition may not immediately be reflected in his overt behavior.) Thus a change in opinion induced within a conference may reverse the operating behaviors of an executive upon his return to his department. Or, it may be that power plays within a board of directors may alter the makeup of coalitions at subsequent meetings of the board.

A definition builder must decide how much he will be influenced by his theories of human behavior. He may simply state that power is the ability to modify behavior, or he may wish to include some mention of the factors which *cause* modifications in behavior. Thibaut and Kelley (1959) have theorized that a person's social behavior is largely determined by the outcomes which he receives in social interaction, and they state their definition of power in terms of outcomes. The Lewinian theorist Cartwright states that an individual's behavior is determined by the psychological forces which act upon him. In the light of this theoretical position, it is not surprising that Cartwright defines power as "the induction of (psychological) forces by one entity b upon another a and the resistance to this induction set up by a" (1959, p. 188). It seems reasonable to state that, with respect to power at least, these definitions are actually in agreement. Both agree that the agent has power over a person, because the agent is able to influence the behavior of the person. The differences lie not in their conception of power, but in their conception of the way in which a person is influenced, i.e., in the causes of human behavior. We have attempted to emphasize this essential agreement among theorists in our previous definition of power by omitting reference to a specific theoretical system of human behavior.

Later, in Chapter Eight, we shall undertake special study of some differences between high and low power persons within groups; now let us consider the *sources* of this power. In this chapter, we consider how influence stems from direct possession of rewards or resources. In Chapter Seven, we shall attempt to understand the more indirect ways that agents gain power in decision-making groups. Although materials in these chapters are for analytical purposes, our readers will be ever-mindful that, in the world of conferences, influencers in decision-making groups use both direct and indirect ways of exercising power over those with less influence.

Sources of Power which Stem from the Agent's Direct Possession of Resources Important to the Other Person

This chapter deals with those situations in which the agent has physical possession of rewards valued by a second person. In the conference situation, the agent may have a vote desired by another. Sometimes the resources involved are less important; it may be merely that the chairman of the group provides another member with immediate recognition, so that his contribution may be placed within the ongoing stream of the discussion, rather than coming as an afterthought. Or, it may be that a group member exercises influence by simply giving a friendly nod of support for another's point. What is important is that many agents have direct physical possession of resources important to conference members and can award or withhold these rewards at will.

PROPOSITION 6.1. Direct control of task-environmental rewards is a source of power.

In this chapter "control of rewards" and "power" have been conceptually separated. Rewards are stimuli which are valued by the person and which have been found to increase the probability of behavior they follow. The foregoing proposition states that persons who have direct control of the reward stimuli (can award or withhold these stimuli) will be able to influence the behavior of other group members. Rewards are the source from which agents gain their power to modify behavioral dispositions.

Butler, Ono, and Miller (1962) directly manipulated the valued resources in the possession of their subjects. Five-man groups passed 100 written messages at a fixed rate in a communication net. The messages were either A (rewards) or B (neutral); subjects were instructed to collect as many of the A messages as possible. Some Ss were originally given only 10 (out of 100) of the valued A messages while others were given 30, 50, 70, or 90 of the valued messages. The total number of messages which an S received was highest for those Ss who originally held the largest stock of valued resources. Subsequent research with different apparatus (Miller and Butler, 1962) repeatedly confirms the relationship between possession of resources and messages received. In addition, "Ratings by each subject of the other subjects on 30 personality traits monotonically increase in favorability with increased power [resources] of the person rated" (Miller and Butler, 1962, p. 36). This finding supports our use of "messages received" as an index of power in this experimental setting.

Cohen (1958) told all subjects that they would be working on a task with another group which was located in another room, and that this second group had the better job. One-half of the subjects were told that they must work on the dull task for the entire experimental session. In contrast, the other half were told that they stood some chance of being "promoted" and that the other group would evaluate their performance and decide who was to be promoted. In the latter condition, the fictitious second group had the ability to reward the members of the first group. Actually, there was no second group and all messages were sent and intercepted by the experimenter. An analysis of the subjects' messages was conducted. Subjects who had been told that another group had the ability to reward them showed concern for the experimental task and indicated a general orientation to the second group. They ignored the other members of their own group. This is evident in the number of messages sent to the second group (more messages and more words per message) and from the content of the messages (fewer messages containing irrelevant content and fewer notes critical of the second group). These measures and several not reported here reflect the high power of the fictitious second group—power which stems from the ability of the second group to control rewards important to the subject, i.e., to promote or not promote.

Bennis, Berkowitz, Affinito, and Malone (1958) presented data from a questionnaire study which directly support this proposition. Data were collected on ninety nurses working in six out-patient departments in a large Eastern city. The experimenter measured the difference between the rewards that *Ss hoped* to receive and rewards they felt they were *likely* to receive, and used this as a measure of the ability of the supervisors to reward the nurses. The power of the supervisor was measured in a similar manner; the *E* determined the difference between the nurses' rating of how they actually spent their time and the supervisor's rating of how he would like them to spend their time. Using these two indices, the authors found that the greater the ability of the supervisor to control resources important to the nurses, the greater was the power of the supervisor. Working in an industrial field situation, Pelz (1951) noted that foremen who could do things for their men had more power over these men.

INTERPERSONAL ATTRACTION AND POWER

The evidence presented in the next proposition (6.2) will suggest that the people we like have a degree of power over us. Before we turn to this evidence, however, let us discuss a few of the reasons *why* interpersonal attraction or liking should be associated with power.

It may be that interpersonal attraction is not a direct source of reward in and of itself. Interpersonal attraction may be nothing more than a symptom or measure of past rewardingness: A liked person has current power, but that power may be due to the rewards which he has provided in the past. In other words, we may value interaction with liked persons because we value the "things" (the task-environmental rewards) which past experience has taught us to expect—not because we value the interaction *per se*.

Even should such be the case, there is evidence to suggest that interaction with liked persons is also rewarding in and of itself. Kelley and Shapiro (1954) found that Ss who were led to believe that they had been accepted by the group indicated a greater "enjoyment of participation in the experiment." This finding provides some support for the assertion that the more a person is accepted, the greater the intrinsic enjoyment of talking with the other group members.

There are many reasons why interaction with friends could be directly rewarding. We value the opinions of the people we like. We are pleased (rewarded) when our friends agree with us, speak well of us and our other friends, and share our disapproval of disliked ideas and people.[1] This extra respect which we grant to the opinions of liked associates gives those friends a special control over our rewards and punishments. Since we value their opinion, they can reward us by merely agreeing with us. This means that liked people can limit our rewards by either (a) withholding all interaction or (b) failing to offer the specific kinds of interaction we desire.

The correlation between attraction and interaction. Our argument has been that interaction with other humans is rewarding and that liking increases the value of the rewards associated with interaction. Now we review the evidence demonstrating the close relationship between interaction and liking (interpersonal attraction).

In an early formulation Homans (1950) asserted an interrelationship between interaction (communication) and sentiment (interpersonal liking): "If the frequency of interaction between two or more persons increases, the degree of their liking for one another will increase, and vice versa" (p. 112). Turner (1957) found that higher than average interaction rates were associated with liked foremen and lower than average interaction rates were associated with unliked foremen. Bovard (1956) discovered dramatic increases in interpersonal liking in his honor classes

---

[1] For general theoretical statements of this position see Festinger (1950, 1957), Heider (1958), Osgood et al. (1957), and Newcomb (1953). For supportive data directly relevant to our interests here, see Newcomb (1961, 1963).

when interaction was encouraged. Dittes and Kelley (1956) found that the introduction of bogus acceptability ratings from other group members (indicating that a S was not liked by other group members) decreased the amount of interaction initiated by that S.[2] Kipnis (1957) reported that both physical closeness and functional closeness (both of which would lead to increased interaction) were positively related to interpersonal liking.

The psychological mechanisms and the direction of causation which underlie this empirical phenomenon are involved and interrelated. For example, Jackson (1959a) found that the effect of high interaction was to increase the *correlation* between (*a*) participants' ratings of value to the group and (*b*) interpersonal attraction in ongoing work groups. Since interaction probably leads to increased accuracy of interpersonal perception (Bieri, 1953; Festinger and Hutte, 1954; Wood, 1948), Jackson's finding may mean that interaction made Ss more aware of the value of the highly liked persons. On the other hand, it may be that interpersonal liking leads to increased interaction. As group members come to like each other and interaction becomes more valuable, they may increase interaction to gain the valued rewards. In either case high attraction would lead to power: the liked person can directly control the rewards which are associated with interaction with him.

So far we have discussed the close relationship between interaction and interpersonal liking, and we have argued that interaction is more rewarding when it takes place between two individuals who like each other. The following propositions specifically discuss interpersonal attraction as a source of power. Proposition 6.2-A discusses personal attraction to a single individual and Proposition 6.2-B focuses on the interpersonal attraction existing among the members of the group.

---

[2] Decrease was significant at (.001) but held only with messages indicating *very low* acceptance. Negative evaluation increased interaction for *low* (N.S.) and *average* (.09) acceptance messages. This suggests that *if there is some likelihood* of increased acceptance, Ss may increase interaction in hopes of becoming liked.

PROPOSITION 6.2. Control of the rewards associated with "friendly interaction" is a source of power.

"Friendly interaction" means interaction with a liked person. This proposition deals with an important class of rewards which are directly under the control of each group member.

PROPOSITION 6.2-A. The greater the personal attraction of other group members to a single individual, the greater the power of that individual.

Several studies in a variety of situations and with a variety of definitions of power have shown that high power persons are liked. Lippitt et al. (1952) had members of three camps rate each other along a power dimension. The campers rated high on power were personally liked by their peers. Hurwitz et al. (1953) sponsored a conference in which the members "were selected by two local people, qualified to judge the prestige of these persons in the eyes of fellow professionals" (p. 484). Those participants who scored highly on this measure of power were also highly liked by the other members of the conference. Lana, Vaughan, and McGinnies (1960) studied two community groups who were engaged in the discussion of mental health films. The members of these discussion groups were asked to nominate members for president and vice president and to choose two members of the group whom they considered most friendly. The correlation between these measures of friendship and power or, as Lana et al. put it, leadership and friendship status, was .65—the highest reported in their study. Borgatta and Bales (1956) and Talland (1957) independently report a similar correlation between member ratings of leadership and popularity. Talland's correlations among the five measures (leadership displayed, contribution to group discussion, dominance of group discussion, general popularity in the group, and friendliness shown to members in the group) ranged from .61 to .87. Hollander and Webb (1955) asked aviation cadets to name three peers that they would like to follow and three they liked. Although the leadership score correlated most highly with other measures of leadership and followership, the correlation between being nominated for leadership and being chosen as a friend was .47, quite significant statistically. These studies are discussed in more detail in Chapter Eleven.

French and Snyder (1959) brought Air Force noncommissioned officers and some of the enlisted men who had been working under them into the laboratory for an experiment on power. First, each group participated in a group discussion in which they were required to judge a number of stimulus figures, and then the enlisted men were assigned to the task of hand-sorting punched cards according to the number of holes in each card. The enlisted men received a number of messages which were supposedly from the noncommissioned officers—in fact, a standard set was substituted. In this way it was possible to study the interaction of leader and follower initially in open interaction and then later to study the reaction of the enlisted men to a standard set of messages. High liking of the leader produced more private opinion change in the open interactions. In the second phase of the experiment, a high degree of liking for the leader was associated with high influence from the standard set of messages.

Finally Horowitz, Lyons, and Perlmutter (1951), by means of a sociometric questionnaire, measured the friendship pattern of twenty persons attending a summer work shop. Then, following a regularly scheduled discussion by the group, the investigators presented to the group three of the assertions made during the discussion, each with the name of its originator. The more highly liked was the author of an assertion, the greater the tendency to agree.

PROPOSITION 6.2-B. The greater the interpersonal attraction among the members of a group, the greater the power of the "group" over the group members.

It would be possible to treat group "cohesiveness" as the sum of the bonds of attraction among all the group members, but it is unlikely that the participant thinks of his "group membership" as a collection of separate friendships. It is likely that a group member abstracts from separate relationships with other group members and forms the concept of a "group." A member may react to a reprimand from the leader differently than he could react to a reprimand from that same person in another context where the person is not a spokesman for the "group." In a similar way, a majority vote can formalize a resolution as the "group decision," and the member might react differently than he would to the same idea supported by the same persons before it was designated as the "group decision." Again, the greater power of cohesive groups is probably due both to (a) the fact that interaction with these group members had been rewarding in the past, and that (b) interaction with liked persons is directly rewarding.

Schachter, Ellertson, and McBride (1951) conducted an early experiment to test the effect of cohesiveness (interpersonal attraction among the group members) on interpersonal influence. Groups of three persons were told that they would be cooperatively producing checker boards with each member performing one operation: cutting the cardboard, pasting it on heavy stock, or painting the squares with a stencil. Actually all Ss were assigned to the job of cutting, all written messages intercepted, and a standard set substituted. Some notes advocated increases and others decreases in productivity. The requests for lower productivity produced greater changes in productivity for those groups in which the experimental instructions had pictured the other group members as congenial. Although Schachter et al. reported that the cohesive groups were *not* more responsive to requests for *increased* production, Berkowitz (1954) reported that the cohesiveness inductions increased the effectiveness of messages advocating both increases and messages advocating a decrease in productivity.[3]

[3] The preponderance of evidence provides fairly strong support for the assertion that groups high in interpersonal attraction have more power over their members. The concept of cohesiveness, however, has been subjected to a great deal of theoretical and empirical criticism. Eisman (1959), for instance, found little relationship among several measures of cohesiveness. See also a discussion of the Eisman paper by Van Bergen and Koekebakker (1959) and a further empirical test by Ramuz-Nienhuis and Van Bergen (1960). Furthermore, Downing (1958) reported negative findings in a study similar to both those of Schachter et al. and Berkowitz reported above. Although Downing's high cohesive Ss did score higher on a question designed to measure cohesiveness, Ss in highly cohesive groups did not show more conformity on a judgmental task.

Kurt Back (1951) demonstrated that cohesiveness can be created at least three different ways. Seventy pairs, each consisting of two different psychology students, were first given (alone) an experimental induction stressing *either* (1) potential interpersonal attraction of his partner, (2) the importance of the task, or (3) the prestige of the group. (Note how all three inductions would increase the value of the group interaction with other group members.) Each subject wrote a story about the three pictures, discussed the pictures with his partner, and finally, independently wrote a second version of the story. Although there were some differences among the three different kinds of cohesiveness, all three inductions produced a larger amount of influence.

In an experiment done with Boy Scout troops, Kelley and Volkart (1952) reported that members who valued their group membership were more resistant to a communication directed against the group norm when attitude change was measured in a private questionnaire than members who did not value their membership.

PUNISHMENT AS A COMPLEMENT TO REWARD

Throughout the earlier parts of this book, we have written implicitly as though punishment were merely the inverse of reward, a kind of "negative reward." But, in many ways, punishment and reward are psychologically distinct processes, not merely reverse images.

Several factors contribute to the fact that learning through punishment is more complex than learning through reward. In the first place, punishment tells the individual only what *not* to do; it does not provide an alternative or substitute for the punished behavior. If there was a "reason" (motive) for the punished behavior, some alternative must be discovered which meets the needs previously satisfied by the punished behavior. Until this happens, there will be psychological forces supporting the behavior while it is being punished. For example, embarrassing a conference member for displaying his self-oriented needs does not eliminate the needs. They can manifest themselves again in some other form such as substantive disagreement which is quite irrational on the surface.

Second, while only the desired responses need be reinforced, it is necessary to punish all undesired behavior. Since the range of undesired behavior is frequently larger than the range of desired behavior, the agent will have to use more punishment or spread it thinner. Miller and Butler (1962) reported that punishment was less effective than reward, possibly for this reason.

In the third place, punishment teaches the person to avoid the punished situation, and this leads to at least two complications. The individual may learn to avoid the whole issue rather than the specifically punished behavior. The participant punished for irrelevant comments may soon learn to avoid all participation, rather than to eliminate merely sidetracking remarks. Furthermore, avoidance learning prevents the individual from gaining further information about the situation he is avoiding. When the group member remains silent, he may never learn the acceptability of his ideas. Avoidance learning is particularly troublesome when the environment is rapidly changing. The individual learns to avoid some part of the environment and thus does not get any information about the changes because he avoids further opportunity to learn.

In the fourth place, punishment works through a learned drive of fear. An individual comes to fear the situations in which he is punished; this creates several problems. Fear is particularly hard to extinguish and may last long after it is appropriate. Fear is an emotion, and excessively high states of emotional involvement decrease the efficiency with which the organism can solve new problems. Perhaps a reason why there is so much controversy about the use of groups in decision-making derives from traumatic experiences individuals encountered in particularly intense and important conferences.

We can cite two examples of punishment effectively used as a source of power. Dittes and Kelley (1956) found evidence suggesting that members threatened with rejection from the group— probably a punishment—showed more conformity, although their results were not entirely straightforward. In an experiment by Raven and French (1958b) subjects received written evaluations from supervisors which requested them to decrease the number of figures they were cutting. In one condition the subjects were told that the supervisor would have the ability to levy fines and the supervisors did levy two 15-cent fines during the course of the experiment. The supervisor did not fine the other half of the subjects, nor were these subjects told that the supervisor could fine them. Messages from the supervisors with ability to punish produced greater change in the cutting productivity than the messages in the no fine condition.

Some work has been done in clarifying the characteristics of situations in which punishment is effective. Two may be asserted as follows:

PROPOSITION 6.3. Control of punishment will be a source of power (a) when the conditions of punishment are clearly specified, and (b) when compliance can be observed.

The mere fact that an agent can punish a person does not insure that the agent will influence the *behavior* of the person. The person must understand what he can do to avoid punishment. Furthermore, if punishment is to be effective as a threat, the person must have learned that the agent can punish him. A conference chairman may exert a great deal of power because of his close personal relationship with the company president; he may have an "informal say-so" on promotions, raises, etc. But unless the new member is aware of his friendship and its consequences, the chairman gains no power from this source. The naive participant cannot be expected to be aware of all the dire consequences which could follow if he angers the chairman. Furthermore, the chairman must make it known that he does not like disagreement. Even if the participant knows the chairman has power, his behavior will not be changed until he knows what price he must pay in order to avoid the wrath of the high power person. Deutsch and Krauss (1960) found that subjects who could not communicate verbally with each other and thus make the conditions for punishment explicit, were unable to use punishment as a source of power. In the experiment Ss operated a trucking line game. Each S had two routes to his destination, a short route and a longer alternate route. In some conditions either or both of the Ss could prevent the other from using the short route by raising a gate, and both could always block the short route with their own "trucks." In the particular circumstances of this experimental game, this ability to punish lowered the payoff (rewards) of the high power Ss as well as that of those with low power. Although many factors were undoubtedly operating in this experiment, the inability of the high power Ss to specify the conditions under which punishment would be applied probably contributed to the results. "Prior research on the role of communication in trust (Deutsch, 1958, 1960; Loomis, 1959) suggests that the opportunity for communication would have made reaching an agreement easier for individualistically-oriented bargainers. This same research (Deutsch, 1960) indicated, however, that communication may not be effective between competitively oriented bargainers" (Deutsch and Krauss, 1960, p. 188).[4]

Not only must the conditions for punishment be clearly specified but it is also necessary that the agent be able to observe the conformity of the low power person. If the agent cannot see whether or not there is compliance, he will be unable to administer punishment for nonconformity. Several studies have demonstrated that public compliance occurs in the face of punishment, but the public compliance was not accompanied by private opinion change. The high power person can observe the public conformity and could punish for nonconformity; but the agent cannot observe private opinion and, therefore, he cannot punish private nonconformity.

In the study by Raven and French (1958b) cited above, the supervisors with ability to punish did produce more public conformity but did not produce more private conformity. Festinger (1957) discusses two dissertations by McBride (1954) and Burdick (1955). These studies suggest that neither reward nor punishment is effective when the high power person cannot observe conformity to his demands.

As part of a larger study, Kelman (1958) manipulated the extent to which compliance could be observed by the agent. Students in a private Negro college listened to a recorded interview between a moderator and a guest (the communicator).

[4] Borah (1963) presents theoretical and empirical criticism of the Deutsch game but the argument above probably still stands.

In one communication the attempt was made to present the communicator in such a way that he would be perceived as possessing high means-control. He was introduced as the president of the National Foundation of Negro Colleges. In the course of the interview it became evident that his foundation had been supporting the college in which the study was being conducted; that he had almost complete control over the funds expended by the foundation; and that he was the kind of person who would not hesitate to use his control in order to achieve conformity. He made it clear that he would withdraw foundation grants from any college in which the students took a position on the issue in question which was at variance with his own position . . . (p. 55). *[One experimental condition completed the questionnaire] under conditions of salience and surveillance. . . . It was made clear—both by the appearance of the questionnaire and by the instructions—that this questionnaire was being administered at the communicator's request and that he would see each subject's answers. Moreover, the subjects were asked to sign their names and to give other identifying information. [In a second experimental condition the questionnaire] was anonymous, and it was made clear to the subjects that their responses would not be seen by the communicator or anyone other than the research staff* (Kelman, 1958, p. 56).

For this communicator with punishment-based power, influence was significantly lower under conditions of nonsurveillance than surveillance.

In our discussion of the differences between punishment and reward, the unanticipated side effects of punishment were mentioned. Two of these are particularly relevant for a social psychology of group process.

PROPOSITION 6.4. Punishment-based power (*a*) will not lead to interpersonal liking, and (*b*) will inhibit the exercise of power based on interpersonal attraction.

As we saw in Proposition 6.2, power and interpersonal liking are usually intercorrelated. In fact, Propositions 6.2-A and 6.2-B assert that interpersonal attraction is a *source* of power. But punishment-based power is an exception to this rule. Raven and French (1958b) found that punishing supervisors did produce more public compliance, but the subjects *liked them less* than nonpunishing supervisors.

This loss of interpersonal liking destroys this basis of power.

Kipnis (1958) reported an experiment in which he varied both lecture versus participatory and rewarding versus punishing styles of leadership. In the "lecture style" condition, the leader merely gave a ten-minute lecture with no discussion; but in the "participation style" condition, the leader outlined his arguments and then invited a general discussion. Within each of these conditions, leaders either offered to reward (give movie passes), punish (take passes away), or made no mention of reward or punishment.

As we would expect from Propositions 6.1 and 6.3, both reward and punishment produced more public compliance. Furthermore, under reward and neutral conditions only, the participatory style of leadership also produced more attitude change (private compliance) and more liking than the lecture style. But under the punishment conditions, the results of the participatory versus lecture comparisons were reversed. Under the punishment manipulations, there was no difference in liking for the two styles of leadership. The participatory leadership style, which had formerly produced *more* attitude change than the lecture style, produced significantly *less* attitude change when associated with punishment. It appears that the extra attraction from the interaction of the participatory leadership style did not bolster the power of leaders who punish.

⁂ ⁂ ⁂

REWARD CONTINGENCIES: FATE CONTROL AND BEHAVIOR CONTROL

Although there has been a minimum of empirical research, the following discussion illustrates some of the complexities which must be faced when an agent who has possession of resources wants to convert his possession into behavioral influences. In *The Social Psychology of Groups*, Thibaut and Kelley (1959) utilized game theory type matrices to analyze social behavior. They stated, "the essence of any interpersonal relationship is *interaction*. Two individuals may be said to have formed a relationship when on repeated occasions they are observed to interact. By interaction it is meant that they emit behavior in each other's presence, they create products for each other, or they communicate with each other" (p. 10). Thibaut and Kelley focused their book on an analysis of the rewards and punishments which an individual, A, receives when he interacts with another individual, B. "The consequences or *outcomes* for an individual participant of any interaction or series of interactions can be stated, then, in terms of the rewards received and the costs incurred . . ." (p. 13). In their discussion of power, Thibaut and Kelley distinguished between fate control and behavior control. "If, by varying his behavior, A can affect B's outcomes *regardless* of what B does, A has *fate control* over B" (p. 102). For example, a group member might have fate control over the entire group. If he chooses to cooperate, the group will be highly rewarded; if he chooses not to cooperate, the group will not be rewarded. In this case, as in all cases of fate control, it does not matter what the group does; the rewards and punishments of the group are entirely dependent upon the behavior of the group member possessing fate control.

"A second kind of power is called *behavior control*. If, by varying his behavior, A can make it desirable for B to vary his behavior too, then A has behavior control over B" (p. 103). In behavior control, the group members have some ability to modify their own rewards and punishments. Through his behavior, the agent can make some alternatives more profitable than others—even if he does not have final control over the rewards and punishments. The group members can make some adjustment to the variations in their environment produced by the agent. To extend the previous example, if the group member decided to cooperate, the rest of the group members can cooperate with him, receiving the reward for the group. If, on the other hand, the group member decides not to cooperate, the group may be able to exclude him from their discussion (see Chapter Eight) and obtain rewards by *other* means. In this way the group will still receive a reward in spite of the individual's decision not to cooperate. Still, the individual has been able to "control" the behavior of the group by making one route to reward more likely than another.

In behavior control, it is easy to see how the individual member has power over the other group members. The individual group member was the agent and his cooperation (or failure to cooperate) was the act through which his influence was exerted. Note that the individual's control over the rest of the group depends upon his ability to control the best route to the outcomes (rewards and punishments) of the rest of the group. If the group does not realize that it can continue discussion among themselves without the group member, or if the group is unable to distinguish between cooperation and noncooperation, the group may fail to change its behavior so that the best course of action is chosen.

The conversion of fate control into behavior control or actualized power is somewhat more subtle. In fate control B's rewards are entirely dependent on the behavior of A. No matter what B does, his outcomes remain constant so long as A's behavior remains constant. If fate control is to be converted into behavior control, A and B must reach some kind of "agreement." For instance, A might agree to behave in a way that rewards B only if B pays some kind of homage to A. In this way B can affect his own rewards indirectly by altering his own behavior. In this kind of relationship it is necessary that both A and B learn the interrelationship among their rewards and punishments, although in behavior control it is only necessary for the inferior member of the power pair to understand (perceive) the power relationship. (See pp. 104–106 in Thibaut and Kelley for a more complete discussion of the conversion of fate control to behavior control.)

CHAPTER SUMMARY

Because they actually possess resources important to other group members, members of decision-making groups can influence other members of their groups. In Propositions 6.1 and 6.3 we saw that the agent's ability to reward or punish another could be a source of power. In Proposition 6.2 we saw that the rewards attached to interaction with a friend are a source of power. This fact is supported by the correlation between power and interpersonal attraction—a large number of studies reporting a positive correlation between interpersonal attraction and influence were cited. It is to be remembered, however, that interpersonal attraction in the present is a symptom of rewards in the past. It is possible that these past rewards could cause both interpersonal attraction and high influence.

Although punishment can be used as a source of power, its usefulness is more limited. In particular, punishment-based power must (a) specify the conditions of punishment clearly and (b) deal with compliance which can be overtly observed (6.3). Furthermore, punishment-based power will inhibit interpersonal liking and then eliminate liking as a source of power.

LIST OF PROPOSITIONS

PROPOSITION 6.1. Direct control of task-environmental rewards is a source of power.

PROPOSITION 6.2. Control of the rewards associated with "friendly interaction" is a source of power.

PROPOSITION 6.2-A. The greater the personal attraction of other group members to a single individual, the greater the power of that individual.

PROPOSITION 6.2-B. The greater the interpersonal attraction among the members of a group, the greater the power of the "group" over the group members.

PROPOSITION 6.3. Control of punishment will be a source of power (a) when the conditions of punishment are clearly specified and (b) when compliance can be observed.

PROPOSITION 6.4. Punishment-based power (a) will not lead to interpersonal liking and (b) will inhibit the exercise of power based on interpersonal attraction.

CHAPTER SEVEN

Indirect sources of power in decision-making groups

In the previous chapter, emphasis was placed upon the power within a group which an individual gains because he physically possesses valued resources. Now we examine the more indirect sources of power in decision-making groups. Some of the ways in which agents influence or mediate rewards and punishments are examined. When an agent does not have direct possession of important rewards, he can often affect or mediate the rewards which are provided by third parties in the task environment. For example, a friend who does not possess money to lend himself may be willing to guarantee a loan from the bank. Here the friend does not have the money which he can either provide or not provide, but his actions influence whether or not someone else rewards or punishes. The agent does not have actual possession of the rewards and punishments important to the person, but he can influence the rewards and punishments provided by some third source.

COMMON FATE

PROPOSITION 7.1. When several individuals are rewarded or punished as an entity,[1] the "group" will have power over the individual members.

[1] Alternately stated, when individuals must locomote into the goal region as an entity.

In many situations people are not rewarded separately, but are treated as a unit. Reward is obtained only when all act together. Such a system would be illustrated in a work group situation where each member of the group is rewarded equally when the single decision of the entire group is evaluated by higher management. We can call this interdependence *common fate* or goal facilitation. Thomas (1957) stated, "we refer to *goal facilitation* . . . when the movement of one person toward a group goal provides movement of all others toward this same goal" (in Cartwright and Zander, 1960, p. 451). Since the environment treats the collection of individuals as a single unit, group members are particularly likely to abstract and think of the individuals collectively as a group and strive for a "group goal."

At this point it will be worthwhile to examine the concept of a "group goal." A group goal can be characterized along two dimensions: (*a*) the nature of the goal itself (whether reward is sought for an individual or the group as a whole) and (*b*) who holds the goal (who seeks or strives). There are, then, four possible combinations: (1) an individual holds a goal for himself, (2) an individual holds a goal for the group, (3) the group holds a goal for an individual, and (4) the group holds a goal for the group as a whole.

Proposition 7.1 is based on data from situations in which all individuals are rewarded as a group; what happens to the group happens to all the individuals within it, and what happens to any individual happens to the group as a whole. Under these conditions of common fate, any member has as much to gain by facilitating the productivity of another group member as he does by increasing his own efforts. Thus a member of a group with common fate has a distinctly different goal from a member who is individually rewarded for his own output. One goal of the individually rewarded member is to increase his own task output. The member in the group with common fate, on the other hand, strives to increase the task output of the group as a whole. Of course, one way for a member to increase the output of the group as a whole is to increase his own contributions. But this similarity should not obscure the differences in motivation between a member of a group with common fate and a member of a group without such a common group goal. Two of the more important consequences of these motivational differences are stated in the two subpropositions which follow.

PROPOSITION 7.1-A. Under conditions of common fate, the individuals will develop interpersonal attraction.

Deutsch (1949) created common fate among his subjects by telling them that the group which did the best job would be excused from one of the term papers and that all members of the group would receive the same grade for group discussion. In other words, the groups as a whole ranked against each other. In contrast to this condition of common fate, competitive subjects were told that one individual in each group was to be excused from writing his term paper, and individuals within the same group were to be ranked against each other in order to determine the grade for group discussion. Both groups worked on two problems —a puzzle problem and a human relations case. Deutsch found that group members with common fate were higher on both his indexes for interpersonal attraction or group cohesiveness. On both tasks the groups with common fate showed more group centeredness (an observer rating) and more group feeling (a participant rating).

Grossack (1954) also created common fate among the group members using the Deutsch technique: "the *Ss* were told that the *group* would be rated as a *group* on its solutions to a human relations problem" (p. 342). A human relations case was distributed to the group, communication was restricted to written messages, and *Ss* communicated at their own discretion. Their notes were intercepted and a standard set substituted. Grossack found that his groups with common fate showed significantly more cohesive behavior (measured through a content analysis of the written messages for such words as "group, we, us, others, etc."). The results of the next study are not so clear. Thomas (1957), in a study to be discussed later, found significant differences between groups with common fate and independent groups only in a subsample which was strongly affected by the experimental inductions and only where there was no division of labor.

The over-all cohesiveness scores were quite high, however, and may have obscured differences.

In summary, the experimental data support our analysis of common fate. When the group is rewarded as an entity, interpersonal attraction (group cohesiveness) develops among the group members.

PROPOSITION 7.1-B. The individual members will have more influence over each other under conditions of common fate.

We already know from Proposition 6.2 that interpersonal attraction and power are highly correlated; so it is to be expected that, since common fate produces high interpersonal attraction, it will also produce high influence. Deutsch (1949) found that groups with common fate demonstrated their high mutual influence on several measures. They were more affected by the ideas of other group members (participant rating) for the human relations problem, they showed greater acceptance of each other's ideas (observer rating) for both problems, and they demonstrated a greater agreement with others (participant rating) for the human relations problem.

When Jackson and Saltzstein (1958) told group members that they would be evaluated as a whole, the *S*s reported that there was more influence among the group members. Grossack (1954), using the same techniques to create common fate, found that members in groups which shared a common fate had greater interpersonal influence on a number of measures.[2] And Thomas (1957) found that group members who share a common fate feel more responsibility toward each other (measured by five questions, such as "If I work too slowly the others would have felt . . .").

Finally, Gerard's (1953) "pressure toward uniformity" had the effect of creating common fate among group members. "To create conditions favorable to the development of strong pressures toward uniformity, the groups were told that the experiment was

---

[2] Grossack's measures were: the number of explicit attempts to modify behavior of communication recipient, the amount of communication which favors reaching a *common agreement* by all members, acceptance of pressures toward uniformity, and the amount of nondirective social influence.

divided into two parts. In the first part the groups would discuss the problem among themselves. In the second part they would discuss the same problem with a group of experienced politicians from the community and they would be observed to see how well they handled themselves. It was indicated that this second discussion would be a severe test of their skill 'because you will be up against considerable opposition. . . . It will be a battle between youth and age' " (Gerard, 1953, p. 253). The members under high pressure toward uniformity then shared a common fate. They showed a greater percentage of changes of opinion and sent more messages to the changers.

In summary, decision-making groups are influenced by the manner in which the task environment rewards its members. When the group is rewarded as a unit, the group—as a reified entity—has power over its members. Once members believe they have a common fate, they develop interpersonal attraction, which, as was pointed out in Chapter Six, increases their power over each other.

Common fate and conformity. The mechanisms operating when groups have a common fate seem closely related to conformity processes in general. Conformity to group norms may influence the rewards and punishments of other group members. In Chapter Two we noted that the superiority of the group over the individual lies in the ability of the group to organize and divide labor. If an individual refuses to abide by the rules established for procedural organization, or if he interrupts the group process with constant disagreement, then the group will be less efficacious and thus less rewarding. A study by Berkowitz and Howard (1959) confirms the interpretation that conformity to the group norms is an indirect source of power within decision-making groups. They found that deviates were sociometrically rejected under conditions of high interdependence, but not when the participants were less dependent upon each other for their rewards. In other words, conformity may be a source of power only when the conformity increases group rewards because the members are interdependent.

Hollander (1960) gathered data from groups in which a paid

confederate was made to appear highly competent. Confederates who had conformed to the group's procedural norms in the past had significantly more influence, i.e., the group adopted the confederate's recommended solution more frequently.

However, as usual, comparisons of homogeneity and conformity versus heterogeneity and disagreement are not simple. As was indicated in Chapters Two and Five, heterogeneity and disagreement in information (i.e., task-related nonconformity) can increase group rewards for some tasks. If the value of these deviant contributions is recognized (unfortunately the vagaries of task-environmental feedback plus a generalized value on conformity can easily mask the task-environmental value of deviant contributions), then *non*conformity would be a source of power.

COMPETENCE AS A SOURCE OF POWER

If an agent has information or skills which can help others to get the things they value, then the agent can modify and mediate the task-environmental rewards and punishments of another person or the group as a whole. Because this competence allows the agent to increase the rewards and decrease the punishment of other individuals, it will be a source of power. Group members can learn about the competence of an agent in several ways; for present purposes two will be considered. First, we shall examine cases in which the group members have directly observed the success of the competent member or group, and then we shall discuss the situation in which an agent has a reputation of competence.

PROPOSITION 7.2. An agent which has been successful in the past will have increased power.

Group success. When the group is rewarded as a whole, the individual members are likely to think of the success as due to the "group's" efforts rather than to the efforts of individuals working separately. Deutsch (1959) varied, among other things, the past success of the group; ". . . all the groups were given a 'group intelligence test.' The test was described to the subjects as 'a measure of group ability . . . a measure of how effectively you people can work together as a group' . . ." (p. 85). One half of the groups were told that they had done well on the "group intelligence test" and the other half were told they had done poorly. The increased power of the supposedly successful group was reflected in several symptoms of power. The members had a greater desire to remain in the group, made more favorable evaluations of the others, had a high perceived capability of the group, expected more cooperation from the others, had a high team spirit, and indicated a high feeling of obligation.

Ziller and Behringer (1960) demonstrated that power based on past success can lead group members to resist the influence of a newcomer. Three-person groups were required to solve two problems through the standard note-passing communication net. After some groups had been told they were successful and others told they were unsuccessful on the first problem, a new member was introduced to the group on the pretext that the experimenter was studying the effects of size. Then the group was presented with a new dot problem which was more difficult than the first. The newcomer (a confederate) communicated the correct answer to the problem and an arithmetic procedure to obtain the answer. The groups which had been successful in the past had a greater resistance to the influence of the knowledgable newcomer who did not share the power deriving from past success.

Individual success. That the individual who has been successful in the past will have increased power in the present is a well-documented empirical phenomenon in the conformity literature (see Campbell, 1961, for review); we cite only a few studies as examples here. Goldberg and Lubin (1958) found that an individual was more influenced by the confederate if he were told that his preliminary estimates were in error. Gilchrist (1952) discovered that an individual was more likely to be chosen as a work partner if he had been a member of a successful team on the previous trial. Furthermore, these preferences generalized to other sociometric questions such as: "With which one would you most prefer to study for examinations?" "Which would you prefer most asking to the co-op for a cup of coffee or a coke?"

Mausner (1954, 1957) reports two studies which demonstrate that *S*s are influenced by partners who have a past history of success on a judgmental task.

But, the competence need not be directly observed in the decision-making situation. Sometimes a reputation of competence may be attached specifically to a particular person. At other times, the reputation stems from an assumption that the agent has power. In the latter case, the reputational halo may be rooted in the fact that the individual has learned to comply to the demands of an entire class of agents, such as chairmen and experts.

PROPOSITION 7.3. An agent with a reputation of competence will have power even if the group members have not directly observed his success.

Haiman (1949) found that the same recorded speech produced more attitude change when college students were told the speaker was the Surgeon General of the United States than when they were told he was Secretary of the American Communist Party. In general, a verbal introduction stressing competence or status will increase the power of an agent. For instance, Levinger (1959) varied, among other things, the information given to the *S*s about the other member of the experimental dyad. In an experiment which involved planning of a model town, "half of the subjects received indications that the partner had somewhat less experience relevant to the task than they" (p. 87), but the other half were led to believe that the partner knew more than they. "The partner said he was majoring in architecture, that in one course he had taken up city planning for several weeks, that he had done well in social studies and art, and that he was pretty confident about this task" (p. 88). Under these conditions the paid assistant had much more power; the subjects perceived him as more powerful, they exerted less influence on their own, were less assertive, and were less resistant to the influence of the assistant.

POWER STEMMING FROM THE FACT THAT
GENERALIZED COMPLIANCE TO THE ACTS OF A
"LEGITIMIZED" AGENT HAS BEEN REWARDED (AND
NONCONFORMITY PUNISHED) IN THE PAST

Some agents have power even though the person has no specific information about this particular agent. A chairman will have power over many people in many situations even though he may be a complete stranger personally. It seems reasonable that this power results from some kind of past experience with chairmen in general. As French and Raven (1959) indicate, this kind of power is accompanied by a conscious attitude that authorities have the right to demand compliance in some situations. This attitude probably stems from a group norm, training in role behavior, and other mechanisms which propagate socially prescribed behavior. We could say that the person has learned to comply to the influence attempts from any member of a general *class* of agents (laws, policemen, chairmen, designated leaders, etc.). Even though a person has never had experience with a particular group rule or specific leader, he *generalizes* from past experience with other rules of procedure and designated leaders when he behaves in the same way toward the new member of the class as he did in the original learning situation. In this way, an agent who is *formally designated* as leader through election or by holding the proper symbols of office gains power from the individual's past learning about the formal position which the agent has been granted.

PROPOSITION 7.4.   Formal designations as a leader, supervisor, boss, etc., will be a source of power.

This proposition is directly supported in an important experiment by Raven and French (1958b). In one condition the subjects were led to believe that they had formally elected their supervisor. In the other condition, however, the subjects were led to believe that the supervisor had not been formally elected.[3]

---

[3] "There were from 8 to 11 members in each experimental group. Three paid participants took part as members of each group. . . . In order to work properly, the experimenter said, the subjects would need a supervisor to

Formal designation was effective in producing high *public* influence (reduction in the rate of cutting figures in response to the slow down messages from the supervisor) only among those subjects who liked the supervisor. Formal designation did increase the *private* conformity among *all* subjects. The same results are reported in a similar earlier study (Raven and French, 1958a).

Torrance (1954) found that pilots had more influence than navigators and navigators more influence than gunners in three-man B-26 bomber crews, even though the crew members were randomly assigned to experimental groups and did not work with the other members of their own crew. There was some tendency for length of time in training to increase this influence. French and Snyder (1959) found that noncommissioned officers had more influence than enlisted men. The men had worked together before, but the experimental task was completely unrelated to previous work experience. Finally, Bass and Wurster (1953) found that high rank in the company was associated with high leadership scores in experimental discussion groups, and Crockett (1955) noted that "emergent" leaders held high rank in their organizations.

Formal designation, however, is only one source of power, and the factors reviewed earlier in these two chapters can either supplement or detract from legitimate power. Evan and Zelditch (1961), for instance, found that formally designated supervisors lost influence if they gave signs of low task competence. Subjects were hired ostensibly to code interview data. After all *S*s had

assure that the subjects were cutting with proper speed and accuracy. The supervisor would be selected through election, a method which had supposedly been accepted as efficient by all previous subjects. . . . The experimenter would present a fictitious tally of the votes on the board and announce that the paid participant had been elected, receiving nearly half again as many votes as her nearest competitor" (Raven and French, 1958b, pp. 84–85). In the formal designation condition the elected supervisor continued acting as supervisor. In the nondesignation condition, two of the paid participants would change positions following a short argument in which the experimenter refused to intervene. Thus, in the nondesignation condition, the acting supervisor was not the one who had been formally elected.

been trained by a "competent" supervisor, they were divided into three groups. Each group received further guidance from "supervisors" who manifested different levels of competence. Subjects exposed to low competence supervisors evidenced more coding errors and were less careful in carrying out the suggestions of the supervisor on "traps" which had been built into the problem so that *S*s would have to consult with the supervisor.[4] Thus, we see that the formal authority system is a source of power in addition to the more informal mechanisms. Power which is based on formal designation of "leader," "group spokesman," "boss," etc., may be called legitimate power.

PROPOSITION 7.4-A. Legitimate power will be weakened when influence attempts are outside the scope specified by formal designation.

The weakened legitimate power will be reflected in decreased personal attraction to the power agent and in smaller amounts of influence. In a previously cited study by Raven and French (1958b) subjects were seated in separate booths and given an incentive to cut printed figures with scissors. The "supervisor" gave the subjects written evaluations requesting a slow down on three occasions. As a measure of the scope of power specified in the formal designation, subjects were asked to indicate the degree to which they felt the supervisor's actions were justified. Group members who did feel that the actions of the supervisor were justified indicated a higher private influence and a greater interpersonal attraction to the supervisor.

Frank's (1944) study is summarized by quoting from his own summary:

Experiments in cracker eating with 62 college subjects who volunteered their services showed that:

1. When the instructions are such that the experiment requires eating, Ss typically eat with full acceptance, as shown by the absence of resistance, rapid eating, and short intervals between crackers. The absence

---

[4] However, neither over-all speed of coding nor total number of errors for the total task was related to the competence manipulations. The performance on areas directly related to supervisor relations is probably a more sensitive measure than total performance.

of resistance to activities supposingly required by the experiment is confirmed with other tasks with preliminary experiments with 27 subjects.

2. Instructions that the experiment does not require eating, but that E will try to make S eat if he refuses tend to arouse resistance to eating (p. 40).

CHAPTER SUMMARY

In Chapter Seven, an attempt was made to gain understanding of the indirect ways that power is assembled within decision-making groups. Conformity processess which operate when groups are subjected to common fate act as a source of power. The second indirect source of power in groups stems from the skill which allows competent agents to mediate rewards to group members. It was noted that at times power is attached to specific agents. At other times, the power was more universal, being associated with reputations and also positions which the social norms of the group define as "legitimate." These indirect bases for power, along with the direct bases indicated in Chapter Six, provide mechanisms through which individuals in groups gain power.

LIST OF PROPOSITIONS

PROPOSITION 7.1. When several individuals are rewarded or punished as an entity, the "group" will have power over the individual members.

PROPOSITION 7.1-A. Under conditions of common fate, the individuals will develop interpersonal attraction.

PROPOSITION 7.1-B. The individual members will have more influence over each other under conditions of common fate.

PROPOSITION 7.2. An agent which has been successful in the past will have increased power.

PROPOSITION 7.3. An agent with a reputation of competence will have power even if the group members have not directly observed his success.

PROPOSITION 7.4. Formal designation as a leader, supervisor, boss, etc., will be a source of power.

PROPOSITION 7.4-A. Legitimate power will be weakened when influence attempts are outside the scope specified by formal designation.

CHAPTER EIGHT

Consequences of small and large amounts of

power for the behavior of group members

In the two previous chapters we discussed studies which give us insight into the source or creation of power. In this chapter we shall discuss studies which give insight into the consequences of power, once it has been created. The previous chapters dealt with the direct and indirect ways in which a person can come to have power; now we shall scrutinize what happens to a person after he has obtained the power in a group.

Before we summarize data on the consequences of power under the following propositions, let us reconsider briefly the problems of empirically defining power. Many studies do not define power in terms of the sources which were discussed in the previous chapter; power instead is defined by asking an observer or fellow group members to rate each person on a scale of "influence," "power," "status," or "prestige." The author then describes the behavior of people who have been rated as powerful. Measuring power through ratings has a significant advantage; it often allows the researcher to observe the operation of power in "real life." On the other hand, some studies create power experimentally by giving subjects access to a source of power similar to those discussed in the previous chapters. For instance, the experimenter could give power to a group member by artificially inflating his appar-

152

ent success on the task. Persons with such experimentally developed power tend to behave in the same way as persons rated high on power by an observer or peer; so there is empirical justification for including data from both types of power definition. The experimental creation of power validates our notions of the way in which power is created; the rating scale measures of power validate our notions of the way powerful persons behave in groups outside the laboratory. Both measures will be used interchangeably in the following propositions.

The distribution of power among individuals in decision-making groups as they move from problem to problem may vary from a concentration within one or two persons to a wide spread of influence among many of the members of the group. Yet, when one examines the power of individuals *vis-à-vis* particular issues, there tends to be a differentiation between those who have large amounts of power versus those who have smaller amounts of power with respect to particular problems. At present, the literature of social psychology tends to be limited to a segmental approach, considering power in groups with respect to issues of limited scope. Thus, it is convenient to group the findings within this chapter in terms of those studies applying to persons with larger amounts of power versus those members with smaller amounts of influence.

One exception to this rule is the interesting work on "expanding influence" reported by Likert (1961). Likert reports an attitude survey in which several levels of management were asked to state the amount of influence which they exerted. For some departments, Likert reports that *both* subordinates and superiors felt they exerted more influence than subordinates and superiors in other departments. It appears that when superiors give subordinates some influence in the actual decision-making both parties increase their reciprocal influence. While subordinates have more influence in decision-making, superiors have more influence in how the decision is carried out.

CONSEQUENCES OF POWER FOR PERSONS
WITH RELATIVELY HIGH POWER

PROPOSITION 8.1. High power persons possess more influence.

Proposition 8.1 is merely a restatement of our definition of power
in Chapter Six. Here we take opportunity to develop the *empirical measures of behavioral influence* which led to the formulation of our definition. High influence is reflected in a cluster of
measures; so the data for Proposition 8.1 will be discussed in
four subpropositions. First, we shall note that high power persons have influence even when they do not make overt behavioral
influence attempts. Second, we shall examine the overt efforts
of the high power person to influence other individuals. Generally, high power persons do a great deal more talking than other
group members. Then we shall note, more specifically, that high
power persons will initiate more communication classified specifically as overt influence. And finally, we shall find that high
power persons will be successful in a larger percentage of the influence endeavors which they do attempt.

Thus, by specifying the empirical means by which high power
persons exert more influence, the tautologically toned Proposition
8.1 is explicated. Let us now examine the evidence supporting
each of these consequences of power for persons of relatively
high power.

PROPOSITION 8.1-A. High power persons exert influence without
making overt behavioral attempts to influence.

A study in summer camps by Lippitt, Polansky, Redl, and
Rosen (1952) was designed largely to test a version of this proposition. Power was measured by asking the campers to rate each
other on questions such as "who is best at getting others to do
what he wants them to do?" Campers high on this measure of
power were imitated by other campers even when they made no
overt behavioral influence attempts. The high power campers,
as we shall see in the next proposition, did have a higher total
activity rate; but the high power members were imitated more
even after the imitation scores are corrected for the higher total
activity of the high power person.

PROPOSITION 8.1-B.   High power-status persons will initiate a greater total number of communications. (Also numbered Proposition 9.3.)

The influence of a power hierarchy on the pattern of communication is so marked that we shall devote a special section to it in the chapter on interaction. Here we merely mention aspects of the interrelationship between power and communication which detail the empirical means by which high power persons actualize their potential influence.

Gerard (1957) reported that *S*s who were told they were the boss and could tell others what to do sent more messages. This experiment suggests that experimentally induced power-status may actually cause participants to initiate more communication. This interpretation is supported by some correlational findings in Borgatta (1954). Persons who expected to receive sociometric choices from others (i.e., who thought they had high status) initiated significantly more interaction than those who did not expect to receive sociometric choices.

The tendency for high power-status persons to initiate more communication is one of the most powerful and reliable phenomena summarized in this book. The relationship is reported in a wide variety of groups. Hurwitz, Zander, and Hymovitch (1953) studied persons who were given a high score on a preconference rating which was completed by "two local people, qualified to judge the prestige of these persons in the eyes of their fellow professionals" (p. 801). Persons given high power ratings initiated a significantly higher number of communications.

Lana, Vaughan, and McGinnies (1960) asked members of two community groups engaged in free discussion sessions concerning mental health to rate their peers on leadership and friendship. Members rated high on leadership, but *not* members rated high on friendship, were characterized by a significantly higher rate of interaction. Mussen and Porter (1959) found that subjects rated effective by their peers after a brief leaderless discussion were characterized by a high frequency of participation. In an experiment where the only communication was through written letters, Shaw and Gilchrist

(1956) found a correlation between number of letters written and leadership rankings. Bates (1952) reported a correlation of .85 between the amount of communications sent and sociometric ranking on who "contributed the most to carrying out the assigned task of the group." Borgatta and Bales (1956) reported a correlation of .50 between similar measures.

Collins (1960) divided a college discussion class into high and low power-status groups on the basis of a questionnaire. Participants were asked to rate fellow group members on the amount of influence they exerted. For the first 12 sessions, all high status Ss initiated a total of 1186 communications, and the low status Ss initiated only 565—somewhat less than half as much. In summary, in spite of wide differences in method of status measurement, a strong tendency for high power-status persons to initiate more communication is demonstrated.

Caudill (1958) reported on the interactions during 63 consecutive administrative conferences held each morning as part of the routine of a mental hospital. Initiations were consistently related to the informal and formal status differences of the participants. Senior doctors initiated the most communication, residents the next most, and nurses were third. Caudill also found the same relationship *within* each of the status groups. "The head of the hospital talked more on the average than the chief resident during the first and second periods. This was true even though it was the chief resident's job actually to run the daily administrative conference" (p. 245). Also the supervisor of nurses talked more than the charge nurses. Initiations from the five residents were also related to their informal status. Informal status was measured by asking the senior doctors to rate the competence of each resident. "There was a considerable correspondence between the amount of a resident physician's participation in the daily conferences and his evaluation by the senior staff" (p. 251). Blau and Scott (1962, pp. 126–127) reported that they replicated the correlation between formal status and initiations in the weekly meetings of two divisions in a county welfare bureau. The relationship between informal status and initiations was replicated in one division, but not the other.

PROPOSITION 8.1-C. High power persons will initiate more communication classified specifically as influence attempts.

Levinger (1959) observed overt influence attempts in his laboratory study at the University of Michigan. Three separate measures of power suggested that high power subjects initiated more influence attempts. Subjects who were told that they were more competent than their partners, subjects whose partner was more accepting of their suggestions, and subjects who had high perceived power were rated by observers as making more influence attempts and having a higher degree of assertiveness.

PROPOSITION 8.1-D. High power persons will be successful in a larger percentage of the influence attempts which they do make than low power persons.

In a study already discussed by Lippitt et al. (1952), campers who were designated as high power by their peers not only had a higher frequency of attempts to influence the behavior of others, but a larger proportion of these attempts were successful. Similarly French and Snyder (1959) found that highly liked (and thus more powerful) noncommissioned officers were more influential. (Influence was measured by post-experimental questionnaires.)

In summary we see that sources of power are empirically correlated with influence effects. This generalization is supported from studies which measure power through participant ratings and in studies which create power experimentally by giving subjects access to a source of power similar to those discussed in the previous two chapters. Furthermore, this high power is reflected in imitation of high power persons, the greater amounts of total communication and specific influence attempts made by high power persons, and, finally, the success of high power persons in their influence attempts.

PROPOSITION 8.2. High power persons will be less affected by the efforts of others to influence them.

Specific influence attempts. As a complement to the fact that high power persons are more successful in their efforts to influ-

ence others, we find that others are less successful in their efforts
to influence high power persons. In the summer camp study
by Lippitt et al. (1952), high power campers were less influenced
than low power campers, and in a conformity experiment by
Harvey and Consalvi (1960) highly liked subjects were least
conformant. According to Proposition 6.2-A, highly liked Ss
have high power. Levinger (1959) found that all three of his
power measures indicated that high power persons were more resistant to the influence attempts of their partners.

Group norms. In the previous paragraph we saw that high power
persons were less influenced by specific communication attempts,
and it follows that, in general, high power persons are relatively
free of influence from group norms. Hollander (1958) entitled
this phenomenon "idiosyncrasy credit." Idiosyncrasy credit is
"the extent to which an individual may deviate from the common
expectancies of the group" (p. 120), in other words, the extent to
which a member is allowed to deviate from the group norm without retaliation. In general, a person builds up idiosyncrasy credit
in the same way that he builds up power, i.e., by increasing the
rewards and decreasing the punishments of other group members;
an individual who has been of service to the group is allowed to
deviate.

As was indicated in the previous chapter, the relationship between power and deviation is complex. High power members do
seem less constrained by group norms, but, on the other hand,
conformity to the group norms is one source of power. The issue
is further complicated by evidence which suggests that group
leaders may better understand the group norms than group members (Chowdhry and Newcomb, 1952). These authors found
that elected leaders of ongoing groups were better able to estimate
group opinion on issues which were relevant, but not on issues
which were irrelevant to the normal interaction in the group.
Talland (1954) noted that leaders had a greater accuracy in
expressing group opinion only after the topic had been discussed.
This suggests that the increased accuracy of the leader may mean
that the group is persuaded to take the leader's position and,

therefore, the group opinion is closer to that of the leader than any other group member. Both factors influence the relationship between power and conformity to group norms. If it is true that low power members have a less accurate perception of the group norms, then they should be less conforming merely out of ignorance of the proper conforming behavior. And if the group opinion is closer to that of the leader because he has had more influence, then leaders should be less deviant because their opinion coincides closely with the group norms. But the data and current theory to be reviewed below (Homans, 1950, p. 416; Hollander, 1958) suggest that over and above these intertwined factors, leaders and other high power persons are *less* constrained by group norms.

We have already cited the study of Harvey and Consalvi (1960) which found the most highly liked subjects to be the least conformant. Blau (1960) conducted a detailed investigation of "patterns of deviations in work groups" for a public assistance agency of a large American city. Both extremes of opinion were considered deviations. That is, subjects who scored a great deal higher than the group norm and subjects who scored a great deal lower were said to "deviate." Subjects whose opinion on a given item was quite close to the group average were categorized as nondeviants. Blau found that three measures, all of which could be considered measures of power, were correlated with deviations from the group norm. Highly integrated workers (other workers reported that they were on a first name basis with the worker), workers with high self-confidence (workers who felt they could work without a supervisor), and workers with high popularity (subject named by two or more persons in the sample as a friend) were all more deviant from the group norm on several measures.

These data suggest that high power group members are less conformant even though the conformity could be used as one source of power. If an individual has proven useful to the group in the past, "he may be thought of as having a degree of group-awarded credits [power] such as to permit idiosyncratic behavior . . . *before* group sanctions are applied" (Hollander, 1958, p.

120). Hollander (1960) observed groups of four subjects and one experimental assistant (who was made to appear highly competent) while 15 problems were solved. The confederate was instructed to fail to conform to the procedural norms agreed upon by the group either early, middle, or late in the sequence of trials. The assistants gained greater acceptance of their proposed solutions if they had conformed to the procedural arrangements in the immediately preceding block of trials. It seems likely that, by virtue of their past reward contributions through conformity to the procedural rules, the conformant members were less restricted by the group.

PROPOSITION 8.3. High power members will tend to form cliques.

In other words, high power members will like their fellow high power members more than other group members and will initiate more communication to fellow high power individuals. In the mental health conference where the participants were preselected for differences in power, high power members liked each other more than they liked low power members (Hurwitz et al., 1953). This finding is partly predictable from the general proposition that high power members are better liked than low power members by *all* members of the group. But when the liking is combined with a tendency for ingroup communication, a variable to be discussed in the chapter on interaction, we expect the high power members to form into a clique.

Mills (1953) analyzed the communication in three-person groups using the Bales interaction process analysis. He found that when the first most active and second most active group members were above average in their support of each other, the coalition remained stable; the third member tended to oppose both members of the coalition without discrimination between them. In summary, high power members will like each other more than low power members and communicate more to each other than to low power members.

CONSEQUENCES OF POWER FOR PERSONS WITH RELATIVELY LOW POWER

PROPOSITION 8.4-A. Low power persons will behave deferentially toward high power persons.

In the camp study reported by Lippitt et al. (1952) the deferential behavior of low power persons is reflected in several observer ratings. Items which reflect this deferential behavior are as follows: "implies superior knowledge or skill in other, asks permission of the other, demonstrates sympathetic or solicitous behavior, shows affection-seeking behavior, and displays negative or hostile behavior."

Although Stotland (1959) studied only low power subjects, he reports that the subjects could be characterized by withdrawal responses to the supervisor, little aggression to the supervisor, and cooperation with unreasonable demands of the supervisor. Finally, the deferential behavior of low power persons is reflected in the fact that they communicate more to high power persons than they do to other low power persons (see Chapter Nine on Communication and Interaction).

Another way that lower power persons indicate their feelings of deference toward those with much influence is by overestimating the performance of high power individuals. Harvey (1953) identified high power-status students in ongoing teen-age cliques through adult rankings on the authority they seemed to wield and the amount of activity they initiated for the group. He then formed three-person experimental groups of the high, middle, and lowest power individual from several high school cliques. Subjects participated in a dart throwing task in which they estimated the performance of each subject, including self, before and after each dart throw. Both high and low power subjects consistently overestimated the performance of high power persons.

PROPOSITION 8.4-B. Low power persons will be *less* deferential and *less* threatened when supported by their peers.

Stotland's (1959) experiment directly tested the effects of peer group relations on reactions to power figures. "The general design of the experiment involved the placement of each subject alone in a position subordinate to a single power figure, while working on a task. The subject's reactions to the supervision and to the supervisor were observed, while the degree of relationship he had with his subordinate was allowed to vary. In one condition, the so-called *alone* condition, he did not meet or know about any other subject besides the supervisor. In the *membership* condition each subject was allowed to have two meetings with another subordinate person who was being given similar treatment by another supervisor in an adjoining room" (pp. 56–57). In both conditions the supervisor frequently disagreed with decisions made by the subject, but never explained his reasons. The subjects' reactions to these "unreasonable" influence attempts were measured through analysis of their interaction with the supervisor and post-experimental ratings. In general, the subjects who met briefly with a peer tended to be less dominated by the supervisor. They showed a greater expression of hostility toward the supervisor, they were more persistent in their efforts to deal with the supervisor's disapproval of their moves, they showed more aggression, less cooperation, and fewer withdrawing responses.

Similarly, Grosser, Polanski, and Lippitt (1951) found that subjects were less constrained in the presence of an *active* collaborator (second child instructed by E to play with toys) than when playing alone.[1]

Many studies in industry have demonstrated the impact of group norms on productivity. These studies have shown how workers, banded together in a group, are able to resist threats and enticements by management to increase productivity. Coch and French (1948) discussed examples of this effect in a Marion, Virginia, pajama factory, and similar examples were found in the Westinghouse studies (e.g., Roethlisberger and Dickson, 1939).

Thus, although low power persons often exhibit deferential behavior toward those with high power, in group situations the

[1] The presence of a *passive* collaborator, however, produced less playing behavior than the alone condition.

existence of support from peers tends to reduce their submissiveness.

PROPOSITION 8.5. Low power persons will be suspicious of high power agents who can arbitrarily award or withhold important resources.

Throughout these propositions on power, we have seen that the high power person can do the things he wants to do even if opposed by other group members. If high power agents can (and do) act in their own interest, we can understand why low power individuals expect this kind of behavior. Furthermore, when low power members can take measures to protect themselves, we expect them to do so.

Solomon (1960) has labeled this behavior "suspicious," and has provided a laboratory demonstration. He used a series of game theory matrices in which each player has two choices: player one can choose between A and B and player two can choose between X and Y. Thus, there are four possible outcomes, and each of the four possible choice combinations provides a specified reward for each player. By varying amounts of these rewards, one player can be given power over another, and one choice can be made much more desirable than another. Solomon found that subjects would protect themselves when playing against a person who stood to gain by exploitation of the subject. In other words, the subjects behave noncooperatively in the expectation that the other person would also be noncooperative especially when the latter had much to gain from noncooperation.

PROPOSITION 8.6. Low power persons will be threatened if ambiguity exists in their relationship with high power agents.

It has sometimes been suggested that the most effective threat or the most effective power is ambiguous. But the experimental evidence offered by Cohen (1959) suggests that ambiguous problem situations provoke threat reactions in low power persons. "The subjects for the experiment were female employees of a public utility company. The experiment was designed so that it would fit into the power structure of the company in that the authority person was to be seen as coming from the supervisory level immediately above that of the subject" (p. 41). "The clarity-unclarity aspect of the situation was created by the kind of problems handed the subject. . . . The problems had been previously established as being 'objectively' clear or unclear. They were word-symbol matching tests in which the subject was asked to match a given word with one of several pictures. In the clear condition, familiar pictures and commonly understood words were presented a few at a time. In the unclear condition vague and unfamiliar pictures and uncommon words were presented in large groups" (p. 43). Working on unclear or ambiguous tasks produced a high threat reaction in low power subjects. This reaction is demonstrated by the low attraction of the subjects to the supervisor, by the high anxiety of the low power person, by negative evaluation of self, by high feelings of aggression, and a longer time spent on the task. Thus, it seems that not only does the power of the member affect others—but even the task itself may contribute to the suspicion with which high power individuals are regarded by low power members of the group.

CHAPTER SUMMARY

Although caution must be used in making a sharp division between high and low power persons (power actually varies in degrees and it is possible to increase the influence of both superior and subordinate), several generalized differences between high and low power persons were documented. Power was measured either by experimentally creating power for a group member by giving him access to a source of power discussed earlier, or by identifying high power persons through questionnaires. The empirical measures through which the influence of high power persons has been shown are reviewed. High power persons are resistant to specific influence by others and less constrained by group norms. Low power persons are generally deferential, although they may be less constrained when supported by their peers. Finally, low power persons are threatened if ambiguity exists in the power relationship.

LIST OF PROPOSITIONS

PROPOSITION 8.1.   High power persons possess more influence.

PROPOSITION 8.1-A.   High power persons exert influence without making overt behavioral attempts to influence.

PROPOSITION 8.1-B.   High power-status persons will initiate a greater total number of communications.   (Also numbered Proposition 9.3.)

PROPOSITION 8.1-C.   High power persons will initiate more communication classified specifically as influence attempts.

PROPOSITION 8.1-D.   High power persons will be successful in a larger percentage of the influence attempts which they do make than low power persons.

PROPOSITION 8.2.   High power persons will be less affected by the efforts of others to influence them.

PROPOSITION 8.3.   High power members will tend to form cliques.

PROPOSITION 8.4-A.   Low power persons will behave deferentially toward high power persons.

PROPOSITION 8.4-B.   Low power persons will be less deferential and less threatened when supported by their peers.

PROPOSITION 8.5.   Low power persons will be suspicious of high power agents who can arbitrarily award or withhold important resources.

PROPOSITION 8.6.   Low power persons will be threatened if ambiguity exists in their relationship with high power agents.

CHAPTER NINE

Communication and interaction

As in the chapters on power, the focus of this chapter is on the behavior of individual group members. Although the topics of communication and interaction have appeared often implicitly and sometimes explicitly in previous chapters, the issues seem important enough in our discussion of group decision-making to warrant a chapter of their own.

As Blau and Scott (1962) suggested, communication and interaction "refer to the same processes but to different aspects of them. The concept of social interaction focuses principally upon the formal characteristics of social relations: such terms as frequency, initiative, superordination, and reciprocity indicate its dimensions. The concept of communication, on the other hand, directs attention to the meaningful content conveyed in the encounter, and its characteristics are described by such terms as flow of messages, obstacles, positive and negative reactions, and exchanges" (p. 116).

As our chapter title implies, we shall consider both aspects of the communication-interaction process; we shall examine both the nature of the information which is transmitted and the more formal characteristics of communication behavior—such as the frequency and direction of communication acts. The first section concerns the initiation or transmission of communication stimuli; the second with the receipt, understanding, or translation of communication stimuli.

We may analyze individual communication behavior in the same way that we have discussed other behaviors in decision-making groups. In the long run, group members learn to initiate communications which are instrumental in obtaining the task-environmental and interpersonal rewards which are valued by an individual. Thus, communication behavior is a function of (a) the nature of the milieu and (b) the kinds of rewards particularly valued by the individual (his motives and needs). A communicator initiates communication when he expects a reward on the basis of his own past experience with this or similar task environments and fellow group members.

The impact of valued rewards on communication is illustrated by several studies. On the assumption that executives who wanted to be promoted would withhold damaging information from their supervisors, Read (1962) predicted and verified that "the stronger the mobility needs among executives, the less accurately they communicate problem-related information" (p. 10). The impact of the behavior of other group members on communication is illustrated in the same study. Untrustworthy interpersonal environments increased this tendency. "The less trust they [the executives] hold for their immediate superiors the greater is this tendency toward inaccurate communication" (p. 10). Another example of the importance of desired rewards is reported by Kelley (1951) in his study on status and communication. Kelley's general hypothesis was that low status persons with no opportunity to improve their own status would use communication (conjectures about the high status job) as a "substitute upward locomotion." Kelley found, however, that this hypothesis held true only for low status persons *who exhibited some desire to move upward.* The importance of motivation for communication is further supported by data from a more general study by Lansing and Heyns (1959). They found that the need for affiliation, as measured by a projective technique, was strongly correlated with the use of the local telephone and somewhat correlated with letter writing.[1] We expect this impact of motivation to operate

---

[1] There was no relationship between need for affiliation and use of the long distance telephone.

in decision-making groups. The communication of each participant will be strongly influenced by the things he wants the conference to accomplish.

❧   ❧   ❧

In 1952 and 1953 S. N. Eisenstadt published two quasi-statistical articles in the *Public Opinion Quarterly* which dealt with communication among immigrants in Israel. His results are discussed in some detail because they are interesting and because these data from a field or "real-life" situation confirm the generalizability of propositions derived in the laboratory.

Eisenstadt studied a group of immigrants who arrived after the State of Israel had been established. The psychological mechanisms which he found as these individuals adapted to a new social environment may be much the same as those which operate when a new group member joins an established conference or when new conferences are formed.

The particular immigrants studied by Eisenstadt were persons whose previous social environments had been characterized by marked status hierarchy and rigid communication patterns built about the "elite"— usually the religious leaders. When they arrived in Israel, they were exposed to unending and strong waves of communication from the new environments into which they entered. The main purpose of this communication was to induce them to perform different roles in this new task environment and to participate in some of its organization.

In the face of this onslaught of communication, a large number of immigrants "disattached" themselves from the old elite (i.e., the impact of the old status system on communication patterns was eliminated). The reasons which Eisenstadt (1952) lists for this "disattachment" can be summarized in one phrase: a change in the "perception" of the old elite. The old elite were no longer "perceived" as a part of the social environment which was likely to reduce the needs of the immigrants. This general proposition is illustrated by Eisenstadt:

1. *"Growing disillusionment about the elites' ability to assure them of various amenities and rights accruing to them in the new social system. . . ."*

2. *"Doubts as to the elites' prestige-position within the new social system. . . ."*

3. *"Disillusionment with the elites' ability to interpret the new social system and its values to the immigrants. . . ."*

4. *"The feeling that attachment to the old elites blocks their achievement of full status within the new society. . . ."*

5. *"The loss of a feeling of participation in the new social system and of belongingness to it as a result of clinging to the old elites . . ."* (Eisenstadt, 1952, pp. 52–53).

This proposition is further strengthened by the finding that the immigrants who did *not* disattach themselves and maintained their old communication patterns about the old elites were either: (1) content to remain in the old social system, or (2) felt that the elites were capable of performing their functions within the new setting and of orienting the immigrants within it.

Two more of Eisenstadt's findings lend support to the importance of participant motives and understandings of the environment. For one thing, he found that the immigrants were much more responsive to "technical communication" than they were to the other types of communication studied. Technical communication concerns the economic roles of the immigrants and, perhaps, may be interpreted as dealing with the most immediate demands of the new task environment and the economic task rewards which are most essential for survival. It is not surprising that, if they respond at all, the immigrants respond to communication relevant to their most basic motives.

The other finding is from the second article (1953) in which Eisenstadt studied a group of about 120 immigrants who seemed to have lost their capacity for communication (had little social position, did not ask for advice, did not discuss personal problems outside the family circle, etc.).

Eisenstadt divided this group of noncommunicants into two groups on the basis of their perceptions of the social environment. The first group maintained a relatively stable, but *narrow* pattern of communication. They participated in the family circle, but the larger social environment seemed to have little relevance to them. For instance, "Almost 90 per cent answered that their present work was very different from their aspirations, and that these aspirations were more or less unrealizable in the new situation" (1953, p. 365). Thus communication was limited to the small family circle—the only portion of the social environment which seemed relevant.

The second (and smaller, about 15 per cent) subgroup of noncommunicants did not feel that either the old or the new elite formed part of a relevant social environment: "The new situation did not provide advice or understanding of the problems in which these people were interested. This was true both of some of their pressing personal and family problems . . . and their 'wider' cultural and social interests. They felt that these problems were of little importance either to their old leaders or to the new ones. . . . Somehow they felt that [neither] the old type of participation . . . nor the new ones could satisfy their needs . . ." (1953, p. 366).

In both subgroups of noncommunicants, a failure to "perceive" a portion of the social environment as potentially instrumental to need satisfaction seems to have resulted in a failure to initiate or to respond to communication from that part of the social environment.

THE INITIATION AND DIRECTIONALITY OF COMMUNICATION AND INTERACTION

The form and the content of interactions in decision-making groups are intimately related in research on communication. In the propositions which follow, the first tend to emphasize the form of the interaction itself. Those appearing later are more concerned with the content of the communications. But, as always in the case of social phenomena, form influences content and vice versa. Hence, the distinctions made in the propositions are analytic, intended to gain more understanding about the nature of communication processes in decision-making groups. In real-life conferences, form and content are present simultaneously.

PROPOSITION 9.1.   Interaction is unevenly distributed among group members.

Several authors have observed that a few people typically do most of the talking in a small group discussion (Bales et al., 1951; Stephan, 1952; Stephan and Mishler, 1952). This tendency becomes stronger as the group increases in size, i.e., the difference between the most active person and the next most active person is greater in large groups (Stephan and Mishler, 1952). In summary, there is a tendency for a few people to dominate the interaction, and this tendency becomes more pronounced with increasing group size.

PROPOSITION 9.2.   The more interactions initiated by a group member, the more interactions will be directed to him by other group members.

This tendency represents, by far, the strongest and most consistent influence on communication flow. If a participant talks, chances are that another participant will react in some way. In 1951 Bales, Strodtbeck, Mills, and Roseborough gathered data using Bales' Interaction Process Analysis. Bales' scheme (Bales, 1950) is a method of communication record taking which notes who sends and who receives each communication. Each communication is further classified into one of twelve content categories.

Bales et al. noted that "The findings reported indicate that if participants in a small group are ranked by the total number of acts they initiate, they will all tend to be ranked: (1) by the number of acts they receive, (2) by the number of acts they address to specific other individuals, and (3) by the number of acts they address to the group as a whole" (p. 468).[2] Collins (1960) reported a correlation of better than .9 between the number of communications initiated and the number received in leaderless classroom discussion.

Bales et al. also reported that incomplete examinations of the data tend to show the top man giving out more information and opinion than he receives, while, on the contrary, low men give out more agreement, disagreement, and requests for information than they receive (Bales et al., 1951, p. 466).

PROPOSITION 9.3. High power-status persons will initiate more communication than low status persons. (This Proposition is also numbered Proposition 8.1-B.)

The extensive data for this proposition were reviewed in Chapter Eight. There are a great many factors, including status, which might cause a particular group member to increase his initiations as well as his receipts. Since initiation tends to provoke reaction (Proposition 9.2), much of the data on the *receipt* of communications by a particular class of persons is completely uninterpretable because the authors did not control for the rate of *initiation*. In particular, since high status persons initiate more communication, nothing can be said about the effects of power-status *per se* on receipts until the high initiations have been controlled for.

---

[2] Further analyses of these same data are reported in two notes by Stephan (1952) and Keller (1951).

COMMUNICATION WITHIN THE FACE-TO-FACE GROUP

Fortunately, we frequently have not had to distinguish between the social processes of the face-to-face group and the processes in larger organizations. Although there are many important differences, we often deal with phenomena which are fundamental in the sense that they operate both in the face-to-face groups and in larger organizations. The impact of status on the direction of communication, however, differs when the focus is shifted from the face-to-face group to the more remote relationships in a larger organization. Physical separation appears to play an important role; no matter how large the status differences in the decision-making conference, all participants can at least see each other and communication is physically possible. In the larger organization, on the other hand, different status groups may be physically separated so that communication is difficult or impossible.

PROPOSITION 9.4. The power-status hierarchy will influence the flow and content of communication within the *face-to-face group*.

PROPOSITION 9.4-A. When there is an *established* power-status hierarchy, all group members will direct more communication to high power-status persons.

Since high power-status persons initiate the most communication, we also expect them to receive the most communication (Propositions 9.2 and 9.3). It is likely that the very high correlation between the number of communications initiated and the number received (Proposition 9.2) has led to decisive overestimation of the effect that status and power, *per se*, exert on communication. But—as a simple descriptive fact—there is no lack of evidence to show that participants direct communication to persons high in power and status (Back et al., 1950; Bates, 1952; Cohen, 1958; Collins, 1960; Festinger, 1948; Hurwitz et al., 1953; Jackson, 1959; Kelley, 1951; Lippitt et al., 1952; Miyamoto, Crowell, and Katcher, 1957; Sherif and Sherif, 1956, p. 226). Although the effect is lessened when the number of initiations is controlled, there may still be some tendency to overcommunicate to high power-status persons (e.g., Hurwitz et al., 1953). Riley, Cohn, Toby, and Riley (1954) used a questionnaire method which may not be contaminated by the effect of initiations. They asked subjects to whom they would go in order to talk over each item in a list of topics, and they also collected an independent measure of power-status. According to their data, subjects prefer discussion with high status persons.

This overcommunication may be another aspect of the general tendency to behave deferentially toward high power persons (Proposition 8.3-A). It is likely that social interaction with high power-status persons is more rewarding in some way than social interaction with others. It should be remembered, however, that it is the high power participants who are in a position to "get things done" within the group. It may be that the participants must direct more of their communication to high power persons because it is necessary for successful work on the task.

PROPOSITION 9.4-B. When a status hierarchy is *still in the process of being developed,* participants who aspire to high status will communicate more to potentially low-status persons than to other aspiring high-status persons.

Interpretation of this proposition rests on two assumptions. In the first place, let us assume that persons who aspire to high status in a newly formed group will communicate in a manner that builds their status rank. Secondly, we join Barnard (1938) and Thibaut and Kelley (1959) in the belief that it is the potentially low-status persons who award this status. In other words, aspiring high-status persons must communicate to potentially low-status persons in order to achieve their goals.

Although they do not suggest the hypothesis under discussion, Larsen and Hill (1958) report data which provide support for this interpretation. The transmission of valued bits of information was studied in two successive camp populations. The direction of the acts of communication which were recorded is summarized in the following chart (same status communications omitted):

	% OF COM-MUNICATION UP STATUS	% OF COM-MUNICATION DOWN STATUS
Group I (little change in status hierarchy)	56	21
Group II (developing status hierarchy)	32	56

Group I shows an excess of *up*-status communication while Group II shows an excess of *down*-status communication. Group I was characterized by a high degree of structure at the opening of the camp—a structure which remained relatively constant throughout the camp period. Group II began with a low degree of structure, but this increased throughout the camp period.

Using the end of camp status measure, communication was up-status in the group with a *fixed* structure. In the group with *developing* structure, communication was down-status. Further analysis revealed that, in spite of the differences in the direction of communication in the two camps, the direction in *changes* in popularity was similar. In both camps the transmitters rose while the receivers (of communication) fell in popularity status.

Collins (1960) conducted an experiment designed, in part, to test Proposition 9.4-B. Interaction was recorded in a college class which was allowed free discussion for three of its four weekly meetings. Although some of the group members did know each other before the class, evidence was obtained to indicate that the status hierarchy became significantly more structured as the course progressed. Throughout the discussion, low status persons initiated more communication to high status persons than to their low status compatriots. This is, of course, exactly what would be expected; since high status persons do more talking, they should receive more initiations from other group members. In order to correct for the difference in the total amount of talking, a special index was computed. Communications received by high (and low) status persons were divided by the total amount which they (the receivers) initiated. In the case of communication from high to low status groups, this index would reflect the *percentage* of total high status initiations answered by a low status group member. In the case of communication from a low status member to a fellow low status member, the index would reflect the *percentage* of the total low status initiations which were answered by another low status person. This index corrects for the difference in the total amount of participation—any difference which remains is due to high status *per se* and not the high initiation always associated with high status. Even after this correction, low status persons sent significantly more communications to high status group members than to low status members.

High status persons also sent significantly more communications to other high status participants than to participants with low status. However, *when these figures are corrected for the number of communications initiated by high status persons,* the high status members initiate significantly more communications to *low* status persons during the early periods of interaction. In further support of Propositions 9.4-A and 9.4-B, this tendency to overcommunicate to low status persons decreased significantly as time passed and the power-status hierarchy became more structured.

In summary, the high rate of initiations of high status persons means that they will receive more communications than low status persons from all group members under all circumstances. If the number of initiations is controlled for, however, a more subtle pattern emerges. (*a*) Even with initiations controlled for, potentially low status persons consistently send more communication to high status group members than to their low status peers. When an adjustment for the large number of initiations from high status persons is made the initiations of these high status members are complex. (*b*) *If the power-status hierarchy is in the process of formation,* high status persons will send extra communications to low status persons—presumably as a means of building their own power-status. This extra communication to the low status group is so small, however, that it cannot be seen until an adjustment is made for the low initiation rate of the low status persons. (*c*) *Once the status hierarchy is formed,* on the other hand, high power-status members send extra communications to their fellow high power-status peers.

PROPOSITION 9.4-C. The content of communication from low to high power-status persons will depend on what the low status person has learned is most likely to obtain reinforcement.

In accord with Proposition 8.3-A, many investigators have found that communication from low status to high status persons is deferential and noncritical. Kelley's (1951) experiment led him to conclude: "This result leads one to expect that the mere introduction of a status difference between the subgroups produces restraints against inter-level criticism" (p. 56). As Campbell summarized the literature with respect to the biasing of communication, "The human . . . [communicator] is usually in the situation of transmitting the message to another human being. And as a rule this relationship will continue in the future and has reciprocal aspects, in which the recipient may be able to act back on the transmitter. In this typical situation, the . . . [communicator's messages] may be expected to deviate from input in the direction of pleasing the recipient, avoiding causing distress, etc." (Campbell, 1958, p. 351).

Kelley (1951) suggested that up-status communication will be noncritical. There are at least two exceptions to this more specific proposition reviewed below which led us to posit the more general wording of Proposition 9.4-C. In overview, the communicator may sometimes feel that critical communication is most likely to win the favor of the high status recipient. Perlmutter and Hymovitch (1954) found that up-status communication was significantly *more* critical when the student thought the unknown receiver had high status (would grade the papers) than when he had low status (would read, but not grade, the papers). They theorize that, in this particular setting, the low status persons thought criticism was most likely to evoke the highest grade (reward).

Cohen (1958) created two kinds of high status positions. In one case, the low status subjects were merely told the other position was more desirable. In the second case, they were also told that the advancement of low status subjects (i.e., themselves) would depend on the high status persons. Thus, some of the high status people had perceived status *and* power. The average number of critical messages to the high status persons without power was three times the average number of the critical messages sent to the position with high status and power (0.97 to 0.33, significant at the .001 level). It seems likely that the low status persons did not think that lack of criticism was likely to increase their rewards when they communicated to "powerless" high status persons.

Cohen's (1958) modification of Kelley's (1951) experiment on status and communication provides further evidence for the *interaction* of the participant's motivation and his understanding of the environment. He found, for instance, that low status subjects engaged in conjectures about the high status job only when motivation and understanding of possible mobility are contradictory. That is, the low status persons used conjectures about the high status job only when (1) there was motivation to move up but such a move was impossible and (2) when the move was possible but not wanted. It did *not* occur when both motivation and environmental possibility were present. In this latter case, *Ss* probably tried to improve their lot directly, and did not bother with conjectures about the other group. One other finding is relevant in this context. Only low status individuals who reported that they believed their communication would have some effect bothered to restrain the criticism in their messages to high status individuals.

Spatial arrangement within the face-to-face group. Data on the effect of spatial arrangement *within* small group discussions are not entirely consistent. Steinzor (1950) found a tendency for people to interact most with persons sitting across from each other rather than with persons sitting immediately to one side or the other. Hearn (1957) replicated this finding in his *"self-motivated"* groups, and then—to the contrary—he found that there was a reverse tendency to interact with neighbors on either side in the *"trainer-induced"* groups. Sommer (1959) found some tendency for groups of two and three to seat themselves across from each other when sent into the hospital cafeteria for discussion, but he found a greater interaction with neighbors than persons across the way during the meals. This latter finding may be due to the fact that friends are likely to sit side by side in a noisy and crowded cafeteria. In summary, there is probably some tendency to direct interaction to the participant across the way in preference to one's immediate neighbor, but the tendency seems weak enough to be reversed by other factors influencing the direction of communication.

COMMUNICATION BETWEEN PERSONS NOT IN THE SAME FACE-TO-FACE GROUP

PROPOSITION 9.5. Communication will be directed toward (a) persons in close physical proximity, (b) persons in the same work group, and (c) the same socio-economic status.

We talk most frequently with those persons whom we see and hear most frequently; we speak most often to those persons who speak to us (Proposition 9.2). And it is persons in close physical proximity, in the same working group, and in the same socioeconomic status who are most likely to talk to us and to offer opportunities for us to talk to them.

Gullahorn (1952) found that distance was the most important variable in accounting for the interaction in an office of 37 workers.   Festinger, Schachter, and Back (1950) found that social visiting relations were more likely to develop if the physical separation was small, and Powell (1952) found the same thing in a Costa Rican village.   Thibaut and Kelley (1959) summarized the studies which "have dealt with the relation between socioeconomic status and direction of sociometric choice in elementary school classes, college student groups, and small communities. . . . In general, the results show that individuals make their choices primarily within their own status level or in adjacent levels" (p. 48).   Note that socio-*economic* status involves large status differences and that members of different status are likely to live in different areas and to be physically distant.   Nonetheless, there is a tendency to communicate excessively to upper status levels which is reminiscent of the previous proposition which dealt with socio*metric* status within face-to-face groups.

The present proposition seems particularly feasible when applied to decision-making groups within the ongoing organization.

As Jackson suggests, "In pursuit of their work goals, people have forces acting upon them to communicate with those who will help achieve their aims, and forces against communicating with those who will not assist, or may retard their accomplishment" (Jackson, 1959b, p. 161). Since differentiation of roles often corresponds to status differences, same-status persons are most likely to reduce work-oriented needs. For example, Simpson (1959) found that communication among first-line supervisors in a textile mill was mainly horizontal. An organizational employee may not even have the *opportunity* to communicate with comparatively high or low status persons. Both Jackson (1953) and Burns (1954) found the most communication within the same status level in their studies of ongoing organizations. There are clearly many exceptions; both the boss-secretary and foreman-worker relationships probably result in work needs which require communication across status levels. But the data reported above seem to indicate that the proposition generally holds.

COMMUNICATION IN THE DEVELOPMENT OF GROUP CONSENSUS

The five propositions developed to this point in Chapter Nine are concerned with the initiation and directionality of communication within groups. Now we turn to studies on the development of consensus in groups.

PROPOSITION 9.6. Communication serves to increase the uniformity of opinion within the group.

When the members of a group are in complete agreement, there seems to be little to talk about. In Chapter Two we discussed the way in which social influence processes allow group members to divide the labor of learning about their task environment; and we have seen how these social sources of knowledge become more important as the "correct" answer becomes objectively ambiguous. As group members come to depend on each other for information about the environment, the uniformity of opinion within the group will increase.

In general, there are two ways that group members increase consensus within their group, and each mechanism is discussed in a subproposition below. First, uniformity can be achieved if either the deviate or the rest of the group change their opinion. As is stated in Proposition 9.6-A, groups striving for unanimity in this way will *increase* the communication directed to the deviate. Second, the group can increase consensus through subgroup formation and by interpersonal rejection of the deviates. Proposition 9.6-B states that interpersonal rejection will be accompanied by a *decrease* in communication to the deviate. Both of these procedures in the end rid the psychological group of its deviates.

Following elaboration of these two subpropositions, we shall discuss some of the variables which determine the relative importance of these two mechanisms for increasing the consensus of opinion within a group.

PROPOSITION 9.6-A. A high number of communications will be addressed to an *accepted* group member who expresses deviate opinions.

Festinger and Thibaut (1951) asked group members to discuss two problems. Opinions could be scaled on a seven-point continuum and each S was asked to display the number corresponding to his opinion on a card; so each S was constantly aware of the exact opinion position of all other Ss. An analysis of the messages written among the Ss revealed that the most messages were sent to subjects who indicated extreme opinions. Gerard (1953) reported the same result in a similar setting. Berkowitz and Howard (1959) and Festinger et al. (1952) also report more written communication to the deviant. Schachter (1951) and Emerson (1954) report similar results for verbal interaction in experiments where paid participants expressed deviant opinions.

PROPOSITION 9.6-B. Rejection of the deviate and subgroup formation will result in a low number of communications addressed to an *unaccepted* group member who expresses deviant opinions.

Although other factors limit the emotional rejection which precedes a decrease in communication, several of the studies cited above report that group members reject *persistent* deviants and consequently decrease their communication to the rejected persons. Schachter (1951) reports an initial increase and then a decrease in communication to the deviant. Festinger and Thibaut (1951) report a decrease in communication to the deviant only when (a) groups felt a low pressure toward uniformity and (b) the participants had been told that they were selected to be as different as possible in their interest and knowledge of the problem. Emerson (1954) and Gerard (1953) did not secure replication of Schachter's decrease in communication to the deviant toward the end of the experiment, but Emerson reports data which suggest that the high school subjects in his experiment were more influenced by the opinions of the deviant (Proposition 9.6-A) and were generally less rejecting of the deviant. This high influence and low rejection would account for the fact that the subjects did not stop communicating with the (paid) deviant.

Factors influencing the relative importance of communication (9.6-A) and rejection (9.6-B) as mechanisms for increasing the uniformity of opinion within the group. Both increased communication to and rejection of the deviate can increase the uniformity of opinion within the group, but they are, to some extent, incompatible; it is psychologically difficult to increase the communication to group members who are rejected from the group. Several variables influence the relative strength of these two mechanisms.

1. In general, we expect the pressure for unanimity and the resistance to subgroup formation to increase with the variables which increase group cohesiveness (common fate, past success, interpersonal attraction, high pressure for agreement, etc.). See Chapter Six.[3]

It may be that members of cohesive groups do not even realize that the deviate disagrees with the other group members. The actual number of arguments expressed may be a poor measure of disagreement. Even though cohesiveness generally is asso-

---

[3] The positive relationship between pressure toward uniformity, group cohesiveness, and communication to the deviant is reported by the studies just discussed (Schachter, 1951; Emerson, 1954; Festinger and Thibaut, 1951; Festinger et al., 1952; Berkowitz and Howard, 1959).

ciated with increased uniformity of opinion, cohesive groups are more vocal in the disagreement which they do have (French, 1941).

2. Another factor which influences the rejection and communication to deviates is the ambiguity of the issue. The communication to the deviant will increase, and the rejection will decrease, as the issues become objectively ambiguous and greater emphasis is placed on social sources of knowledge (Festinger and Thibaut, 1951).

3. A third factor closely related to objective ambiguity is the extent to which group opinion is structured. The group will be more rejecting and send less communication to the deviate on issues on which they have fixed and structured opinions (Festinger and Thibaut, 1951; Emerson, 1954).

4. The group will be less rejecting of high power group members (Proposition 8.2).

All through the book, an attempt has been made to indicate the complicated nature of interlocking social mechanisms. Usually our data allow us only to indicate exceptions to more general findings. These apparent exceptions should alert us to potentially opposing mechanisms which can operate in decision-making groups. Unfortunately the data do not always allow us to detail the specific interrelations among juxtaposed processes. In this section on the development of group consensus, we have a clear illustration of the complexity and intricacy which are involved in the social psychology of groups. Whether a group will achieve consensus by further communication with the deviate or by excluding him from the group *depends* . . . ! It depends upon how other factors treated in earlier chapters—such as common fate, past success, interpersonal attraction, pressure toward uniformity, perception of disagreement, the ambiguity of the task, and the distribution of power within the group—operate within the complex of interrelated processes.

RECEIPT OF COMMUNICATION

In general, the way that a conference participant "perceives" or understands the meaning of a communication stimulus is essentially the same way he "perceives" or understands any other stimulus. Campbell (1958) examined the psychological literature in an attempt to identify systematic errors on the part of human links in communication systems. He collected a list of the ways in which human beings are less than perfect as they try to assimilate the information contained in their environment. In this section we shall list and briefly discuss those of Campbell's principles which are relevant to the decision-making group. Readers interested in experimental documentation of these principles are referred to the original Campbell paper (1958).

1. The conference participant's understanding of the stimulus inputs "if imperfect, will on the average be shorter, simpler, and less detailed than [the objective] input" (p. 342). We have already seen in Proposition 2.2 and 2.2-A the way that conference members retain and assimilate only a small portion of the total amount of information possessed by all participants.

2. ". . . The middle portion of the message will be the least well retained" (p. 343). Handbooks on group discussion and public speaking have long recognized that the strongest positions in a speech or contribution are at the beginning and at the end. The application of this principle would stress the importance of clear introductory and summarizing statements for each contribution of any length.

3. There is some tendency to mold the stimulus "in the direction of regularized, more symmetrical output" (p. 344). There is a tendency to distort the stimulus message "in the direction of dividing the content into clear-cut 'entities,' reducing gradations both by exaggerating some differences and losing others" (p. 344). This principle may partially explain the tendency of conference participants to see the world as either black or white. This kind of thinking may lead them to ignore subtle differences in degree which could become vital for group decision.

4. "An imperfectly transmitted message will be distorted in the direction of important past messages, both *rewarding* and *punishing* past messages. . . . The older simpler notion of wishful distortion, leading to the suppression of messages of unpleasant association, does not seem to hold up except in those situations where the transmitter fears the reaction of a human recipient to the message itself" (Campbell, 1958, pp. 350–351). This

principle stresses the way that we pay closest attention to those messages which have important consequences to us. The evidence seems to indicate that the messages associated with both reward and punishment from the task environment or from the interpersonal reaction will influence our future understanding of other messages.

5. A new message stimulus tends to be modified so that it takes on meaning similar or identical to previous stimulus messages. "This tendency . . . is probably the most pervasive of the systematic biases" (p. 346). We have frequently seen how the behavior of conference members is, to a large extent, reasonably consistent from time to time and situation to situation. There is some reason then for group participants to expect their fellow members to communicate currently in much the same way as they have communicated previously. Nonetheless, we should recognize that this tendency interferes when the sender is trying to modify his position or in some other way say something different from his previous communication in a conference situation.

6. Errors will, in general, be in the direction of making the meaning of a stimulus message similar to the meaning expected by the receiver. Many communication breakdowns in groups may well be due to the fact that participants simply do not listen; many participants are so sure that they know what other members will say that they do not feel obligated to pay close attention. But, as we have seen in Chapters Two and Five, the most important part of conference communication may occur when another member says something that we do not expect, and thus offers us a perspective or possible solution which would not have occurred to us while working alone.

7. The recipient of a communication stimulus will understand or "perceive" the message so that it is similar or compatible to the receiver's own attitudes. A study by Burns (1954) is interesting both for its results and its methodology. Burns developed a system in which the executives recorded the time, direction, and content of their own communications. He found that, in 20 per cent of the communication between persons of different status, there was a consistent difference in the interpretation of the purpose of the communications. For the highest ranking executive studied, fully one-half of the messages he classified as "instruc-

tion or decision giving" were classified as "advice or information received" by the subordinate. The mistake was almost never made in the opposite direction. Since the "giving of instructions or decisions" is probably a cue of high status, Burns hypothesizes that these discrepancies were due to a need to protect status.

8. Participants tend to reduce the content of messages so that they mean little more than "this is good" or "this is bad." "There is a tendency to distort coding assignments in the direction of an affective or evaluative coding. The most natural coding of any input by the human operator seems to be of the general nature of 'like' versus 'dislike,' 'approach' versus 'avoid,' 'good' versus 'bad,' 'beautiful' versus 'ugly,' etc. The general finding of psychologists is that whatever assignment is given tends to be distorted in the direction of this evaluative assignment. This is shown repeatedly as a 'halo' effect, or general factor in rating assignments" (Campbell, 1958 p. 357). This principle is represented in the decision-making group by the quick evaluation of ideas as either completely good or completely bad. This kind of thinking or "perception" of communication messages obscures other important aspects of the message. If we examine the contribution to see whether it is "good" or "bad," we probably ignore other important aspects of the message.

9. "There is a strong tendency toward overdependence on a single source [of communication] and a neglect of all other sources. This one source is usually the most valid one, but not necessarily so" (p. 360).

10. "When a group of persons are exposed to a message stimulus and asked to state its meaning (size, degree of movement, amount of prejudice, etc.), they will distort their individual interpretations in the direction of their fellows" (p. 361). This proposition assumes, of course, that the participants are in a position to know, or think they know, the interpretation of their fellows. The possibility that this distortion can work to the advantage of the group was discussed in Proposition 2.5-C.

11. This series of principles is concluded with two propositions not explicitly included in Campbell's list. In general, we expect that these human "biases" or "distortions" of the message's stimulus meaning will be greatest when the message is unclear or ambiguous. In many respects, this principle is the converse

of Proposition 2.5-A: "The more evidence which is presented in favor of a verbal sentence, the greater its internal consistency, and the more consistent it is with past experience, the more likely is the group to accept it." Thrasher (1954) reported a clear increase in conformity as the stimulus being judged becomes less structured; and Solomon Asch stated, "In agreement with other investigators, we find that the majority effect grows stronger as the situation diminishes in clarity" (Guetzkow, 1951, p. 189).

12. Working in a laboratory setting, Triandis (1960a, 1960b) found that when individuals have similar cognitive profiles, as measured on Osgood's semantic differential, they are able to communicate more effectively. Could it be that the greater the similarity in cognitive structures of the initiator and recipient, the greater is the accuracy with which the recipient understands the meaning intended by the initiator? Further evidence on this issue is provided by Runkel (1956) when he found that students who thought in similar ways to their instructors received higher grades on quizzes. Yet the "data provided evidence that the higher grades [of students cognitively similar to instructor] on the part of the co-linear [similar] students could not be accounted for by differences in scholastic ability as measured by A.C.E. scores, nor by conformity to a common attitude norm, nor by preference for the same attitude position as that held by the teacher" (Runkel, 1956, p. 191). In other words, the higher grades of students similar to the instructor are not caused by scholastic ability, conformity to a common attitude norm, or agreement with the instructor on a *specific* attitude.

The superior communication between persons with similar cognitive backgrounds is probably one of the mechanisms which operates to produce superior productivity on some tasks in homogeneous groups. It is to be remembered, however, that this accuracy of communication may be bought at a high price. In fact, the price may be so high that homogeneity leads to *inferior* performance on complex tasks, as was mentioned in Point 10 above. Although homogeneous groups may understand each other, there is no assurance that the members have the necessary knowledge to communicate. As we asserted in Chapter Five, heterogeneous groups are more likely to eliminate random errors, have a greater number of alternatives available for consideration, and have a superior critical potential.

LIST OF PROPOSITIONS

PROPOSITION 9.1.   Interaction is unevenly distributed among group members.

PROPOSITION 9.2.   The more interactions initiated by a group member, the more interactions will be directed to him by other group members.

PROPOSITION 9.3.   High power-status persons will initiate more communication than low status persons. (This Proposition is also numbered 8.1-B.)

PROPOSITION 9.4.   The power-status hierarchy will influence the flow and content of communication within the face-to-face group.

PROPOSITION 9.4-A.   When there is an established power-status hierarchy, all group members will direct more communication to high power-status persons.

PROPOSITION 9.4-B.   When a status hierarchy is still in the process of being developed, participants who aspire to high status will communicate more to potentially low status persons than other aspiring high status persons.

PROPOSITION 9.4-C.   The content of communication from low to high power-status persons will depend on what the low status person has learned is most likely to obtain reinforcement.

PROPOSITION 9.5.   Communication will be directed toward (a) persons in close physical proximity, (b) persons in the same work group, and (c) the same socio-economic status.

PROPOSITION 9.6.   Communication serves to increase the uniformity of opinion within the group.

PROPOSITION 9.6-A.   A high number of communications will be addressed to an accepted group member who expresses deviate opinions.

PROPOSITION 9.6-B.   Rejection of the deviate and subgroup formation will result in a low number of communications addressed to an unaccepted group member who expresses deviant opinions.

CHAPTER TEN

Participant satisfaction with the conference

The psychological investigation of work groups in industry has long been concerned with the worker's affective or emotional evaluation of his job. The topic of industrial morale, job satisfaction, or job attitudes has been the subject of much speculation and appreciable research (Herzberg, Mausnor, Peterson, and Capwell, 1957). The "Human Relations" psychologists have insisted that industrial management policy must consider the morale of workers as well as the efficient use of the machines. All in all, participant satisfaction has held a central place in early psychological studies of industrial settings.

It has become quite apparent, however, that the experimental data do not fit the traditional theoretical conceptualizations. The positive relationship between satisfaction and productivity, for instance, which is stated and implied by many writers appears not to be a relationship at all (Brayfield and Crockett, 1955). In general, these negative results seem to have discouraged further experimental research on participant satisfaction. Although two theoretical reconceptualizations (Thibaut and Kelley, 1959, pp. 23–24, 80–89; and March and Simon, 1958, pp. 47–52, 119–121, 182–183) are available, little new experimental data have been published. After a theoretical overview, we shall review the empirical data on participant satisfaction.

Satisfaction represents an individual's subjective evaluation or judgment of the rewards that he has received. Several terms are used almost interchangeably with *satisfaction;* a highly satisfied person has high *morale* and the satisfied worker has *job satisfaction* or favorable *job attitudes.* If it is necessary to specify what satisfaction *is*, most researchers define it as a judgment of a subjective state of feeling or evaluation. It can be most directly measured by asking the person to answer such questions as: "How satisfied are you?," "Do you like your job?," "Are you satisfied with the conference?"

Many other research measures are highly correlated with self-report measures of satisfaction. Campbell and Tyler (1957) report high correlations between a group's ratings of its own morale and the ratings of the same group by other work groups in two quite separate situations. Campbell (1955) asked three yeomen in the headquarters squadron to rank the ten submarines of the squadron on a scale of happiness. The combined rankings of these three "informants" correlated very highly (.9) with the rankings produced by a thirty-item questionnaire completed by the men in the submarines themselves.

As we shall see in the propositions to follow, one of the major determinants of satisfaction is the reinforcement provided in the situation. This close relation between rewards received and satisfaction has led several authors to define satisfaction in terms of these rewards: "Morale is an index of the extent to which an individual perceives a probability of satisfying his own motives through cooperation with the group" (Stagner, 1958, p. 64). "Morale is the extent to which an individual's needs are satisfied and the extent to which the individual perceives that satisfaction as stemming from his total job situation" (Guion, 1958, p. 62).

SATISFACTION AS A JUDGMENT

When an individual is asked to estimate his degree of satisfaction with a decision-making conference, he is being asked to make a psychological judgment. In other words, "How satisfying was this conference?" is quite similar to asking, "How heavy was this weight?" or "How much prejudice is indicated by this statement?" From its early beginnings in psychophysics, psychology has a long history of interest in the principles of judgment. Do these time-honored principles apply to judgments of satisfaction as they apply to judgments of pitch, prejudice, and pungency?

One of the most important laws which has emerged from the psychology of judgment is that such judgments are relative. That is, a stimulus object will be evaluated in comparison with either an internal standard, such as the "adaptation level" (Helson, 1959), or an external object which serves to "anchor" the subjective ruler used to make the judgments. One of the important determinants of these touchstones of evaluation is the past experience of the judge. If an executive has always worked in a company in which conferences usually end without decisions, he will probably rate the conference which completes a third of its agenda as "very high." On the other hand, had the same executive worked in a company where conferences were usually quite productive, he might rate the same output as either "average" or even "very low."

A participant's rating of satisfaction will, then, depend on at least two factors. His satisfaction will be *high* (1) if the "absolute" quality of the present decision-making group is *high*, and (2) if the quality of other conferences he has participated in is generally *low*. The level of rewards which an individual has learned to expect in a particular situation can be called his level of aspiration.[1]

Regardless of the actual size of the reward, the individual will be satisfied if it is larger than his level of aspiration or expectations and dissatisfied if it is lower than his level of aspiration. Stouffer and his associates (1949) find several examples of this effect in their studies of the American soldier. Noncombat troops overseas showed higher satisfaction with Army life than did noncombat troops in the United States, presumably because the overseas troops have a lower standard of comparison. In other words, noncombatant troops overseas compared their fate against

---

[1] For a more complete discussion of satisfaction, level of aspiration, and related phenomena see March and Simon (1958, pp. 47–52, 119–121, 182–183), Thibaut and Kelley (1959, pp. 23–24, 80–89), Lewin, Dembo, Festinger, and Sears (1944), Harvey and Sherif (1951), Johnson (1946), and Helson (1959).

a standard of combat troops or civilians in a war-torn area. This standard would be lower than the standard used by troops in the United States. Similarly Negro troops stationed in the North were less satisfied than the Negro troops stationed in the South presumably because *relative to the welfare of surrounding civilian Negroes,* the troops stationed in the South fared better.

SATISFACTION AS A JUDGMENT OF REWARDS RECEIVED

Two studies experimentally demonstrated that high rewards increase satisfaction. Collins, Davis, Myers, and Silk (1964) told *S*s that they were to participate in a five-man communication net experiment. In fact, all messages written by the *S*s were intercepted and the experimenter wrote all messages actually received by the *S*s. The messages which the *S*s received encouraged him to accept a relayer role. In other words, "Yellow," or the self-nominated keyman played by the experimenter, asked each subject to relay his own and his neighbor's information to Yellow. (See discussion of relayer role in Guetzkow's experiments in Chapter Three.) Although it was impossible for the *S* personally to solve the problem with the information he was given, he was told that the group had solved the problem whenever he enacted the relayer role, i.e., whenever he passed both his and his neighbor's information on to Yellow. Presumably, Yellow then solved the problem and the entire group was given credit for a success. A successful trial constitutes a task-environmental reward and should increase the satisfaction of group members.

At the end of four trials, the number of rewards (inductions of group success) was significantly correlated with such questions as: "To what extent did you enjoy your experience in this experiment?" and "How satisfied were you with your job in helping the group to solve the problem?" That these correlations disappeared at the end of the experiment after ten trials will be discussed later. For the moment, we see that the *number* of experimentally applied rewards in an operant conditioning experiment increased subjects' reports of enjoyment and satisfaction.

Collins (1963) demonstrated that the *magnitude* of the rewards also increases satisfaction. *S*s were assigned an intrinsically dull and uninteresting task—cutting out simple designs from sheets of paper. On some trials, Ss received a card which stated that the group had been successful on the last trial and had earned a monetary prize. The subject's own share of the prize was physically taped to the card, and Ss were assured that the money was theirs to keep. Some Ss received rewards of 10¢ per card and others received 50¢ per card.

A satisfaction questionnaire was administered at the end of the experiment which included such items as "How well did you like your job?," "How pleasurable was your participation in the experiment?," and "How satisfied were you with the other members of the group?" A factor analysis of the eight item scale revealed that the first unrotated factor accounted for 87 per cent of the common variance. This means that all eight questions measured a general and unidimensional over-all evaluation of experience in the group.

Ss who had received high magnitude rewards were generally more satisfied and happy. The positive relationship between satisfaction and rewards was quite stable. It held for both the college undergraduates and telephone operators who served in the experiment. Furthermore, the reward contingencies did not alter the causal relationship between rewards and satisfaction. One half of the Ss were told that the rewards they received would depend on the group's performance; and—in fact—they were rewarded whenever they cut out seven or more houses. The other half of the Ss were told that their performance would have no effect on the rewards they received; and—in fact—they were rewarded on a random basis unrelated to their productivity. Both groups of Ss reported more satisfaction with 50¢ rewards than with 10¢ rewards.

Salience of rewards. An outside observer can never be sure that a particular stimulus is rewarding to a specific group member at a certain time. True, we can note that similar stimuli were rewarding to similar people in similar situations; but generalization to new situations is never more than a statistically probable prediction. In particular, outside observers should be careful when we assume that the group success is rewarding to the individual member. Although Collins, Davis, Myers, and Silk (1964) found that inductions of *group* success were related to individual satisfaction at the end of four trials, this correlation had disappeared at the end of ten trials. The reason for this breakdown may be explained as follows. At the end of ten trials the number of rewards was still correlated with measures of group success, group cooperation, and group morale, yet the number of rewards then was completely unrelated to the question, "How successful were *you* personally in helping to solve the problem?" Apparently the *S*s, who were generally quite confused throughout the experiment, came to feel that the inductions of group success had little or nothing to do with them personally. Group success did not function as a reward for those *S*s. Evidence for this interpretation can be found if *S*s are divided into an "aware" sample, who indicated that they knew Yellow was solving the problems—presumably with their help, and an "unaware" sample, who did not think anyone was solving the problem. Thirteen out of 13 correlations between number of rewards and a satisfaction item were higher for the aware sample. This relationship even holds for the nonsignificant correlations between number of group successes and individual satisfaction at the end of trial ten.

A particularly tempting mistake is to assume that the industrial worker and the conference participant are rewarded by their task productivity. The individuals may be completely indifferent to the amount of work accomplished or the quality of the decision. Their concern may lie more with "keeping one's reputation clean," "impressing the boss," or "showing you can stick with your friends." Under these circumstances group success and individual productivity would *not* constitute a task-environmental reward. Then task success would not increase individual satisfaction. Leaders who stress productivity and quality may make *management* happy, but—in many cases—the conference *participant* "couldn't care less."

Homans describes a thesis by L. B. Barnes (1958) illustrating that some rewards offered by the company were not salient or important to the employees.

In a study of a research laboratory attached to a manufacturing company, L. B. Barnes found he could divide the engineers in the laboratory into two different categories, which he called professionals *and* organizationals, *according to differences in their backgrounds. In their past experience, including lengthy technical training at universities, the professionals had acquired the values of academic, research scientists. The past experience of the organizationals was apt to have been somewhat different, and they tended to identify themselves with business and look forward to a career in the company. In point of fact the laboratory was asked to do little true research, and spent much of its time running routine tests and providing other services for the ongoing manufacturing operations of the company. Not surprisingly, the organizationals were much better satisfied than the professionals. By the acquired values of the latter, the rewards they got from the job itself were small. They were not doing what they were trained to do and liked to do* (Homans, 1961, p. 271).

The variety of stimuli which are rewarding in practical settings. In the situations presented to this point, the researches were completed in circumstances where only one class of stimuli proved rewarding. Thus, it was possible to observe that when the salience of the reward is low, satisfaction is low, even though the objective stimuli constituting "rewards" are present. But in practical situations a gamut of stimuli are often presented simultaneously, at least some of which may be rewarding. The factor analytic studies of satisfaction exhibit the large variety of stimuli which may be salient for participants in work situations. The authors of these studies administer a questionnaire containing several specific questions on satisfaction. "Factors," or groups of items which tend to be answered in the same way by a particular employee, are then identified. Each factor, or common element in each cluster of questions, provides some information about the different sources of rewards between which the employees discriminate.

Wherry (1958) reported such factors which were identified in four separate samples of industrial employees; his reports of each of the four analyses yielded (1) a general factor and five group factors, (2) working conditions, (3) financial reward, (4) supervision, (5) management, and (6) personal development. Wherry further reported that "the invariance of morale factors compares favorably with that of ability factors" (p. 83). Roach (1958) reported similar factors in his sample of clerical and management employees.[2]

Although these factor analytic studies increase the credibility of our postulated close relationship between reward and satisfaction, they also demonstrate the multifactored or complex nature of participant satisfaction. Apparently, a participant can be very happy with one aspect of group interaction (the consideration of the leader, for example) and unsatisfied with another aspect (e.g., the domination of the conference by a few participants). A global or general measure of satisfaction will reflect the combination of many different rewards and satisfactions—some of which will be high and some lower than the general over-all rating.

PROPOSITIONS ABOUT SATISFACTIONS PRODUCED BY TASK-ENVIRONMENTAL REWARDS

The following propositions uniformly reflect the fact that satisfaction in decision-making groups is produced by the rewards associated with interaction in the conference. There are several sources of rewards from interaction in a group, and the data will be discussed in three sections. The two initial classes deal with sources of reward for the whole group. The first source of rewards to the group as a whole is the task-environment (Propositions 10.1 and 10.2). The second class of rewards to the entire group is interpersonal rewards (Proposition 10.3). For the final section we turn our attention from the group as a whole and examine sources of rewards for individual members within the group. We study interpersonal and task rewards which are contingent on a particular position within a group (Propositions 10.4 and 10.5).

[2] ". . . A 62-item employee opinion survey was subjected to a modified centroid factor analysis. This survey had previously been filled out by 2,072 clerical and management employees. Twelve factors emerged from the analysis. One of the factors was identified as a general bias or 'halo' factor, and another was identified as a general attitude toward supervision. The remaining ten factors were identified as: Pride in company, intrinsic job satisfaction, and satisfaction with each of the eight following conditions —setting up and enforcing job standards, supervisory consideration, work load and pressure, interest in and treatment of the individual, administration of salaries, communications, development and progress, and co-workers" (Roach, 1958, p. 419).

As we argued in Chapter Four, since the task-environmental feedback is so remote from the immediate task efforts of committee members, it is likely that most behaviors in decision-making conferences are immediately supported by interpersonal rewards. Substantive agreement is primarily symptomatic of a task accomplishment but that does not mean it cannot also be an interpersonal reward. In fact, one of the important functions of interpersonal rewards is to give immediate support to task activities which do not elicit any *immediate* feedback from the task environment. It would be a serious mistake, however, to overlook the task environment in which a conference works; ultimately, the test of a decision-making group is reflected in task-environmental rewards. We maintain the distinction between the task-environmental and interpersonal rewards in order to emphasize the role of the task environment in the decision-making conference.

PROPOSITION 10.1. Success on the group task will produce satisfaction.

The participants in the 72 conferences in business and government studied by the University of Michigan (Marquis, Guetzkow, and Heyns, 1951) rated their satisfaction with several aspects of the conference. The empirical correlates of these measures will be reported throughout these propositions, but here we are concerned with the reasons the participants gave for their ratings. These reasons throw some light on the factors which conference members themselves consider determinants of satisfaction. Participants see their degree of satisfaction with the conference as a function of the adequacy of the problem solving. Typical comments were: "Discussion was thorough and frank," "Decisions reached were good," "Good exchange of opinion and ideas," "We got a lot accomplished."

Similar opinions were expressed by 75 top level executives (Kriesberg, 1950) who were asked what things made a conference effective. These men, who spend an average of ten hours a week in conference, stressed factors which were leader functions: adequate preparation of the agenda, and keeping the problem in focus during discussion. They rarely mentioned the more fundamentally interpersonal rewards such as status, social approval, and "shooting the bull," which are discussed in the next section. The paucity of comments on this score clearly reflects the executive's conception of conferences as instruments serving only his own administrative needs. In Proposition 10.1 we see that participants and executives are correct in stressing task success as a source of attraction, but it is important to remember the *interpersonal* determinants of attraction discussed in the next two propositions.

Several studies have included an objective measure of task success and have found that high satisfaction was associated with high task effectiveness. Medalia and Miller (1955) measured the efficiency of fifty radar sites in the Air Defense Command through ratings of the division commander. Groups high on this measure of efficiency indicated significantly higher satisfaction. Hoffman (1959) also found that high-quality group decision was associated with high satisfaction. And as would be suspected, even when there is no objective measure of task success, if the participants believe they have been successful, they are satisfied. Berkowitz and Levy (1956) found that groups who were told they had done well by E had a high pride in group performance even though they had not actually been successful. Deutsch (1959) found that members of groups who were told that they had been successful on a preliminary task were significantly more satisfied than members of groups who were told they had failed. Satisfaction was measured by participant ratings on this question which followed each of the five tasks: "If the experimenter said that you could leave now if you wished, what would you do— leave now or continue working with this group?" In summary, the data from laboratory studies strongly support the proposition that success, actual or perceived, on the group task will produce satisfaction with the group.[3]

Several measures in the field study of 72 conferences in busi-

[3] Raven and Rietsema (1957) reported a study in which subjects listened to a tape recording simulating group interaction but thought they were actually interacting with students in another room. In one condition the script of the tape recording was written so that the subject could clearly understand the group goal, but in the other condition the group goal was unclear. The clear group goal resulted in a greater attraction to the goal-related task but did *not* cause the participants to rate the group more favorably.

ness and government reflect the heightened satisfaction produced by success on the group task. The larger the percentage of agenda completed in a meeting, the more the participants are satisfied with it. Satisfaction is also higher in meetings where the agenda topics are completed with dispatch. The longer it takes to reach a decision on the substantive topic, the lower the satisfaction. Meetings in which the observers rated the problem solving as orderly, efficient, and rapidly paced also showed higher member satisfaction. Shorter meetings leave the participant more satisfied than long ones.

If efficient problem solution leads to higher satisfaction, then groups with easy problems should be more satisfied.[4] Unfortunately no direct measure of problem difficulty was obtained in the field study of 72 conferences. The observers did, however, make a rating of the degree to which the problems before a conference demanded an integrative type of solution. If a conference was concerned with a few over-all policy decisions, it was given a high rating on this variable. If, on the other hand, the meeting was devoted to a number of independent routine administrative decisions, it received a low rating on "problem integration." Although this index can hardly be considered a pure measure of problem difficulty, in these conferences faced with over-all policy decisions, the problems may have been more difficult.

Satisfaction was significantly lower in meetings which dealt with problems requiring integration. As the difficulty of the problems confronting a conference increases, we find an alteration in a number of other variables which were related to satisfaction in the field study of 72 conferences. Signs of strain appear in almost all aspects of the group functioning. More difficult problems are more time consuming, and conferences faced with such problems find themselves with considerable unfinished business at the end of the meeting. This is obviously one source of lowered

---

[4] It would be possible that group members have higher *expectations* (aspiration levels) when working on easy problems and, since satisfaction results from rewards that *exceed* expectations, easy problems may not always be related to satisfaction. Success on an easy task may not be as satisfying as success on a difficult task.

satisfaction, since members are more likely to be satisfied with meetings in which the problems are disposed of rapidly and completely.

More difficult problems are those which require considerable discussion and are likely to bring out differences of opinion in a group. Groups faced with such problems showed significantly more conflict and signs of frustration. Participants showed more aggressive and self-oriented need behavior unrelated to the realities of the problems at hand. Furthermore, the unity of the group was threatened. The observers noted that the congruence of motivations among members was lower when the problems were difficult; and the participants perceived their group as less unified. All in all, the results suggest that increased problem difficulty resulted in lower productivity (Proposition 3.1) for a variety of reasons, and that this lower productivity was associated with low satisfaction.

Rapid and efficient problem solving in a group is possible only with adequate communication; so it is not surprising to find that the communication measures have a positive relation both to problem-solving measures and to satisfaction. The highest correlation is between the observer rating of "understandability" of what was said in the meeting and satisfaction.

Participant ratings reflecting the success of the group task are also correlated with satisfaction. It is hardly surprising to find that when members think their decisions are good, they are also highly satisfied at the end of the meeting ($r = .73$). Another measure reflecting the participant's evaluation of task success is their agreement with the final decision. In those meetings where the members showed substantial agreement with the decisions, satisfaction was high; disagreement with the decisions was accompanied by lower satisfaction. Furthermore, agreement with decisions was an important determinant of satisfaction *within* a conference group. In these conferences the participant who expressed the most complete agreement with the decisions was likely to be the most satisfied member of his group. It appears, in summary, that success on the task will produce satisfaction.

PROPOSITION 10.2. Success in solving problems of interpersonal relations will produce satisfaction.

In Chapter Five we elaborated on the necessity for a patterning of interpersonal relations within the group. Propositions 3.2 and 3.3 and Chapter Five assert that inefficiency in meeting problems of internal interpersonal organization is reflected in lower productivity. Now we document the increased satisfaction with the higher task productivity which results from adequate handling of interpersonal problems. Smith's (1956) study on the threat induced by ambiguous role expectations was discussed in some detail in Proposition 3.3. It will be remembered that he introduced an interpersonal obstacle into his groups working on a "forty questions" task by instructing two paid participants to remain silent throughout the group interaction. The impact of this problem was lessened for some groups by informing them that some subjects thought of themselves as "listeners." When compared with a control group, both the presence of two silent members and the failure to clarify their roles significantly lowered the satisfaction of the subjects with the group. Both manipulations lowered the success of the group in solving the problems of the internal system and thus lowered satisfaction.

The rest of the data for this proposition will be discussed under two subpropositions which specify two of the specific problems of interpersonal relations which will affect the satisfaction of the group members.

PROPOSITION 10.2-A. Congruence of member motivation and a lack of self-oriented needs will produce satisfaction.

Several findings from the field observation of 72 conferences in business and government provide support here. One observer rating of participant characteristics which showed a significant positive relation to satisfaction was that of "congruence of member goals." Whenever the participants saw eye to eye about the objectives of the meeting and agreed as to the means for obtaining these objectives, they tended to leave the meeting feeling satisfied. A similar rating made by the participants on "congruence of means" was also significantly related to satisfaction.

The participants' ratings of their own motivation, as contrasted with those made by the observers, all showed positive relationships to satisfaction, although some of the correlations were quite low. When the participants felt that the problems being discussed were important and that they had considerable stake in the way the problems were settled, they tended to be more satisfied with the meetings.

The data gathered by the self-oriented needs observer (Fouriezos, Hutt, and Guetzkow, 1950) throw further light on the relation between motivation and satisfaction. This observer kept a record of the instances in which the behavior of each participant in a conference seemed to be dominated more by a strong ego need than by the demands of the immediate situation (see Chapter Five). Dissatisfied groups showed significantly more of this sort of behavior than did the satisfied groups.[5]

One of the measures which shows the highest relation to satisfaction was computed from the data obtained in the interview with the chairman at the conclusion of the conference. He was asked to indicate the cliques which existed in his conference group. There was a marked tendency for satisfaction to be lower in conferences where the leader was aware of a large number of cliques. The observers also recorded the number of cliques they saw during the conference. This measure bears a similar relationship to satisfaction. If we reason that an incongruity of motivation and resultant conflict would be reflected in the

---

[5] The self-oriented needs variable was related to several variables other than satisfaction; the following list should help to place it in context. The self-oriented needs observer rating is related to:

r	VARIABLE
.37	Low participant satisfaction
.32	Low group productivity
.55	Low group solidarity
.73	High group conflict
.46	Personal involvement of participants with problem being considered

formation of cliques, this evidence supports the proposition that such incongruity leads to dissatisfaction. This interpretation is supported by the fact that clique formation in these conference groups was found to be a function of the amount of conflict and frustration manifested in the meetings. All of these disruptive factors—conflict, frustration, and cliques—have adverse effects upon satisfaction and when one of them is present in the conference others tend to be manifest also.

PROPOSITION 10.2-B. Agreement on leadership will produce satisfaction.

Shelley (1960) reports a direct test of this proposition. Members of thirteen girls' clubs selected the three group members who did the most in helping the group attain its goals; and then they rated their groups on satisfaction or its effectiveness in attaining group goals. Groups with a high consensus on leadership were significantly more satisfied.[6]

Many of the findings in the field study of 72 conferences can be interpreted in this light.[7] For example, several variables [8]

[6] The proposition is supported at both individual and group levels. When all subjects who disagree with the majority are collected irrespective of their group membership, Ss who disagree with the majority are less satisfied. And when high consensus groups are separated from low consensus groups, both individuals who agree with the majority *and* individuals who do not agree are less satisfied if they are members of a low consensus group.

[7] Most of the following data are reported in Berkowitz (1953).

[8] The following variables are correlated with high satisfaction:

r	VARIABLE
.29 *	Leader has control of process—postmeeting Observer Rating
.33 †	High functional differentiation of leader, Observer Rating
.33 †	Low per cent of participation by members
.31 †	High per cent of functional units of communication addressed to leader
.30 †	Few solutions proposed by members, Observer tally

* Significant at the .05 level.
† Significant at the .01 level.

suggest that when the chairman is the sole behavioral leader, the participants are satisfied; but this finding must be interpreted in the light of the correlation between member participation and conflict. The more the participants tended to talk to each other rather than the leader (and thus the less the behavioral leadership of the chairman), *the higher the conflict.*

It seems likely that conference participants in business and government settings have fairly definite opinions as to how conferences should be run. When a conference conforms to this opinion, the members are satisfied; when the conference departs from this pattern, satisfaction is lowered. In general, as we state in Proposition 10.2, any factor which makes interpersonal relations more difficult will decrease satisfaction. In particular, we might expect that factors which disrupt or alter the preferred pattern of conference procedure will be associated with lowered member satisfaction; any factor which tends to keep the leader in the center of the conference process will be associated with greater satisfaction if group members expect the leader to assume a directive role. This may mean that it is interpersonal rewards that are involved.

SATISFACTIONS PRODUCED BY INTERPERSONAL REWARDS

PROPOSITION 10.3.   Interaction with persons we like and persons who like us will produce satisfaction.

In Proposition 6.2 we discussed the inter-relationship between interaction and interpersonal liking and argued that high interpersonal attraction increases the rewardingness of interaction. We also saw how the rewards from interaction produced power. Now we see that these rewards also increase satisfaction with the group experience. Exline (1957) told some groups that they were congenial (i.e., that they stood high on a scale of congeniality and that they should get along well together) and some groups that they were noncongenial. The congeniality induction produced a high liking among the co-workers and a greater satisfaction with the progress of the groups. Kelley and Shapiro (1954) asked the members in their experimental groups to rate each other on acceptability; they then passed out fake messages indicating varying degrees of group acceptance of each member. Group members who were led to believe that they were accepted by the group indicated a high desire to remain in the group and an enjoyment of participation in the experiment. These two experiments suggest that interaction with liked and accepting group members produced satisfaction with the group processes. The association of high morale with high interaction in the Bavelas communication nets is discussed in Proposition 10.5 below.[9]

Proposition 7.1-A specifies that individuals will develop interpersonal attraction when they share a common fate, and here we note that this interpersonal attraction is reflected in high satisfaction. Deutsch (1949) reported that a group graded as a unit expressed a higher evaluation of the group and its products.

SATISFACTIONS PRODUCED BY REWARDS
TO INDIVIDUALS CONTINGENT ON THEIR
POSITION WITHIN THE GROUP

PROPOSITION 10.4.   A position of high power will produce satisfaction.

If a person is in a position where he can influence the behavior of others, be uninfluenced by other group members, be unrestrained by group norms, and be a member of a high status clique, then that person is clearly in a position which has advantages. To state that high power members are more satisfied with their experience in the group is, in a sense, to summarize all that has been said about power to this point. Gerard (1957) found that subjects who were told that they were the boss and could tell others what to do were more highly satisfied, and Haythorn (1953) observed that members who received high sociometric choice (and thus also had high power) rated themselves and were rated by observers as high on "morale." This

---

[9] The field study of 72 conferences found a negative relationship between the amount of communication and the degree of satisfaction; but interaction was also associated with high conflict and this conflict may have offset the pleasures of interaction.

general state of satisfaction found in high power persons is reflected in the fact that high power campers desire little change in others and express some tendency to desire little change in themselves (Rosen, Levinger, and Lippitt, 1960).

PROPOSITION 10.5. A position of centrality and autonomy will produce satisfaction.

One source of experimentation which has provided data on participation satisfaction is the work done in the Bavelas (1950) communication nets. It will be remembered that Bavelas designed a procedure in which Ss were isolated in separate, but adjoining, stalls. In that way it is possible to control the potential channels of communication by opening or closing the slots between the stalls. A diagram of the nets referred to in the following discussion is reproduced below.

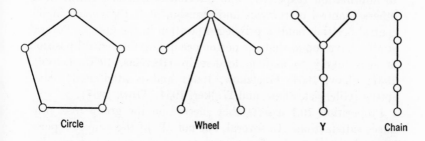

Circle Wheel Y Chain

In the first study reporting extensive data from this procedure, Leavitt (1951) recorded that subjects were more satisfied with interaction in some nets than in others. In general, the greater the number of open communication channels, the higher the satisfaction; the circle was highest in satisfaction, followed by the chain, the "Y," and then the wheel. The circle participants were significantly more satisfied than the wheel participants. We shall argue that the high satisfaction in these nets is a function of the positions of the participants and not a characteristic of the entire net; nets with a large number of desirable positions, of course, will be generally more satisfied. This interpretation is supported by Leavitt's analysis of the different positions within all nets: "The most central positions in other patterns enjoy their jobs more than any circle position. Peripheral positions, on the other hand, enjoy the job less than any circle position" (p. 45).

These results have been largely confirmed by subsequent research although the literature is not without contradictions. Nonetheless, we are still left wondering what it is about a central and independent position which produces high satisfaction; so we shall explore the intervening mechanisms which could produce satisfaction in the Bavelas net before turning to the evidence directly supporting the proposition.

There are any number of factors which could operate to make the central positions more satisfying. According to Proposition 10.4, a person with high power is better able to satisfy his needs whatever they might be. A person in a central position would be in much the same situation; by virtue of his greater access to information (expertise) and his control of communication to others (control of rewards and punishments), the person in the central position holds a privileged position in the group. Several studies have found that the person occupying the central position is more likely to assume leadership (Bavelas, 1950; Leavitt, 1951; Shaw, 1954; Guetzkow, 1960) and is attributed higher status (Gilchrist, Shaw, and Walker, 1954; Trow, 1957).

Proposition 10.1 asserts that success on the group task produces satisfaction. In several, but not all, of the studies reporting higher satisfaction for independent positions and groups, independence was also associated with increased success or increased perceptions of success (Shaw, 1954, 1955; Shelly and Gilchrist, 1958). One way in which independent groups and positions could produce high satisfaction is through increased success on the group task.

The effect of centrality and independence may also be mediated by the rewards contingent on the interpersonal system discussed in Propositions 10.2 and 10.3. To begin with, the independence of group and position can affect the rewards intrinsic in interaction. In Chapter Six on power, we argued that there are rewards intrinsic to interaction and that the rewardingness of interaction is increased by interpersonal attraction. Nearly every study reported that persons in central-independent positions send and receive more messages; and at least one (Gilchrist, Shaw, and Walker, 1954) found that central positions receive more sociometric choices. Since centrality-independence leads to increased interaction and sociometric choice, it seems likely that independent positions may receive more of the rewards frequently intrinsic in interaction.

Centrality-independence may not always lead to *increased* interpersonal rewards; in some circumstances centrality could be correlated with the punishments of the internal system. Bales' suggestion that task leadership may provoke interpersonal antagonism is discussed in Chapter Eleven. Shaw, Rothschild, and Strickland (1957) offered the following interpretation for their experiments in which centrality is sometimes associated with disagreement with other group members. Ss were asked to estimate the number of clicks presented through earphones. "The findings with respect to ratings of satisfaction are understandable if it be assumed that the increased satisfaction resulting from a favorable position in the net is counteracted by being in disagreement with others in the group. In Condition III [central position and only 1 other S heard different stimulus] these effects are both in the same direction and the expected significant differences [in satisfaction] among Ss were found; in Condition I [central position, but other 3 Ss heard different stimulus] the two influences are in direct opposition and no differences were found; and in Condition II [central position but 2 of other 3 Ss heard different stimulus] the issue is confused, but slight insignificant differences in the expected direction were found" (p. 327).

Even after all these possible mediating variables are considered, there is still room to argue that autonomy or independence, *per se*, is a source of satisfaction. At least in our American culture it is reasonable to speak of a need for autonomy or independence which would be directly satisfied by interaction in an autonomous position. Vroom (1959) found that persons with a high need for independence were most highly satisfied with their job in real-life situations when it allowed them a degree of independent action.[10]

[10] Vroom (1959) administered an attitude questionnaire to 108 first-, second- and third-line supervisors in a company whose basic function is the delivery of small parcels. Some of the 16 items measuring need for independence

The notion that centrality produces satisfaction because it satisfied a need for independence is supported in an insightful study by Trow (1957). Working with the Bavelas nets, Trow created a condition of autonomy which was *not* correlated with centrality. High autonomy, *but not high centrality*, was associated with high satisfaction. Furthermore, the relationship between autonomous positions and satisfaction appears heightened for subjects with a high need for autonomy.[11]

CHAPTER SUMMARY

Depending upon the motives of the participants in decision-making groups, particular stimuli generated from group interaction may or may not have reward value. Thus, whether a group yields satisfactions to its members depends upon the salience of the supposed rewards for its members. When members are motivated toward productivity, then the rewards originating in the task environment—or at least thought to originate therefrom—will create satisfaction within the group (10.1, 10.2-A, 10.2-B).

"refer to frequency with which the S regularly engages in independent behavior . . . while others deal with the satisfaction he gets from this behavior" (p. 323). The following are two of the four questions used to measure "psychological participation": (a) "In general, how much say or influence do you have on what goes on in your station?" (b) "Do you feel you can influence the decision of your immediate superior regarding things about which you are concerned?" (p. 323).

In general, high psychological participation was correlated with satisfaction with job ($r = .36$, $p < .05$); but this same correlation was significantly higher among supervisors with a high need for independence than among supervisors with a low need for independence (.55 versus .13). The differences between the two correlations is significant at .02).

[11] Trow (1957) used three-person nets. In the central position, the S could communicate with both other Ss. In the peripheral position he could communicate with only one other S. Each S was given a number of outlines to cut out, but was warned that other Ss might be assigned the same task. The subjects could communicate with each other through the prescribed channels, but could use only special code names for the outlines. In the autonomous condition, the S received the translations necessary to decode the messages. In the dependent condition, another S had the translations and that S told the other "Ss" what to work on. In fact the experimental S was the only "group" participant, and the other messages were written by the experimenter.

Because of the remoteness of most group outputs to individual behavior, most satisfactions stem from the interpersonal rewards directly provided by interaction among participants. When there is congruence among member motivations and when there is agreement upon leadership, then satisfactions are generated. When participants interact with persons they like and who like them, they tend to be satisfied. Given needs for power and autonomy, it was noted that individuals who occupy roles which permit the exercise of power and autonomy tend to gain more satisfaction than those who occupy group roles which do not permit such access to such role-related rewards.

Because the objective output of the group may or may not be correlated with the rewards which generate satisfaction among participants in decision-making groups, the widespread tendency to judge the success of conferences only in terms of their member's satisfaction would seem quite fallacious.

LIST OF PROPOSITIONS

PROPOSITION 10.1. Success on the group task will produce satisfaction.

PROPOSITION 10.2. Success in solving problems of interpersonal relations will produce satisfaction.

PROPOSITION 10.2-A. Congruence of member motivation and a lack of self-oriented needs will produce satisfaction.

PROPOSITION 10.2-B. Agreement on leadership will produce satisfaction.

PROPOSITION 10.3. Interaction with persons we like and persons who like us will produce satisfaction.

PROPOSITION 10.4. A position of high power will produce satisfaction.

PROPOSITION 10.5. A position of centrality or autonomy will produce satisfaction.

CHAPTER ELEVEN

Leadership: Leadership traits and the

differentiation of leadership roles

To find a discussion on leadership at the *end* of a social psychology of group processes for decision-making is a bit unusual! Leadership was one of the first areas in social psychology to be examined empirically. Even a casual glance at bibliographies on small group research quickly documents the dominant part leadership has played in the history of experimental social psychology. Many entire books—Bass' *Leadership, Psychology, and Organization Behavior* (1960), for instance—have used leadership as a major conceptual framework. The many inter-related definitions of leadership have given leadership concepts both a flexibility and a lack of precision. Yet, in our view, the empirical study of leadership—no matter which definition is used—boils down to a highlighting or emphasis on some of the more fundamental group processes. Since several of these processes have been reviewed in earlier chapters, it may be fruitful to examine some of the empirical research on leadership and see how it cuts across, in a variety of ways, the fundamental, underlying social processes in group decision-making.

A large variety of meanings assigned to the term "leadership" were carefully reviewed by Gibb (1954) in his comprehensive summary of research on leadership. As the different conceptions of leadership suggested by Gibb are examined, one notes that, while we have rejected the concept of leadership as a basic organizational topic in this book, *research* on leadership has been ever-present in our preceding chapters. For example, if leaders are defined as "those members of a group who influence their fellows more than they are influenced by them" (Gibb, p. 882), then the three chapters on power would also be chapters on leadership.

According to Gibb (1954) the " 'popular' answer to the question: 'Who is leader?' suggests that whoever occupies a leader's office is a leader" (1954, p. 880). Following this definition, the leadership would be formally designated or legitimate power. One problem with this definition is illustrated by Caudill's (1958) research on decision-making conferences in a psychiatric hospital, which was discussed in the chapter on Communication and Interaction. Caudill found that the head of the hospital talked more and had more of his suggestions accepted than the chief resident. "This was true even though it was the chief resident's job actually to run the daily administrative conference" (Caudill, 1958, p. 245). Raven and French (Chapter Seven) found that mere designation of an individual as "boss" increased his influence over the other members. Nonetheless, both Chapters Six and Seven indicate that there are many other sources of power than that derived from formal designation.

Another of the many conceptualizations reviewed by Gibb illustrates how definitions of leadership tend to emphasize one or another kind of influence of one member over the others, namely, "definition of the leader in terms of sociometric choice" (Gibb, 1954, p. 881). Certainly "liking" is an important source of power (Proposition 6.2-A). Yet, as will be seen below in the section on peer nominations, such processes are but one facet of the leadership process.

Other of Gibb's definitions have also appeared in earlier chapters. The impact of a member on the group's sense of entity (Gibb, p. 883) was included in our discussion of the role of common fate in Chapter Seven. Research on leadership style was included in the chapter on Interpersonal Relations, as was done in our discussion of the Haythorn et al. study of personality. The dominant influence of substantive contribution by high status group members was discussed in Chapter Two on group and individual productivity.

In summary, it seems that many of the topics usually devoted to leadership—along with their accompanying bibliography—have been presented in earlier chapters. Before concluding this book, however, it seems worthwhile to examine two treatments of the leadership problem in more detail. First, the few positive results which have emerged from the quest for leadership traits will be reviewed; for this approach may be of greater relevance for groups having common characteristics—like the group used in decision-making—than has been allowed to date. Second, some theories of leadership have developed which distinguish interpersonal and task-environmental facets of behavior, paralleling the basic conceptual scheme used in the development of this book. Examination of this material should give further insight into the nature of group processes.

LEADERSHIP TRAITS

No matter how they defined their terms, early researchers diligently searched for a set of personal characteristics which would distinguish the leader from the nonleader. Typical of the findings on leadership traits is the fact that Bird (1940) was able to collect a long list of leadership characteristics, but only 5 per cent of the items on the list were common to four or more investigations. "On the whole, the attempt to discover the traits that distinguish leaders from non-leaders has been disappointing" (Cartwright and Zander, 1960, p. 490).

These studies, however, were made over a wide variety of groups, presenting a wide variety of different task demands. Yet, when we conceptualize the findings broadly, we discover that the specific findings can be grouped into a number of categories as Stogdill (1948) has done: He asserted that characteristics associated with leadership in one situation or another may be classified as follows:

1. Capacity (intelligence, alertness, verbal facility, originality, judgment).

2. Achievement (scholarship, knowledge, athletic accomplishments).
3. Responsibility (dependability, initiative, persistence, aggressiveness, self-confidence, desire to excel).
4. Participation (activity, sociability, cooperation, adaptability, humor).
5. Status (socio-economic position, popularity).

(Stogdill, 1948, reprinted in Browne and Cohn, 1958, p. 58).

Note how each of these personal characteristics could contribute to overcoming task-environmental and interpersonal obstacles, and that the importance of a particular characteristic depends upon the particular interpersonal relations and task environment. Originality would be important for the proliferation of alternative solutions; knowledge would aid in development of evidence for decision; persistence could prevent the group from giving up on its task before interpersonal conflicts were solved; cooperation has appeared to release energy devoted to interpersonal problems for attack upon the group task; and popularity might add enough power to an individual so that his suggestions would be accepted.

Despite present discouragement in finding traits which separate leaders from nonleaders, Fiedler (1960) disregarded characteristics which get a man into a position of leadership (such as family connections or popularity) and focused on a trait associated with effectiveness once the leaders are already established in their position. Fiedler measured a personal characteristic of leaders in quite a wide variety of situations, which seems to distinguish those who are effective from those who are less successful.

Fiedler asked his leaders to estimate similarities between their fellow group members. The scale sheet used for these ratings consists of a listing of 20 pairs of personality adjectives and their antonyms, such as "quits easily" versus "keeps trying," and "easygoing" versus "quick-tempered." Fiedler thus had the leader fill out one scale describing his most preferred co-worker and one describing his least preferred co-worker. Through comparison of the similarity between these two profiles, Fiedler could identify two kinds of leaders: (a) leaders who assume most and least preferred co-workers to be quite similar, and (b) leaders who assume most and least preferred co-workers to be quite dissimilar. The latter kind of leader is "psychologically distant and rejecting to those with whom he cannot work easily," while the former kind of leader is "either more tolerant of poor co-workers, or he accepts or rejects individuals on bases other than their ability to work" with him (Fiedler, 1960, p. 591).

If a leader is accepted by his group members (i.e., his activities influence their performances), then Fiedler finds that the style of the leader's interpersonal relations influences the group's effectiveness, be it a basketball team or an open hearth steel crew. Those leaders who are distant probably tend to induce an "emphasis on the task" and therewith *increase* productivity. Those leaders who regard followers as similar in their personal characteristics "tend toward warmer, psychologically closer, interpersonal relations with their subordinates" and thereby are significantly *less* effective in promoting productivity in their task groups (Fiedler, 1960, pp. 602–604). Despite these encouraging findings, some qualifications from Fiedler's own findings and the general negative findings on trait research should restrain our optimism.

Our inability to discover personal traits which are productive across many and widely differing situations would seem to derive from the fact that the interpersonal relations and task-environmental obstacles of groups vary a great deal. Thus, it seemed useful in the development of this book to describe the processes involved in group decision-making—inasmuch as the quest for characteristics which set the "great man" apart from the rest has failed in general.

DIFFERENTIATION OF ROLES IN THE SMALL GROUP: A TASK SPECIALIST AND A SOCIAL-EMOTIONAL SPECIALIST

Leadership is a scattered activity—one member being influential at one time because of a particular combination of environmental demands and personal characteristics, and another being influential at another time because of a different congruence of demand and trait. If our distinction between task and interpersonal obstacles is fundamental, it may be that two separate "specialists," a task-environmental and an interpersonal leader, will emerge in the same group.

In a series of articles reporting an ongoing research program at the Laboratory for Social Relations at Harvard University, R. F. Bales postulated a fundamental tendency for leadership to be differentiated into two kinds of leaders: a "task specialist" and a "social-emotional specialist" (Bales, 1950, 1955, 1956, 1958; Bales and Slater, 1955; Borgatta and Bales, 1953; Slater, 1955). In the following section we shall review data from several investigators which are relevant to such a theoretical distinction. With the data in hand, we will then comment briefly on Bales' formulation.

1. *Single status order.* One of the first findings that led Bales to reject the hypothesis of a "single status order" was the fact that the correlation between ratings of (a) liking and (b) task leadership is generally low. The single status order hypothesis implies that the most liked member will also be seen as the best at meeting interpersonal obstacles, best at suggesting effective approaches to the task, and superior at working on the task. According to the single status hypothesis, "no matter which . . . criteria the researcher takes, he will come out with the same rank order of members" (Bales, 1958, p. 439).

We have already reviewed considerable data to indicate that interpersonal liking is one source of power (Proposition 6.2-A) and that task competence is another (Proposition 7.2). Although liking and task leadership are correlated to some extent, the correlations are low enough that we are led to postulate two separate concepts. Hollander and Webb (1955) reported that while leadership and followership nominations were correlated .92, friendship nominations correlated with leadership only .47 and with followership only .55.[1] Similarly, Gibb (1950) found correlations in the

[1] The data are subject to methodological concern: the cadets chose the three most favored *and* the three *least* favored peers for both the leadership and followership questions.   Only the three *most* liked friends were chosen. This may be why the friendship rating reliability was much lower than the

low and middle forties between observer ratings of leadership and sociometric questions which asked group members to choose (a) whom they would like to participate with in further similar activities and (b) whom they liked. Bales has consistently found strong relations between participant rankings, "Who contributed the best ideas for solving the problem?" and "Who did the most to guide the discussion and keep it moving effectively?" On the other hand, the correlations between these two questions and "How well did you like each of the other members?" are much lower. Taken together, these sets of findings suggest that, although they are related, "leadership" and liking can be empirically separated.

2. *"Like" ratings of most frequent interactor.* There is some tendency for the most frequent interactor in the group to be (a) less liked and (b) more disliked than would be expected on the basis of a simple linear relationship between interaction and liking. Also, the second most frequent interactor may be rated lower than would be expected on a ranking for contributing ideas. This conclusion stems from a chart presented in Bales (1953, p. 146) which is based on only four separate five-man groups which met for twelve sessions; and, unfortunately, the cumulative data do not meet the assumptions required for a statistical test. None the less, the suggestion that the highest interactor may be lower on liking measures and higher on disliking measures did lead Bales to ask, "Is the top man doing something to lose likes and provide dislikes?" (Bales, 1958, p. 440). Furthermore, "Liking seems to be centered on the second and third man in activity, and they both seem to be lower than expected on idea ranking. Can it be that these men are tending to avoid too heavy an emphasis on the task area for fear of being disliked?" (Bales, 1958, p. 441).

leadership and followership ratings (.41 for friendship as compared to .94 for followership and .91 for leadership). While this lower reliability of the friendship measure may reflect the fact that no single person was a friend to all cadets, it may also mean that the friendship measure was less precise. Is it this lower precision in the measure of liking which produces the low correlation? In any event, the leadership and followership ratings have a common method's variance not shared by the friendship ratings.

Similar results appear when the total amount of communication initiated, the total communication received, and the three rankings—Ideas, Guidance, and Liking—are analyzed in a correlation matrix. The correlations among (a) Talking, (b) Receiving, and rankings of (c) Ideas, and (d) Guidance are highly intercorrelated—especially in groups for which there is high agreement on who is the leader (Bales and Slater, 1955, p. 286). The correlations of all these measures with (e) Liking, however, are much lower than the correlations among the four "task-related" measures.

3. *Decrease over time of the correlation between liking and ideas.* The likelihood that the best-liked person will also be highest on both Liking and Ideas decreases over time. The percentage of sessions in which the same person held the top rank in both Ideas and Liking over the four sessions are 56 per cent for the first session, 12 and 20 per cent for the second and third sessions, and only 8 per cent for the last session. According to Bales, this suggests that the high initiators are doing something to alienate the other group members.

4. *Behavioral differences.* Best-Liked men who are not also rated tops on Ideas behave differently than Idea men who are not best Liked. Bales and Slater (1955) report that the 56 sessions of the total sample were reduced to 23 sessions by eliminating all sessions in which (1) there was a tie for either the Idea or the Like ranking and (2) all sessions in which the same man was top in both the Idea and Like rankings. In each of these sessions, then, there was one person who was tops on the Like ranking, but not tops on the Ideas rankings (the "social-emotional specialist") and another person who was tops on Ideas, but not Likes (the "task specialist"). The interactions initiated by these two kinds of group members were then compared. In general, "The top man in the Idea position is higher in giving suggestions and opinions whereas the man in the top Liked position is higher in giving and receiving solidarity and tension release" (Bales and Slater, 1955, p. 280).

5. *Reactive nature of the "social-emotional specialist."* The behavior of the "social-emotional specialist" closely resembles a profile of reactive interactions. A reactive statement immediately follows a communication of another group member. If a member continues to talk so that his remarks immediately follow one of his own previous communications, the communication was proactive. Proactive communications, of course, must take place toward the end of an extended contribution of a single member, while reactive communications always immediately follow the comments of another group member. All extended task contributions, therefore, would be classed as proactive; many interpersonally rewarding communications such as approval would be classed as reactive. Bales suggests that the similarity between the interactions of the "social-emotional specialist" and the reactive profile further bolsters the distinction between a "task" and a "social-emotional" specialist in most groups, since the "social-emotional" specialist contributions are primarily reactive.

6. *Feedback.* As part of his interpretation of the earlier findings, Bales postulated that task communication created a certain amount of antagonism in his groups. According to Bales, the task specialist "tends to be liked because he is satisfying needs in relation to the task area. But he also tends to arouse a certain amount of hostility because his prestige is rising relative to the other members, because his suggestions constitute proposed new elements to be added to the common culture, to which all members will be committed if they agree. Whatever readjustments the members have to make in order to feel themselves committed will tend to produce minor frustrations, anxieties, and hostilities. These are centered to some degree on the object most active in provoking the disturbance—the task specialist" (Bales and Slater, 1955, p. 297).

Bales has tried to isolate some more specific factors which would explain the dislike which is provoked by the task specialist. Since the task specialist initiates much substantive communication, he may be disliked because he does not give the other group members time to react. Bales cites two studies which suggest that the inability to react to or comment on communication provokes dislike. Leavitt and Mueller (1951) found an initial reaction of hostility to the communication sender when the receiver could not reply. Thibaut and Coules (1952) reported similar results. According to Proposition 10.3, "Interaction with persons we like and who like us will produce satisfaction." Perhaps it is not enough if another person talks to us; we may not be satisfied unless we also have an opportunity to participate—at least to the extent of an occasional agreement, question, or clarification.

In order to test this hypothesis, Bales (1956) divided group members into three groups on the basis of their feedback ratio. The feedback ratio is the number of communications received divided by the number initiated. It reflects the amount of communication which a person received in relation to the amount he initiated. High initiators with low feedback ratios tend to be disliked. No such trend appears for high initiators with medium and high feedback ratios.

It may be, as Bales suggests (1956, 1958), that some high initiators talk so much that other group members are deprived of their opportunity to participate through feedback. When the top Idea man deprives others of an opportunity to comment, he could keep his top Idea ranking. But, some other group member —who allowed the group members to participate through feedback—would then gain the top Like ranking. According to Bales, the low feedback ratio caused the dislike.

On the other hand, the causation might be going in the other direction; the dislike may be causing the low feedback ratio. Other group members may send more communications to those people they like. We know from Proposition 9.4-A that high status people received more communication, and liking is an ingredient of generalized status.[2] It is possible, then, that the low feedback ratio of disliked high initiators is an effect rather than a cause.

[2] Negative evidence is provided by French and Snyder (1959) who reported a correlation of only .12 (not significant) between the degree a noncommissioned officer is liked and the "influence attempts" which he receives. No data, however, on the total communication rates are presented.

7. Industrial factor analyses. Factor analytic studies in industrial settings (Fleishman, Harris, and Burtt, 1955) have identified two factors similar to Bales' distinction. The research is summarized by Fleishman and Harris (1962):

Consideration *includes behavior indicating mutual trust, respect, and a certain warmth and rapport between the supervisor and his group. This does not mean that this dimension reflects a superficial "pat-on-the-back," "first name calling" kind of human relations behavior. This dimension appears to emphasize a deeper concern for group members' needs and includes such behavior as allowing subordinates more participation in decision making and encouraging more two-way communication.* Structure *includes behavior in which the supervisor organizes and defines group activities and his relation to the group. Thus, he defines the role he expects each member to assume, assigns tasks, plans ahead, establishes ways of getting things done and pushes for production. This dimension seems to emphasize overt attempts to achieve organizational goals.*

Since the dimensions are independent, a supervisor may score high on both dimensions, low on both, or high on one and low on the other. . . .

. . . Production supervisors rated high in "proficiency" by plant management turned out to have leadership patterns high in Structure and low in Consideration. . . . On the other hand, this same pattern of high Structure and low Consideration was found to be related to high labor turnover, union grievances, worker absences and accidents, and low worker satisfaction (pp. 43–44).

Summary. The correlation between liking and idea leadership is positive. But, because it is moderate, we are encouraged to look for cases in which Liking and Idea leadership function separately. In particular, there is suggestive data from a few groups to indicate that the most frequent initiator is not as well liked as would be expected if liking and leadership were highly correlated. Although the Idea leader stands better than a 50–50 chance of also being the best-liked man at the end of a group's *first* session, it is very unlikely that he will maintain his top ranking on both Liking and Ideas by the fourth session. Bales suggests that the task leaders do things which alienate the affection of other group members. In particular, Bales suggests that the high initiator may not allow the other group members ample opportunity to react, comment, or feedback their reactions to the contributions of the idea leader.

COMMENT ON BALES' DIFFEREN-
TIATION OF LEADERSHIP ROLES

In an illustrative way, perhaps the following two sets of comments on Bales' imaginative work will indicate how our previous description of the underlying processes in decision-making groups is useful in understanding leadership phenomena. Bales stressed that many of the things which group members must do to achieve task-environmental rewards create frustrations, and —since the task leader is most immediately responsible—the leader will be blamed. But, the "social-emotional specialist" may also be doing things (providing interpersonal rewards such as approval and interaction) which gain the liking of other group members for him. A differentiation of roles could reflect a *gain* in popularity of the best-Liked man instead of a *loss* of the popularity of the Idea man.

Bales conceives of the social-emotional specialist as one member of a two-member team which moves the group on to task-environmental rewards. The "task specialist" focuses on task-environmental obstacles. Perhaps we can extend this analysis, however, and note that an excessive desire for liking can become an interpersonal obstacle in itself.

Behavior designed to secure liking from other group members is an example of "Individual Prominence and Achievement Behavior" (Carter, 1954), behavior which is directed toward an individual's own private goals. Far from helping the group move toward the common goal, an Individual Prominence Behavior may actually hinder the group progress (See the section in Chapter Five on "The Disruption of Interpersonal Relations through Individualistic Motivation"). It is to be stressed that satisfaction of the social and emotional needs of members is not always to be equated with the performance of "group maintenance functions" as has been implied by many writers (see, for instance, Cartwright and Zander, 1960, p. 496). Interpersonal rewards may be used to support task activities (Chapter Four), but the social-emotional specialist who buys friendship with interpersonally rewarding interaction may lead the group to *disintegration*.

It is consistent with Bales' presentation to state that the "task specialist" is liked because he provides task-environmental rewards, and the "social-emotional specialist" is liked because he provides interpersonal rewards. Viewed from this perspective, it is interesting to note that Bales has worked in an experimental setting in which task-environmental rewards probably play a minimal role. The participants discuss problems which have no clearly "correct" answer; so there are no obvious task-environmental rewards. Furthermore, since the groups are newly formed, individual group members are not closely identified with the group as a whole. Since the *low* Idea contributor is not identified with the group as a whole, he may see no reason why the contributions of the *top* Idea man should benefit him (the "low" Idea man) personally. In other words, contributions of the Idea man may not be salient rewards to other group members and, therefore, even the best idea may buy only minimal liking for the contributor.

It is likely that the Idea man would be better liked if the task-environmental rewards were more distinct. If the experimenter gave the groups information on the quality of the discussions, for instance, the group members might increase their appreciation of the idea contributions of the "Task Specialist." The importance of task-environmental accomplishments would also be increased by placing the group as a whole into competition with other groups as did Deutsch (1949). As we indicated in Chapter Four, however, Bales' experimental setting is probably quite typical of decision-making conferences: task-environmental rewards in decision-making conferences are usually vague, undifferentiated, late in coming, and relatively unimportant to the momentary satisfactions of the group members.

Bibliography

Adams, S. Status congruency as a variable in small group performance. *Social Forces,* 1953, 32, 16–22.

Allport, F. H. The influence of the group upon association and thought. *J. exp. Psychol.,* 1920, 3, 159–182.

———. *Social Psychology.* Boston: Houghton Mifflin, 1924.

Allport, G. W. The historical background of modern social psychology. In Gardner Lindzey (Ed.), *Handbook of social psychology: Theory and method, Vol. I,* Cambridge, Mass.: Addison-Wesley, 1954, 3–56.

Altman, I., & McGinnies, E. Interpersonal perception and communication in discussion groups of varied attitudinal composition. *J. abnorm. soc. Psychol.,* 1960, 60, 390–395.

Asch, M. J. Nondirective teaching in psychology: an experimental study. *Psychol. Monogr.,* 1951, 65, 1–23.

Asch, S. E. Studies of independence and conformity: I. A minority of one against a unanimous majority. *Psychol. Monogr.,* 1956, 70, 1–70.

Atthowe, J. M., Jr. Interpersonal decision making: the resolution of a dyadic conflict. *J. abnorm. soc. Psychol.,* 1961, 62, 114–119.

Back, K. W. Influence through social communication. *J. abnorm. soc. Psychol.,* 1951, 46, 9–23.

———, Festinger, L., Hymovitch, B., Kelley, H., Schachter, S., & Thibaut, J. The methodology of studying rumor transmission. *Hum. Relat.,* 1950, 3, 307–312.

Bales, R. F. *Interaction process analysis: A method for the study of small groups.* Cambridge, Mass.: Addison-Wesley, 1950.

———. The equilibrium problem in small groups. In T. Parsons, R. F. Bales, & E. A. Shils (Eds.), *Working papers in the theory of action.* Glencoe, Ill.: Free Press, 1953, 111–161.

———. Adaptive and integrative changes as sources of strain in social systems. In A. P. Hare, E. F. Borgatta, & R. F. Bales (Eds.), *Small groups: Studies in social interaction.* New York: Knopf, 1955, 127–131.

223

Bales, R. F. Task status and likeability as a function of talking and listening in decision-making groups. In L. D. White (Ed.), *The state of the social sciences.* Chicago: University of Chicago Press, 1956, 148–161.

———. Task roles and social roles in problem solving groups. In Eleanor E. Maccoby, T. M. Newcomb, & E. L. Hartley (Eds.), *Readings in social psychology.* (3rd ed.) New York: Holt, Rinehart & Winston, 1958, 396–413.

———, & Slater, P. E. Role differentiation in small decision-making groups. In T. Parson, R. F. Bales, et al., *The family, socialization, and interaction process.* Glencoe, Ill.: Free Press, 1955, 259–306.

———, & Strodtbeck, F. L. Phases in group problem solving. *J. abnorm. soc. Psychol.,* 1951, 46, 485–495.

———, Strodtbeck, F. L., Mills, T. M., & Roseborough, Mary E. Channels of communication in small groups. *Amer. sociol. Rev.,* 1951, 16, 461–468.

Barnard, C. I. *The functions of the executive.* Cambridge, Mass.: Harvard University Press, 1938.

Barnes, L. B. An industrial laboratory. Unpublished M. B. A. thesis, Harvard Graduate School of Business Administration, 1958.

Barnlund, D. C. A comparative study of individual, majority, and group judgment. *J. abnorm. soc. Psychol.,* 1959, 58, 55–60.

———, & Haiman, F. S. *The dynamics of discussion.* Boston: Houghton Mifflin, 1960.

Bass, B. M. *Leadership, psychology, and organizational behavior.* New York: Harper, 1960.

———, & Dunteman, G. Behavior in groups as a function of self-, interaction, and task orientation. *J. abnorm. soc. Psychol.,* 1963, 66, 419–428.

———, & Wurster, C. R. Effects of the nature of the problem on LGD performance. *J. appl. Psychol.,* 1953, 37, 96–99.

Bates, A. P. Some sociometric aspects of social ranking in a small, face-to-face group. *Sociom.,* 1952, 15, 330–341.

Bavelas, A. Communication patterns in task-oriented groups. *J. acoust. Soc. Amer.,* 1950, 22, 725–730.

Bennis, W. G., Berkowitz, N., Affinito, M., & Malone, M. Authority, power, and the ability to influence. *Hum. Relat.,* 1958, 11, 143–155.

Berkowitz, L. Sharing leadership in small, decision-making groups. *J. abnorm. soc. Psychol.,* 1953, 48, 231–238.

———. Group standards, cohesiveness, and productivity. *Hum. Relat.,* 1954, 7, 509–519.

———, & Howard, R. C. Reactions to opinion deviates as affected by affiliation need(n) and group member interdependence. *Sociom.,* 1959, 22, 81–91.

———, & Levy, B. Pride in group performance and group-task motivation. *J. abnorm. soc. Psychol.,* 1956, 53, 300–306.

Berkowitz, L., Levy, B. I., & Harvey, A. H. Effects of performance evaluations on group integration and motivation. *Hum. Relat.,* 1957, 10, 195–
208.

Bieri, J. Changes in interpersonal perceptions following social interaction.
J. abnorm. soc. Psychol., 1953, 48, 61–66.

Bird, C. *Social psychology.* New York: Appleton-Century, 1940.

Blake, R. R., & Brehm, J. W. The use of tape recording to simulate a group
atmosphere. *J. abnorm. soc. Psychol.,* 1954, 49, 311–313.

Blau, P. M. *The dynamics of bureaucracy.* Chicago: University of Chicago Press, 1955.

———. Patterns of deviation in work groups. *Sociom.,* 1960, 23, 245–261.

———, & Scott, W. R. *Formal organizations: A comparative approach.* San
Francisco: Chandler, 1962.

Borah, L. A. The effects of threat in bargaining: Critical and experimental
analysis. *J. abnorm. soc. Psychol.,* 1963, 66, 37–44.

Borgatta, E. F. Analysis of social interaction and sociometric perception.
Sociom., 1954, 17, 7–32.

———, & Bales, R. F. Sociometric status patterns and characteristics of
interaction. *J. soc. Psychol.,* 1956, 43, 289–297.

Bovard, E. W., Jr. Interaction and attraction to the group. *Hum. Relat.,*
1956, 9, 481–489.

Brayfield, A. H., & Crockett, W. H. Employee attitudes and employee performance. *Psychol. Bull.,* 1955, 52, 396–424.

Browne, C. G., & Cohn, T. S. (Eds.) *The study of leadership.* Danville,
Ill.: The Interstate Printers and Publishers, 1958.

Bruce, R. S. Group judgments in the fields of lifted weights and visual
discrimination. *J. Psychol.,* 1935, 1, 117–121.

Burdick, H. The compliant behavior of deviates under conditions of threat.
Unpublished Ph.D. dissertation, University of Minnesota, 1955.

Burns, T. The directions of activity and communication in a departmental
executive group. *Hum. Relat.,* 1954, 7, 73–97.

Butler, D. C., Ono, H., & Miller, N. *"Power to reinforce" as a determinant
of communication.* Mimeograph, 1962.

Campbell, D. T. The informant in quantitative research. *Amer. J. Sociol.,*
1955, 60, 339–342.

———. Systematic error on the part of human links in communication
systems. *Information and control,* 1958, 1, 334–369.

———. Methodological suggestions from a comparative psychology of
knowledge processes. *Inquiry,* 1959, 2, 152–182.

———. Conformity in psychology's theories of acquired behavioral dispositions. In I. A. Berg & B. M. Bass (Eds.), *Conformity and deviation.* New York: Harper, 1961, 101–142.

———. Social attitudes and other acquired behavioral dispositions. In
S. Koch (Ed.), *Psychology: A study of a science.* Vol. 6. *Investigations of man as socius: Their place in psychology and the social sciences.* New York: McGraw-Hill, 1963.

Campbell, D. T., & Tyler, Bonnie B. The construct validity of work-group morale measures. *J. appl. Psychol.*, 1957, 41, 91–92.

Cartwright, D. Power: A neglected variable in social psychology. In D. Cartwright (Ed.), *Studies in social power.* Ann Arbor: University of Michigan, 1959, 1–14.

————, & Zander, A. (Eds.) *Group dynamics: Research and theory.* (2nd ed.) Evanston, Ill.: Row, Peterson, 1960.

Cathcart, R. S. An experimental study of the relative effectiveness of selected means of handling evidence in speeches of advocacy. Ph.D. Dissertation, Northwestern University, 1953.

Caudill, W. A. *The psychiatric hospital as a small society.* Cambridge, Mass.: Harvard University Press, 1958.

Chowdhry, K., & Newcomb, T. M. The relative abilities of leaders and non-leaders to estimate opinions of their own groups. *J. abnorm. soc. Psychol.*, 1952, 47, 51–57.

Coch, L., & French, J. R. P., Jr. Overcoming resistance to change. *Hum. Relat.*, 1948, 1, 512–532.

Cohen, A. R. Upward communication in experimentally created hierarchies. *Hum. Relat.*, 1958, 11, 41–53.

————. Situational structure, self-esteem, and treat-oriented reactions to power. In D. Cartwright (Ed.), *Studies in social power.* Ann Arbor: University of Michigan, 1959, 35–52.

Cohen, M. R., & Nagel, E. *An introduction to logic and scientific method.* New York: Harcourt, Brace, 1934.

Collins, B. E. The interaction of status and communication: Some hypotheses and an empirical test. Unpublished M.A. thesis, Northwestern University, 1960.

————. An experimental study of satisfaction, productivity, turnover, and comparison levels. Unpublished Ph.D. dissertation, Northwestern University, 1963.

————, Davis, H. L., Myers, J. G., & Silk, A. J. An experimental study of reinforcement and participant satisfaction. *J. abnorm. soc. Psychol.*, 1964, in press.

Cooper, L. *The rhetoric of Aristotle.* New York: Appleton, 1932.

Crockett, W. H. Emergent leadership in small, decision-making groups. *J. abnorm. soc. Psychol.*, 1955, 51, 378–383.

Dashiell, J. F. Experimental studies of the influence of social situations on the behavior of individual human adults. In C. Murchison (Ed.), *Handbook of social psychology.* Worcester, Mass.: Clark University Press, 1935, 1097–1158.

Davis, J. H., & Restle, F. The analysis of problems and prediction of group problem solving. *J. abnorm. soc. Psychol.*, 1963, 66, 103–116.

DeSoto, C. B. Learning a social structure. *J. abnorm. soc. Psychol.*, 1960, 60, 417–421.

Deutsch, M. An experimental study of the effects of co-operation and competition upon group process. *Hum. Relat.*, 1949, 2, 199–231.

——. Trust and suspicion. *J. Conflict Resolution*, 1958, 2, 265–279.

——. Some factors affecting membership motivation and achievement motivation in a group. *Hum. Relat.*, 1959, 12, 81–95.

——. The effect of motivational orientation upon trust and suspicion. *Hum. Relat.*, 1960, 13, 123–139.

——, & Krauss, R. M. The effect of threat upon interpersonal bargaining. *J. abnorm. soc. Psychol.*, 1960, 61, 181–189.

Dittes, J. E., & Kelley, H. H. Effects of different conditions of acceptance upon conformity to group norms. *J. abnorm. soc. Psychol.*, 1956, 53, 100–107.

Downing, J. Cohesiveness, perception, and values. *Hum. Relat.*, 1958, 11, 157–166.

Eisenstadt, S. N. Communication processes among immigrants in Israel. *Publ. Opin. Quart.*, 1952, 16, 42–58.

——. Conditions of communication receptivity. *Publ. Opin. Quart.*, 1953, 17, 363–374.

Eisman, Bernice. Some operational measures of cohesiveness and their inter-relations. *Hum. Relat.*, 1959, 12, 183–189.

Emmerson, R. M. Deviation and rejection: An experimental replication. *Amer. Sociol. Rev.*, 1954, 19, 688–693.

Evan, W. M., & Zelditch, M., Jr. A laboratory experiment on bureaucratic authority. *Amer. Sociol. Rev.*, 1961, 26, 883–893.

Exline, R. V. Group climate as a factor in the relevance and accuracy of social perception. *J. abnorm. soc. Psychol.*, 1957, 55, 382–388.

——, & Ziller, R. C. Status congruency and interpersonal conflict in decision-making groups. *Hum. Relat.*, 1959, 12, 147–162.

Farnsworth, P. R., & Williams, M. F. The accuracy of the median and the mean of a group of judgments. *J. soc. Psychol.*, 1936, 7, 237–239.

Faust, W. L. Group versus individual problem-solving. *J. abnorm. soc. Psychol.*, 1959, 59, 68–72.

Festinger, L. The role of group belongingness in a voting situation. *Hum. Relat.*, 1948, 1, 154–180.

——. Informal social communication. *Psychol. Rev.*, 1950, 57, 271–282.

——. *A theory of cognitive dissonance.* Evanston, Ill.: Row, Peterson, 1957.

——, Gerard, H., Hymovitch, B., Kelley, H., & Raven, B. The influence process in the presence of extreme deviates. *Hum. Relat.*, 1952, 5, 327–346.

——, & Hutte, H. A. An experimental investigation of the effect of unstable interpersonal relations in a group. *J. abnorm. soc. Psychol.*, 1954, 49, 513–522.

——, Schachter, S., & Back, K. *Social pressures in informal groups: A study of human factors in housing.* New York: Harper, 1950.

Festinger, L., & Thibaut, J. Interpersonal communication in small groups. *J. abnorm. soc. Psychol.*, 1951, 46, 92–99.

——, Torrey, Jane, & Willerman, B. Self-evaluation as a function of attraction to the group. *Hum. Relat.*, 1954, 7, 161–174.

Fiedler, F. E. The leader's psychological distance and group effectiveness. In D. Cartwright and A. Zander (Eds.), *Group dynamics: Research and theory.* (2nd ed.) Evanston, Ill.: Row, Peterson, 1960, 586–606.

Fleishman, E. A., & Harris, E. F. Patterns of leadership behavior related to employee grievances and turnover. *Personnel Psychol.*, 1962, 15, 43–56.

——, Harris, E., & Burtt, H. *Leadership and supervision in industry: An evaluation of a supervisory training program.* Columbus: Ohio State University Bureau of Educational Research, 1955.

Fouriezos, N. T., Hutt, M. L., & Guetzkow, H. Measurement of self-oriented needs in discussion groups. *J. abnorm. soc. Psychol.*, 1950, 45, 682–690.

Frank, J. D. Experimental study of personal pressure and resistance: I. Experimental production of resistance. *J. gen. Psychol.*, 1944, 30, 23–41.

French, J. R. P., Jr. The disruption and cohesion of groups. *J. abnorm. soc. Psychol.*, 1941, 36, 361–377.

——, Israel, J., & Ås, D. An experiment on participation in a Norwegian factory: Interpersonal dimensions of decision-making. *Hum. Relat.*, 1960, 13, 3–19.

——, & Raven, B. The bases of social power. In D. Cartwright (Ed.), *Studies in social power.* Ann Arbor: University of Michigan, 1959, 150–167.

——, Ross, I. C., Kirby, S., Nelson, J. R., & Smyth, P. Employee participation in a program of industrial change. *Personnel*, 1958, 16–29.

——, & Snyder, R. Leadership and interpersonal power. In D. Cartwright (Ed.), *Studies in social power.* Ann Arbor: University of Michigan, 1959, 118–149.

Gerard, H. B. The effect of different dimensions of disagreement on the communication process in small groups. *Hum. Relat.*, 1953, 6, 249–272.

——. Some effects of status, role clarity, and group goal clarity upon the individual's relations to group process. *J. Pers.*, 1957, 25, 475–488.

Ghiselli, E. E., & Lodahl, T. M. Patterns of managerial traits and group effectiveness. *J. abnorm. soc. Psychol.*, 1958, 57, 61–66.

Gibb, C. A. The sociometry of leadership in temporary groups. *Sociom.*, 1950, 13, 226–243.

——. Leadership. In G. Lindzey (Ed.), *Handbook of social psychology.* Reading, Mass.: Addison-Wesley, 1954.

Gibb, J. R. The effects of group size and of threat reduction upon creativity in a problem solving situation. *Amer. Psychologist*, 1951, 5, 324.

Gilchrist, J. C. The formation of social groups under conditions of success and failure. *J. abnorm. soc. Psychol.*, 1952, 47, 174–187.

Gilchrist, J. C., Shaw, M. E., & Walker, L. C. Some effects of unequal distribution of information in a wheel group structure. *J. abnorm. soc. Psychol.*, 1954, 49, 554–556.

Glanzer, M., & Glaser, R. Techniques of the study of group structure and behavior: II. Empirical studies of the effects of structure in small groups. *Psychol. Bull.*, 1961, 58, 1–27.

Goldberg, S. C., & Lubin, A. Influence as a function of perceived judgment error. *Hum. Relat.*, 1958, 11, 275–281.

Gordon, Kate H. Group judgments in the field of lifted weights. *J. exp. Psychol.*, 1924, 7, 398–400.

Greenspoon, J. The reinforcing effect of two spoken sounds on the frequency of two responses. *Amer. J. Psychol.*, 1955, 68, 409–416.

Grossack, M. M. Some effects of cooperation and competition upon small group behavior. *J. abnorm. soc. Psychol.*, 1954, 49, 341–348.

Grosser, D., Polansky, N., & Lippitt, R. A laboratory study of behavior contagion. *Hum. Relat.*, 1951, 4, 115–142.

Guetzkow, H. (Ed.) *Groups, leadership and men; Research in human relations.* Pittsburgh: Carnegie Press, 1951. Reissued, New York: Russell & Russell, 1963.

———. Conversion barriers in using the social sciences. *Admin. Sci. Quart.*, 1959, 4, 68–81.

———. Differentiation of roles in task-oriented groups. In D. Cartwright and A. Zander (Eds.), *Group dynamics: Research and theory.* (2nd ed.) Evanston, Ill.: Row, Peterson, 1960, 683–704.

———, & Dill, W. R. Factors in the organizational development of task-oriented groups. *Sociom.*, 1957, 20, 175–204.

———, & Gyr, J. An analysis of conflict in decision making groups. *Hum. Relat.*, 1954, 7, 367–382.

———, Kelley, E. L., & McKeachie, W. J. An experimental comparison of recitation, discussion, and tutorial methods in college teaching. *J. educ. Psychol.*, 1954, 45, 193–207.

———, & Simon, H. A. The impact of certain communication nets upon organization and performance in task-oriented groups. *Mgmt Sci.*, 1955, 1, 233–250.

Guilford, J. P. *Fundamental statistics in psychology and education.* (2nd ed.) New York: McGraw-Hill, 1950.

Guion, R. M. Industrial morale (a symposium): 1. The problem of terminology. *Personnel Psychol.*, 1958, 11, 59–64.

Gullahorn, J. T. Distance and friendship as factors in the gross interaction matrix. *Sociom.*, 1952, 15, 123–134.

Gurnee, H. Maze learning in the collective situation. *J. Psychol.*, 1937, 3, 437–443.

Haiman, F. S. An experimental study of the effects of *ethos* in public speaking. M. A. thesis, Northwestern University, 1948.

Hare, A. P. *Handbook of small group research*. Glencoe, Ill.: Free Press, 1962.

Harvey, O. J. An experimental approach to the study of status reactions in informal groups. *Amer. Sociol. Rev.*, 1953, 18, 357–367.

———, & Consalvi, C. Status and conformity to pressures in informal groups. *J. abnorm. soc. Psychol.*, 1960, 60, 182–187.

———, & Sherif, M. Level of aspiration as a case of judgmental activity in which ego-involvements operate as factors. *Sociom.*, 1951, 14, 121–147.

Haythorn, W. A. The influence of individual members on the characteristics of small groups. *J. abnorm. soc. Psychol.*, 1953, 48, 276–284.

———, Couch, D. H., Haefner, D., Langham, P., & Carter, L. The behavior of authoritarian and equalitarian personalities in groups. *Hum. Relat.*, 1956, 9, 57–74.

Hearn, G. Leadership and the spatial factor in small groups. *J. abnorm. soc. Psychol.*, 1957, 54, 269–272.

Heider, F. *The psychology of interpersonal relations*. New York: Wiley, 1958.

Heinicke, C., & Bales, R. F. Developmental trends in the structure of small groups. *Sociom.*, 1953, 16, 7–38.

Helson, H. Adaptation level theory. In S. Koch (Ed.), *Psychology: A study of a science. Vol. I. Sensory, perceptual, and physiological formulations*. New York: McGraw Hill, 1959.

Herring, P. The social sciences in modern society. *Social Science Research Council items*, March, 1947.

Herzberg, F., Mausner, B., Peterson, R. O., & Capwell, Dona F. *Job attitudes: Review of research and opinion*. Pittsburgh: Psychological Service of Pittsburgh, 1957.

Hoffman, L. R. Similarity of personality: A basis for interpersonal attraction? *Sociom.*, 1958, 21, 300–308.

———. Homogeneity of member personality and its effect on group problem-solving. *J. abnorm. soc. Psychol.*, 1959, 58, 27–32.

———, Harburg, E., & Maier, N. R. F. Differences and disagreement as factors in creative group problem solving. *J. abnorm. soc. Psychol.*, 1962, 64, 206–214.

Hollander, E. P. Conformity, status, and idiosyncrasy credit. *Psychol. Rev.* 1958, 65, 117–127.

———. Competence and conformity in the acceptance of influence. *J. abnorm. soc. Psychol.*, 1960, 61, 365–369.

———, & Webb, W. B. Leadership, followership, and friendship: An analysis of peer nominations. *J. abnorm. soc. Psychol.*, 1955, 50, 163–167.

Homans, G. C. *The human group*. New York: Harcourt, Brace, 1950.

———. *Social behavior: Its elementary forms*. New York: Harcourt, Brace & World, 1961.

Hoppe, R. A.   Memorizing by individuals and groups: A test of the pooling-of-ability model.   *J. abnorm. soc. Psychol.*, 1962, 65, 64–71.

Horwitz, M.   The recall of interrupted group tasks: An experimental study of individual motivation in relation to group goals.   *Hum. Relat.*, 1954, 7, 3–38.

———, Lyons, J., & Perlmutter, H. V.   Induction of forces in discussion groups.   *Hum. Relat.*, 1951, 4, 57–76.

Hunt, E. B., & Rowe, R. R.   Group and individual economic decision making in risk conditions.   In D. W. Taylor (Ed.)   *Experiments on decision making and other studies.*   Armed services Technical Information Agency, 1960.   Pp. 21–25.   (Tech. Rept. No. 6, AD 253952.)

Hurwitz, J. I., Zander, A. F., & Hymovitch, B.   Some effects of power on the relations among group members.   In D. Cartwright & A. Zander (Eds.), *Group dynamics: Research and theory.*   Evanston, Ill.: Row, Peterson, 1953, 800–809.

Husband, R. W.   Cooperative versus solitary problem solution.   *J. soc. Psychol.*, 1940, 11, 405–409.

Jackson, J. M.   Analysis of interpersonal relations in a formal organization.   Ph.D. thesis, University of Michigan, 1953.

———.   Reference group processes in a formal organization.   *Sociom.*, 1959a, 22, 307–327.

———.   The organization and its communication problems.   *J. Communication*, 1959b, 9, 158–167.

———, & Saltzstein, H. D.   The effect of person-group relationships on conformity processes.   *J. abnorm. soc. Psychol.*, 1958, 57, 17–24.

Johnson, D. M.   How a person establishes a scale for evaluating his performance.   *J. exp. Psychol.*, 1946, 36, 25–34.

Keller, J. B.   Comment on "Channels of communications in small groups."   *Amer. Sociol. Rev.*, 1951, 16, 842–843.

Kelley, H. H.   Communication in experimentally created hierarchies.   *Hum. Relat.*, 1951, 4, 39–56.

———, & Shapiro, M. M.   An experiment on conformity to group norms where conformity is detrimental to group achievement.   *Amer. Sociol. Rev.*, 1954, 19, 667–677.

———, & Volkart, E. H.   The resistance to change of group-anchored attitudes.   *Amer. Sociol. Rev.*, 1952, 17, 435–465.

Kelman, H. C.   Compliance, identification, and internalization: Three processes of attitude change.   *J. Conflict Resolution*, 1958, 2, 51–60.

Kipnis, Dorothy McB.   Interaction between members of bomber crews as a determinant of sociometric choice.   *Hum. Relat.*, 1957, 10, 263–270.

———.   The effects of leadership style and leadership power upon the inducement of an attitude change.   *J. abnorm. soc. Psychol.*, 1958, 57, 173–180.

Klugman, S. F.   Group judgment for familiar and unfamiliar materials.   *J. genet. Psychol.*, 1945, 32, 103–110.

Knight, Hazel C. A comparison of the reliability of group and individual judgments. Unpublished M.A. thesis, Columbia University, 1921.

Krasner, L. Studies of the conditioning of verbal behavior. *Psychol. Bull.,* 1958, 55, 148–170.

Kriesberg, M. Executives evaluate administrative conferences. *Advanc. Mgmt,* 1950, 15, 15–18.

———, & Guetzkow, H. The use of conferences in the administrative process. *Public Administration Rev.,* 1950 (Spring), 10, 93–98.

Lana, R. E., Vaughan, W., & McGinnies, E. Leadership and friendship status as factors in discussion group interaction. *J. soc. Psychol.,* 1960, 52, 127–134.

Lansing, J. B., & Heyns, R. W. Need affiliation and frequency of four types of communication. *J. abnorm. soc. Psychol.,* 1959, 58, 365–372.

Lanzetta, J. T., & Roby, T. B. Effects of work-group structure and certain task variables on group performance. *J. abnorm. soc. Psychol.,* 1956, 53, 307–314.

———, & Roby, T. B. Group learning and communication as a function of task and structure "demands." *J. abnorm. soc. Psychol.,* 1957, 55, 121–131.

———, & Roby, T. B. The relationship between certain group process variables and group problem-solving efficiency. *J. soc. Psychol.,* 1960, 52, 135–148.

Larsen, O. N., & Hill, R. T. Social structure and interpersonal communication. *Amer. J. Sociol.,* 1958, 63, 497–505.

Leavitt, H. J. Some effects of certain communication patterns on group performance. *J. abnorm. soc. Psychol.,* 1951, 46, 38–50.

———, & Mueller, R. A. H. Some effects of feedback on communication. *Hum. Relat.,* 1951, 4, 401–410.

Levinger, G. The development of perceptions and behavior in newly formed social power relationships. In D. Cartwright (Ed.), *Studies in social power.* Ann Arbor: University of Michigan, 1959, 83–98.

Lewin, K. Studies in group decision. In D. Cartwright and A. F. Zander (Eds.), *Group dynamics: Research and theory.* Evanston, Ill.: Row, Peterson, 1953, 287–301.

———, Dembo, T., Festinger, L., & Sears, P. Level of aspiration. In J. McV. Hunt (Ed.), *Personality and the behavior disorders.* New York: Ronald, 1944, 333–378.

Likert, R. *New patterns of management.* New York: McGraw-Hill, 1961.

Lippitt, R., Polansky, N., Redl, F., & Rosen, S. The dynamics of power. *Hum. Relat.,* 1952, 5, 37–64.

Lonegran, B. G., & McClintock, C. G. Effects of group membership on risk-taking behavior. *Psychol. Rep.,* 1961, 8, 447–455.

Loomis, J. L. Communication, the development of trust, and cooperative behavior. *Hum. Relat.,* 1959, 12, 305–315.

Lorge, I., Fox, D., Davitz, J., & Brenner, M. A survey of studies contrasting the quality of group performance and individual performance, 1920–1957. *Psychol. Bull.*, 1958, 55, 337–372.

———, & Soloman, H. Two models of group behavior in the solution of eureka-type problems. *Psychometrika*, 1955, 20, 139–148.

———, Tuckman, J., Aikman, L., Spiegel, J., & Moss, Gilda. Solutions by teams and by individuals to a field problem at different levels of reality. *J. educ. Psychol.*, 1955, 46, 17–24.

Maier, N. R. F. *Psychology in industry.* (2nd ed.) Boston: Houghton Mifflin, 1955.

March, J. G. An introduction to the theory and measurement of influence. *Amer. polit. sci. Rev.*, 1955, 49, 431–451.

———, & Simon, H. A. *Organizations.* New York: Wiley, 1958.

Marquis, D. G. Individual responsibility and group decision involving risk. *Industr. Mgmt Rev.*, 1962, 3.

———, Guetzkow, H., & Heyns, R. W. A social psychological study of the decision-making conference. In H. Guetzkow (Ed.), *Groups, leadership and men: Research in human relations.* Pittsburgh: Carnegie Press, 1951, 55–67.

Mausner, B. The effect of one partner's success in a relevant task on the interaction of observer pairs. *J. abnorm. soc. Psychol.*, 1954, 49, 557–560.

———, & Bloch, B. L. A study of the additivity of variables affecting social interaction. *J. abnorm. soc. Psychol.*, 1957, 54, 250–256.

Maynard, H. B., Stegmerten, G. J., & Schwab, J. L. *Methods-time measurement*, New York: McGraw-Hill, 1948.

McBride, Dorothy. The effects of public and private changes of opinion on intragroup communication. Unpublished Ph.D. dissertation, University of Minnesota, 1954.

McGinnies, E., & Altman, I. Discussion as a function of attitudes and content of a persuasive communication. *J. appl. Psychol.*, 1959, 43, 53–59.

Medalia, N. Z., & Miller, D. C. Human relations leadership and the association of morale and efficiency in work groups: A controlled study with small military units. *Soc. Forces*, 1955, 33, 348–352.

Miller, N., & Butler, D. C. Intragroup interaction and the reinforcement structure. Unpublished progress report to the National Institutes of Health, Research Grant: MH 04840-02, 1962.

Mills, T. M. Power relations in three-person groups. *Amer. Sociol. Rev.*, 1953, 18, 351–357.

Mintz, A. Non-adaptive group behavior. *J. abnorm. soc. Psychol.*, 1951, 46, 150–159.

Miyamoto, S. F., Crowell, Laura, Katcher, A. Communication behavior in small discussion groups. *J. Communication*, 1957, 7, 151–160.

Mukerji, N. P. An investigation of ability in work in groups and in isolation. *Brit. J. Psychol.*, 1940, 30, 352–356.

Mussen, P. H., & Porter, L. W. Personal motivation and self-conceptions associated with effectiveness and ineffectiveness in emergent groups. *J. abnorm. soc. Psychol.*, 1959, 59, 23–27.

Newcomb, T. M. An approach to the study of communicative acts. *Psychol. Rev.*, 1953, 60, 393–404.

———. The acquaintance process. New York: Holt, Rinehart, & Winston, 1961.

———. Stabilities underlying changes in interpersonal attraction. *J. abnorm. soc. Psychol.*, 1963, 66, 376–386.

Osborn, A. F. *Applied imagination.* New York: Scribners, 1957.

Osgood, C. E., Suci, G. J., & Tannenbaum, P. H. *The measurement of meaning.* Urbana, Ill.: University of Illinois, 1957.

Parnes, S. J., & Meadow, A. University of Buffalo research regarding development of creative talent. In Calvin W. Taylor (Ed.), *The third University of Utah research conference on the identification of creative scientific talent.* University of Utah, 1959.

Pelz, D. C. Leadership within a hierarchical organization. *J. soc. Issues,* 1951, 7, 49–55.

———. Some social factors related to performance in a research organization. *Administrative Sci. Quart.*, 1956, 1, 310–325.

Pepinsky, Pauline N., Pepinsky, H. B., & Pavlik, W. B. The effects of task complexity and time pressure upon team productivity. *J. appl. Psychol.*, 1960, 44, 34–38.

Perlmutter, H. V., & Hymovitch, B. Communication to high and low power foreign and domestic authorities. *J. Psychol.*, 1954, 38, 281–289.

Powell, R. M. Sociometric analysis of informal groups—their structure and function in two contrasting communities. *Sociom.*, 1952, 15, 367–399.

Pryer, M. W., & Bass, B. M. Some effects of feedback on behavior in groups. *Sociom.*, 1959, 22, 56–63.

Radke, Marian, & Klisurich, D. Experiments in changing food habits. *J. Amer. Dietetics Assoc.*, 1947, 23, 403–409.

Ramuz-Nienhuis, Wilhelmina, & Van Bergen, Annie. Relations between some components of attraction-to-group: A replication. *Hum. Relat.*, 1960, 13, 271–277.

Raven, B. H., & French, J. R. P., Jr. Group support, legitimate power, and social influence. *J. Pers.*, 1958a, 26, 400–409.

———, & French, J. R. P., Jr. Legitimate power, coercive power, and observability in social influence. *Sociom.*, 1958b, 21, 83–97.

———, & Rietsema, J. The effects of clarity of group goal and group path upon the individual and his relation to the group. *Hum. Relat.*, 1957, 10, 29–45.

Read, W. H. Upward communication in industrial hierarchies. *Hum. Relat.*, 1962, 15, 3–15.

Riecken, H. W., & Homans, G. C. Psychological aspects of social structure.

In L. Gardner (Ed.), *Handbook of social psychology: Special fields and application, II.* Reading, Mass.: Addison-Wesley, 1954, 786–832.

Riley, Matilda W., Cohn, R., Toby, J., & Riley, J. W., Jr. Interpersonal orientations in small groups. *Amer. Sociol. Rev.,* 1954, 19, 715–724.

Roach, D. E. Dimensions of employee morale. *Personnel Psychol.,* 1958, 11, 419–431.

Robinson, K. F. An experimental study of the effects of group discussion upon the social attitudes of college students. *Speech Monogr.,* 1941, 8, 34–57.

Roby, T. B., & Lanzetta, J. T. A laboratory task for the study of individuals or groups. Lackland Air Force Base, Tex.: Air Force Personnel and Training Research Center, October, 1957. (*Res. Rept.* AFPTRC-TN-57-124, ASTIA Document No. AD 134 256.)

———, & Lanzetta, J. T. Considerations in the analysis of group tasks. *Psychol. Bull.,* 1958, 55, 88–101.

Roethlisberger, F. J., & Dickson, W. J. *Management and the worker.* Cambridge, Mass.: Harvard University Press, 1939.

Rosen, S., Levinger, G., & Lippitt, R. Desired change in self and others as a function of resource ownership. *Hum. Relat.,* 1960, 13, 187–193.

Rosenberg, S. Cooperative behavior in dyads as a function of reinforcement parameters. *J. abnorm. soc. Psychol.,* 1960, 60, 318–333.

———, Erlick, D. E., & Berkowitz, L. Some effects of varying combinations of group members on group performance measures and leadership behaviors. *J. abnorm. soc. Psychol.,* 1955, 51, 195–203.

Runkel, P. J. Cognitive similarity in facilitating communication. *Sociom.,* 1956, 19, 178–191.

Schachter, S. Deviation, rejection, and communication. *J. abnorm. soc. Psychol.,* 1951, 46, 190–207.

———, Ellertson, N., McBride, Dorothy, & Gregory, Doris. An experimental study of cohesiveness and productivity. *Hum. Relat.,* 1951, 4, 229–238.

Schonbar, Rosalea A. The interaction of observer-pairs in judging visual extent and movement: The formation of social norms in "structured" situation. *Arch. Psychol.,* 1945, 299.

Schramm, W. Utilization of the behavioral sciences. *Report of a planning review for the Behavioral Sciences Division.* New York: 1954.

Schutz, W. C. What makes groups productive? *Hum. Relat.,* 1955, 8, 429–465.

———. *FIRO: A three-dimensional theory of interpersonal behavior.* New York: Rinehart, 1958.

Sengupta, N. N., & Sinka, C. P. N. Mental work in isolation and in group. *Indian J. Psychol.,* 1926, 1, 106–109.

Shaw, M. E. Group structure and the behavior of individuals in small groups. *J. Psychol.,* 1954, 38, 139–149.

Shaw, M. E. A comparison of two types of leadership in various communication nets. *J. abnorm. soc. Psychol.*, 1955, 50, 127–134.

———. Some effects of irrelevant information upon problem-solving by small groups. *J. soc. Psychol.*, 1958a, 47, 33–37.

———. Some motivational factors in cooperation and competition. *J. Pers.*, 1958b, 26, 155–169.

———. Acceptance of authority, group structure and the effectiveness of small groups. *J. Pers.*, 1959a, 27, 196–210.

———. Some effects of individually prominent behavior upon group effectiveness and member satisfaction. *J. abnorm. soc. Psychol.*, 1959b, 59, 382–386.

———. A note concerning homogeneity of membership and group problem solving. *J. abnorm. soc. Psychol.*, 1960, 60, 448–450.

———. Some effects of varying amounts of information exclusively possessed by a group member upon his behavior in the group. *J. gen. Psychol.*, 1963, 68, 71–79

———, & Gilchrist, J. C. Intra-group communication and leadership choice. *J. soc. Psychol.*, 1956, 43, 133–138.

———, & Penrod, W. T., Jr. Validity of information, attempted influence, and quality of group decisions. *Psychol. Reports*, 1962, 10, 19–23.

———, Rothschild, G. H., & Strickland, J. F. Decision processes in communication nets. *J. abnorm. soc. Psychol.*, 1957, 54, 323–330.

Shelley, H. P. Status consensus, leadership, and satisfaction with the group. *J. soc. Psychol.*, 1960, 51, 157–164.

Shelly, M. W., & Gilchrist, J. C. Some effects of communication requirements in group structures. *J. soc. Psychol.*, 1958, 48, 37–44.

Sherif, M., & Sherif, C. W. *An outline of social psychology.* (Rev. ed.) New York: Harper, 1956.

Shevitz, R. N. *Leadership acts: IV. An investigation of the relation between exclusive possession of information and attempts to lead.* Columbus, Ohio: Ohio State University Res. Found., 1955.

Shure, G. H., Rogers, M. S., Larsen, I. M., & Tassone, J. Group planning and task effectiveness. *Sociom.*, 1962, 25, 263–282.

Simpson, R. L. Vertical and horizontal communication in formal organizations. *Administrative Sci. Quart.*, 1959, 4, 188–196.

Sims, V. M. The relative influence of two types of motivation on improvement. *J. educ. Psychol.*, 1928, 19, 480–484.

Slater, P. E. Role differentiation in small groups. *Amer. Sociol. Rev.*, 1955, 20, 300–310.

Smith, E. E. *Effects of threat induced by ambiguous role expectations on defensiveness and productivity in small groups.* Group Process Lab., Univ. of Colorado, 1956, Tech. Rept. #1, Contract No. 1147 (03), Office of Naval Research.

———. The effects of clear and unclear role expectations on group productivity and defensiveness. *J. abnorm. soc. Psychol.*, 1957, 55, 213–217.

Smith, M. Group judgments in the field of personality traits. *J. exp. Psychol.*, 1931, 14, 562–565.

Solomon, L. The influence of some types of power relations and game strategies upon the development of interpersonal trust. *J. abnorm. soc. Psychol.*, 1960, 61, 223–230.

Sommer, R. Studies in personal space. *Sociom.*, 1959, 22, 247–260.

Spence, R. B. Lecture and class discussion in teaching educational psychology. *J. educ. Psychol.*, 1928, 19, 454–462.

Stagner, R. Industrial morale (a symposium): 2. Motivational aspects of industrial morale. *Personnel Psychol.*, 1958, 11, 64–70.

Steinzor, B. The spatial factor in face to face discussion groups. *J. abnorm. soc. Psychol.*, 1950, 45, 552–555.

Stephan, F. F. The relative rate of communication between members of small groups. *Amer. Sociol. Rev.*, 1952, 17, 482–486.

———, & Mishler, E. G. The distribution of participation in small groups: An exponential approximation. *Amer. Sociol. Rev.*, 1952, 17, 598–608.

Stogdill, R. M. Personal factors associated with leadership: A survey of the literature. *J. Psychol.*, 1948, 25, 35–71.

Stonner, J. A. F. A comparison of individual and group decisions involving risk. Unpublished M. A. thesis, Massachusetts Institute of Technology, School of Industrial Management, 1961.

Stotland, E. Peer groups and reactions to power figures. In D. Cartwright (Ed.), *Studies in social power*. Ann Arbor: University of Michigan, 1959, 53–68.

Stroop, J. R. Is the judgment of the group better than that of the average member of the group? *J. exp. Psychol.*, 1932, 15, 550–560.

Stouffer, S. A., Suchman, E. A., DeVinney, L. C., Star, Shirley A., & Williams, R. M. *The American soldier.* Vol. I. *Adjustment during army life.* Princeton: Princeton University Press, 1949.

Taffel, C. Anxiety and the conditioning of verbal behavior. *J. abnorm. soc. Psychol.*, 1955, 51, 496–501.

Talland, G. A. The assessment of group opinion by leaders, and their influence on its formation. *J. abnorm. soc. Psychol.*, 1954, 49, 431–434.

———. Role and status structure in therapy groups. *J. clin. Psychol.*, 1957, 13, 27–33.

Taylor, D. W., Berry, P. C., & Block, C. H. Does group participation when using brainstorming facilitate or inhibit creative thinking? *Admin. Sci. Quart.*, 1958, 3, 23–47.

———, & Faust, W. L. Twenty questions: Efficiency in problem solving as a function of size of group. *J. exp. Psychol.*, 1952, 44, 360–368.

Thibaut, J. W., & Coules, J. The role of communication in the reduction of interpersonal hostility. *J. abnorm. soc. Psychol.*, 1952, 47, 770–777.

Thibaut, J. W., & Kelley, H. H. *The social psychology of groups.* New York: Wiley, 1959.

——, & Riecken, H. W. Authoritarianism, status, and the communication of aggression. *Hum. Relat.,* 1955, 8, 95–120.

Triandis, H. C. Cognitive similarity and communication in a dyad. *Hum. Relat.,* 1960a, 13, 175–183.

——. Some determinants of interpersonal communication. *Hum. Relat.,* 1960b, 13, 279–287.

Thie, T. W. The efficiency of the group method. *English J.,* 1925, 14, 134–137.

Thomas, E. J. Effects of facilitative role interdependence on group functioning. *Hum. Relat.,* 1957, 10, 347–366.

Thorndike, R. L. On what type of task will a group do well? *J. abnorm. soc. Psychol.,* 1938a, 33, 409–413.

——. The effects of discussion upon the correctness of group decisions, when the factor of majority influence is allowed for. *J. soc. Psychol.,* 1938b, 9, 343–362.

Thrasher, J. Interpersonal relations and gradations of stimulus structure as factors in judgmental variation: An experimental approach. *Sociom.,* 1954, 17, 228–241.

Timmons, W. M. *Decisions and attitudes as outcomes of the discussion of a social problem.* New York: Teach. Coll., Contr. Educ., No. 777, Columbia Univ., Bureau of Publications, 1939.

——. Can the product superiority of discussors be attributed to averaging or majority influences? *J. soc. Psychol.,* 1942, 15, 23–32.

Tomeković, T. Level of knowledge of requirements as a motivational factor in the work situation. *Hum. Relat.,* 1962, 15, 197–216.

Torrance, E. P. Some consequences of power differences on decision making in permanent and temporary 3-man groups. *Research studies,* State College of Washington, 1954, 22, 130–140. Reprinted in Hare, A. P., Borgatta, E. F., & Bales, R. F. (Eds.), *Small Groups.* New York: Knopf, 1955.

Trow, D. B. Autonomy and job satisfaction in task-oriented groups. *J. abnorm. soc. Psychol.,* 1957, 54, 204–209.

Tuckman, J., & Lorge, I. Individual ability as a determinant of group superiority. *Hum. Relat.,* 1962, 15, 45–51.

Turner, A. N. Foreman, job, and company. *Hum. Relat.,* 1957, 10, 99–112.

Underwood, B. J., Duncan, C., Taylor, J., & Cotton, J. *Elementary Statistics.* New York: Appleton-Century-Crofts, 1954.

Van Bergen, Annie, & Koekebakker, J. "Group cohesiveness" in laboratory experiments. *Acta Psychologica,* 1959, 16, 81–98.

Vroom, V. H. Some personality determinants of the effects of participation. *J. abnorm. soc. Psychol.,* 1959, 59, 322–327.

Wallach, M. A., Kogan, N., & Bem, D. Group influence on individual risk taking. *J. abnorm. soc. Psychol.,* 1962, 65, 75–86.

Wapner, S., & Alper, T. G. The effect of an audience on behavior in a choice situation. *J. abnorm. soc. Psychol.,* 1952, 47, 222–229.

Watson, G. B. Do groups think more efficiently than individuals? *J. abnorm. soc. Psychol.,* 1928, 23, 328–336.

Wherry, R. J. Industrial morale: (a symposium). 4. Factor analysis of morale data: Reliability and validity. *Personnel Psychol.,* 1958, 11, 78–89.

Whyte, W. H., Jr. *The organization man.* New York: Simon & Schuster, 1956.

Wood, H. G. An analysis of social sensitivity. Unpublished Ph.D. dissertation, Yale University, 1948.

Yuker, H. E. Group atmosphere and memory. *J. abnorm. soc. Psychol.,* 1955, 51, 17–23.

Zajonc, R. B. The effects of feedback and probability of group success on individual and group performance. *Hum. Relat.,* 1962, 15, 149–161.

Ziller, R. C. Scales of judgment: A determinant of the accuracy of group decisions. *Hum. Relat.,* 1955, 8, 153–164.

———, & Behringer, R. D. Assimilation of the knowledgeable newcomer under conditions of group success and failure. *J. abnorm. soc. Psychol.,* 1960, 60, 288–291.

A bibliography from conference research*

Department of Psychology
University of Michigan
1947–1951

Berkowitz, L. Some effects of leadership sharing in small decision-making conference groups. Abstract of doctoral dissertation, University of Michigan, *Microfilm Abstracts*, 1951, 11, 729–730; and *University Microfilms*, Ann Arbor, Mich., Publication No. 2573.

———. Sharing in small, decision-making groups. *J. abnorm. soc. Psychol.*, 1953, 48, 231–238.

Bovard, E. W., Jr. Conformity to social norms in stable and temporary groups. *Science*, 1953, 117, 361–363.

Crockett, W. H. Emergent leadership in small, decision-making groups. *J. abnorm. soc. Psychol.*, 1955, 41, 378–383.

Fouriezos, N. T., Hutt, M. L., and Guetzkow, H. The measurement of self-oriented needs in the discussion situation, and their relationship to satisfaction with group outcome. *J. abnorm. soc. Psychol.*, 1950, 45, 682–690.

Guetzkow, H. Unitizing and categorizing problems in coding qualitative data. *J. clin. Psychol.*, 1950, 6, 47–58.

———. Interagency committee usage. *Pub. Administration Rev.*, 1950, 10 (3), 190–196.

———. An exploratory empirical study of the role of conflict in decision-making conferences. *Int. Soc. Sci. Bull.*, 1953, 5, 286–300.

———, & Gyr, J. An analysis of conflict in decision-making groups. *Hum. Relat.*, 1954, 7, 367–382.

———, & Kriesberg, M. Executive use of the administrative conference. *Personnel*, 1950, 26, 318–323.

* Office of Naval Research (N6 ONR-232, T.O. 7).

Gyr, J. Analysis of committee member behavior in four cultures, *Hum. Relat.,* 1951, 4 (2), 193–202.

Henry, W. E., & Guetzkow, H. Group projection sketches for the study of small groups. *J. soc. Psychol.,* 1951, 33, 77–102.

Heyns, R. W. Effects of variation in leadership on participant behavior in discussion groups. Abstract of doctoral dissertation, University of Michigan, *Microfilm Abstracts,* 1949, 9 (2), 161–163; and *University Microfilms,* Ann Arbor, Mich., Publication No. 1172.

Kriesberg, M. Executives evaluate administrative conferences. *Adv. Mgmt.,* 1950, 15, 15–17.

———, & Guetzkow, H. The use of conferences in the administrative process. *Pub. Administration Rev.,* 1950, 10, 93–98.

Levin, H. Personal influence and opinion change in conferences. Abstract of doctoral dissertation, University of Michigan, *Microfilm Abstracts,* 1951, 11 (2), 424–425; and *University Microfilms,* Ann Arbor, Mich., Publication No. 2411.

Marquis, D. G., Guetzkow, H., & Heyns, R. W. A social psychological study of the decision-making conference. In H. Guetzkow (Ed.), *Groups, Leadership and Men.* Pittsburgh, Pa.: Carnegie Press, 1951. Reissued, New York: Russell & Russell, 1963.

Peterman, J. N. Satisfaction with conference decisions. Abstract of doctoral dissertation, University of Michigan, *Microfilm Abstracts,* 1951, 11, 748–749; and *University Microfilms,* Ann Arbor, Mich., Publication No. 2634.

Shelley, H. P. The role of success and failure in determining attitude toward the group as a means to member goals. Abstract of doctoral dissertation, University of Michigan, *Microfilm Abstracts,* 1951, 11 (2), 436–437; and *University Microfilms,* Ann Arbor, Mich., Publication No. 2462.

Sperling, P. I. Attitude dispersion and its perception as related to satisfaction with a group product. Abstract of doctoral dissertation, University of Michigan, *Microfilm Abstracts,* 1949, 9 (2), 171–173; and *University Microfilms,* Ann Arbor, Mich., Publication No. 1259.

Author Index

243

246 AUTHOR INDEX

Perlmutter, H. V., 129, 176
Peterson, R. O., 188
Polansky, N., 154, 162
Porter, L. W., 155
Powell, R. M., 178
Pryer, M. W., 62, 63, 71, 72

Radke, Marian, 51
Ramuz-Nienhuis, Wilhelmina, 130
Raven, B. H., 132, 134, 135, 148, 149, 150, 197, 211
Read, W. H., 167
Redl, F., 154
Restle, F., 21, 31
Riecken, H. W., 76
Riesman, D., 13
Rietsema, J., 197
Riley, J. W., Jr., 173
Riley, Matilda W., 173
Roach, D. E., 194, 195
Robinson, K. F., 51
Roby, T. B., 15, 71, 73, 75
Roethlisberger, F. J., 49, 162
Rogers, M. S., 79
Roseborough, Mary E., 171
Rosen, S., 154, 205
Ross, I. C., 49
Rossenberg, S., 58, 77
Rothschild, G. H., 207
Rowe, R. R., 42, 43
Runkel, P. J., 186

Saltzstein, H. D., 143
Schachter, S., 130, 178, 180, 181
Schonbar, Rosalea A., 20
Schramm, W., 3
Schutz, W. C., 92, 93, 94, 104
Schwab, J. L., 64
Scott, W. R., 83, 84, 156, 166
Sears, P., 190
Sengupta, N. N., 35
Shapiro, M. M., 126, 203
Shaw, M. E., 29, 35, 39, 91, 100, 104, 105, 155, 206, 207
Shelley, H. P., 100, 202

Shelley, M. W., 206
Sherif, C. W., 172
Sherif, M., 172, 190
Shevitz, R. N., 39
Shure, G. H., 79, 85
Silk, A. J., 191, 193
Simon, H. A., 63, 64, 188, 190
Simpson, R. L., 179
Sims, V. M., 35
Sinka, C. P. N., 35
Slater, P. E., 215, 217, 218
Smith, E. E., 66, 70, 71, 98, 200
Smith, M., 21
Smyth, P., 49
Snyder, R., 129, 149, 157, 219
Soloman, H., 20, 21, 31
Solomon, L., 163
Sommer, R., 177
Spearman, C., 20
Spence, R. B., 52
Stagner, R., 189
Stegmerten, G. J., 64
Steinzor, B., 177
Stephan, F. F., 170, 171
Stogdill, R. M., 212, 213
Stonner, J. A. F., 42, 44
Stotland, E., 161
Stouffer, S. A., 190
Strickland, J. F., 207
Strodtbeck, F. L., 62, 171
Stroop, J. R., 19

Taffel, C., 75
Talland, G. A., 128, 158
Tassone, J., 79
Taylor, D. W., 25, 26, 32
Taylor, J., 10
Thibaut, J. W., 104, 122, 136, 137, 138, 173, 178, 180, 181, 182, 188, 190, 219
Thie, T. W., 51
Thomas, E. J., 141, 142, 143
Thorndike, R. L., 22, 47
Thrasher, J., 186
Timmons, W. M., 47
Toby, J., 173

Subject Index[1]

[1] Page numbers which refer to footnotes are followed by the letter "n." Proposition numbers are set in boldface type. The number before the period refers to the chapter number and the number following the period refers to the proposition number within the chapter. Subject Index prepared by Mrs. Marilynne J. Adler.